hestnuts chicken chocolate cod cookies corn blue crabs soft-shell crabs cucumbers curry duck eggplant eggs fennel grapefruit halibut ham
imp skate red snapper spaghetti strawberries sweet potatoes swiss chard swordfish tomatoes truffles tuna veal watermelon yogurt zucchini

acorn squash anchovies apples arugula green asparagus white asparagus black beans green beans beef beets broccoli cabbage cheese c
lamb lemons lobster mackerel mussels olive oil olives oranges oysters parmesan peas pork potatoes quail rabbit raspberries salmon sca

GEOFFREY ZAKARIAN'S
TOWN *Country*

GEOFFREY ZAKARIAN'S

TOWN *Country*

150 RECIPES FOR
LIFE AROUND THE TABLE

GEOFFREY ZAKARIAN
WITH DAVID GIBBONS
PHOTOGRAPHS BY QUENTIN BACON

CLARKSON POTTER/PUBLISHERS
NEW YORK

Published in the United States by Clarkson Potter/Publishers,

an imprint of the Crown Publishing Group,

a division of Random House, Inc., New York.

www.crownpublishing.com

www.clarksonpotter.com

Library of Congress Cataloging-in-Publication Data

Zakarian, Geoffrey.

Geoffrey Zakarian's town/country : 150 recipes for life around the table /

Geoffrey Zakarian with David Gibbons.—1st ed.

1. Cookery. I. Gibbons, David, 1957–. II. Title.

TX714.Z35 2006

641.5—dc22 2005020410

ISBN-13: 978-1-4000-5468-8

ISBN-10: 1-4000-5468-0

Printed in China

Design by Level, Calistoga, CA

10 9 8 7 6 5 4 3 2 1

First Edition

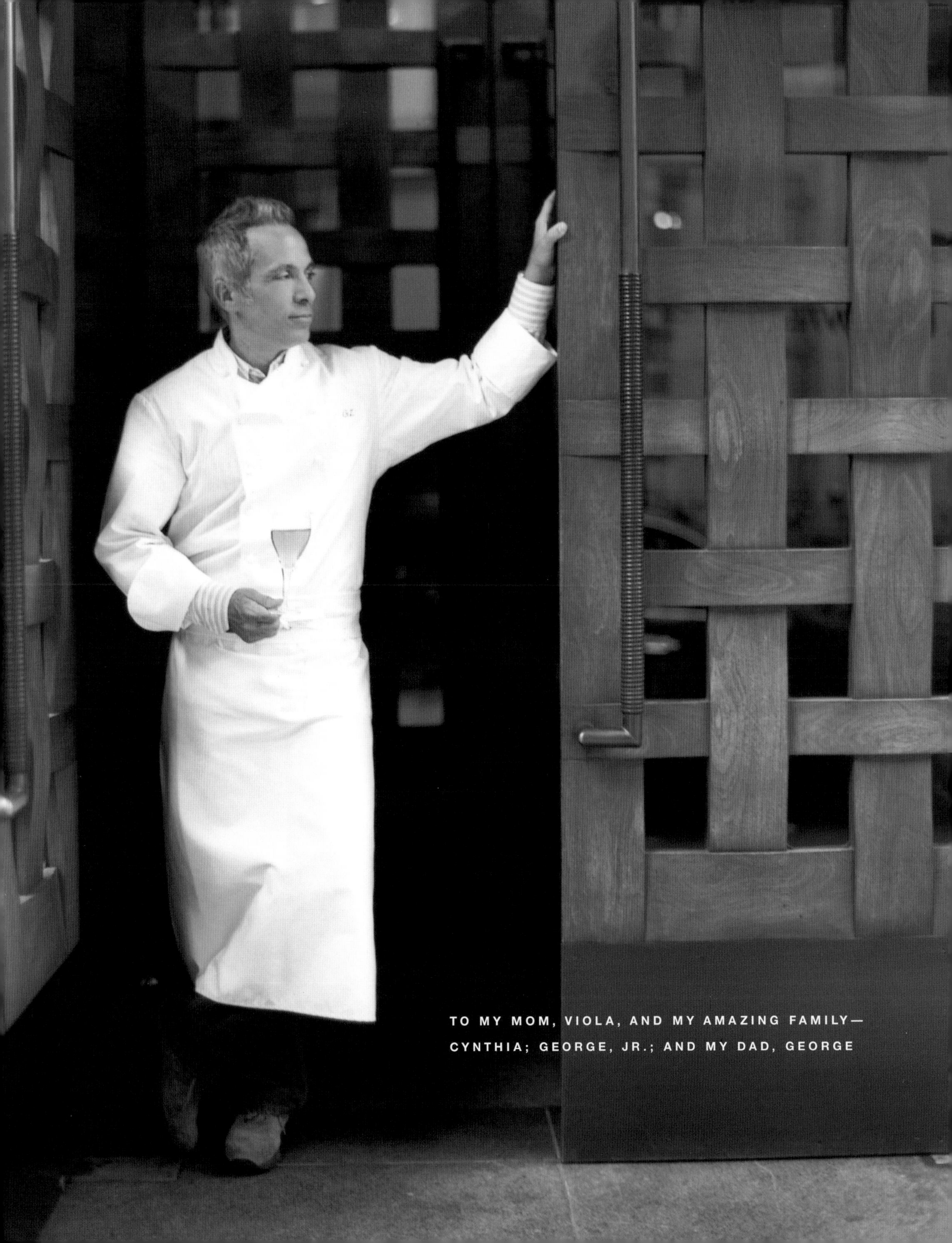

TO MY MOM, VIOLA, AND MY AMAZING FAMILY—
CYNTHIA; GEORGE, JR.; AND MY DAD, GEORGE

contents

introduction

"WHAT DO I WANT TO COOK FOR DINNER TONIGHT?"

acorn squash
anchovies
apples
arugula
green asparagus
white asparagus
black beans
green beans
beef
beets
broccoli
cabbage
cheese
cherries
chestnuts
chicken
chocolate

It's the burning question in the minds of people who cook and the principal reason they turn to cookbooks for inspiration and help. In conceiving this book—one I've contemplated enthusiastically for a long time—I thought about how I tackle this most fundamental of all kitchen questions. My approach is simple, and it's one I believe works whether you're a professional chef like me, looking to attract customers and impress critics, or a home cook just searching for a good recipe to liven up a weeknight meal. I keep a pantry list of favorite ingredients in my head at all times. Whenever the "what to cook" question arises, I scroll down this mental list. In a few minutes, a particular ingredient will strike just the right chord for the occasion.

I think of the list as my personal inventory of nature's best ingredients. These are the foods that get me excited, arouse my passion and send me charging into the kitchen to start slicing and dicing. They aren't necessarily all of a particular type or category—you'll notice that beef and spaghetti, apples and cheese are all there—but each is an ingredient that holds a special memory, association, or irresistible allure for me, and they do share a common trait: they all possess what I call the "Yummy Factor." I know it sounds a little silly, but this is my mantra in the never-ending quest for culinary nirvana: Searching for the Yummy Factor. It's about my most deeply felt connections to certain ingredients, and it's also about a childlike delight and feeling of discovery—which makes sense because, after all, I first experienced those sensations as a kid and they still return deliciously whenever I eat my favorite foods.

My basic approach is to create flavorful twists on proven classics to bring out the essential character of ingredients. For example, my aim is to create a pea soup that's more "pea soupy" than any other one on the planet. I want to deliver the flavor of fresh asparagus loud and clear, glorious and melodious. I'm not trying to impress anybody with fancy, complex preparations. But I do like to delight people with intense, focused, essential flavors, to give them the pure joy of fresh asparagus in springtime. I'm looking to amuse them and maybe (occasionally) keep them guessing: "How did he get that asparagus to taste so . . . *asparagussy?"* This is what I mean by the Yummy Factor. If a dish doesn't have that, I won't put it on my menu, and you won't see it in this book. If it doesn't immediately provoke a *wow reaction*—the pure joy of recognizing a familiar taste in a new and exciting presentation—then it's not worth pursuing.

Starting from my personal pantry list, the next question was how to organize the book so readers could jump quickly from the "what to cook" question to some viable and delicious answers. So I whittled it down to about sixty-five key favorites, which are listed in alphabetical order in pairs. Just run your finger down the Contents. Maybe it feels like a veal night, or perhaps you're wondering what to do with all those beautiful ripe cherries now in season. Stop when an ingredient jumps out at you, then turn to its page. You'll find two recipe options: one an elegant town preparation, and the other a more casual—but equally delicious—country one.

Since I have a propensity to tackle most of life's important questions (including cooking) by sorting everything into pairs, that's how I decided to organize this book. My dishes almost always start off with a couple of basic ingredients that represent an intriguing pairing—or contrast—of flavors or textures: sweet *vs.* sour, smooth *vs.* crunchy, hot *vs.* cold. Pairings or partnerships are what make a recipe dynamic. The best ones start off with this dualism or contrast, eventually harmonizing to achieve balance. I find breaking down everything into pairs is a great way to simplify and streamline the sometimes overly complicated and preciously analyzed world of modern cuisine.

The concept for this book grew out of another fundamental pairing that informs the way I look at all sorts of lifestyle issues—including how I come up with my recipes and how I named my restaurants. It's represented by two geographical poles: town and country. I live in Tribeca, a Manhattan neighborhood that embodies the spirit of casual sophistication. It's a bustling urban setting with a strong country, or casual, feel to it. In the late 1990s, when I was searching for a new restaurant location, I wanted to focus on the downtown area, from Twenty-third Street all the way down to the Financial District, including Tribeca. But my real-estate brokers kept showing me spaces in midtown. I eventually settled on the best one, which was in the Chambers Hotel, run by my friend Ira Drukier, the highly successful hotelier (who had also developed the Mercer, the Stanhope, and the Elysée). Shortly after we inked the deal, I was telling a friend how excited I was about the new place. I told him where it was, smack in the middle of midtown. He said, "But I thought you wanted to be downtown." My response was, "Hey, it's not midtown or downtown, it's just *town*." The phrase stuck. (Technically, the restaurant's name is Town at the Chambers Hotel, since nobody's allowed to own the word *town.*) The name wasn't just a whim, though; it stuck for a reason: because it was shorthand for an approach I really believe in.

Town would be the ultimate in urban sophistication, minus the pretension. There was no preconceived notion about having to be in a certain neighborhood, or conform to any particular trend. It is ultramodern, artsy, and hip, but also mainstream and located centrally enough to appeal to a wide audience.

Beginning with the food and encompassing every detail we could imagine, Town was designed to make diners feel cool, urbane, and confident without taking on snooty airs. My new restaurant, Country, has a more homey accent. The two types of dining—town and country—are not so much opposites as two routes to the same destination. Country style is a natural extension of town style because man does not live by caviar alone; sometimes he must have a bowl of pasta. Just as "town" is somewhat formal and sophisticated yet unpretentious, so "country" is casual and relaxed yet never haphazard.

mackerel
mussels
olive oil
olives
oranges
oysters
parmesan
peas
pork
potatoes
quail
rabbit
raspberries
salmon

Although I maintain a typically intense, high-energy Manhattan lifestyle, I try to spend a lot more time in the Country mode than I do in the Town one. I think of Town as a special-occasion or restaurant style of dining, whereas Country is akin to what you'll experience in a neighborhood café or bistro. In a restaurant context, Country means no reservations, a simpler menu, and quicker service; it means serving dishes family-style on platters to pass around and a decor worthy of country inns. It does not mean any less delicious food, less carefully selected ingredients, less planning, or less attention to detail. In your home cooking and entertaining, you can expect to dine Town style maybe once or twice a month, and Country style once or twice a week. When diners go to my restaurant Country, it should be like going to the house of a friend who is a great home cook; likewise, when your friends dine at your home and you cook a Town recipe, their experience will be akin to dining at my restaurant.

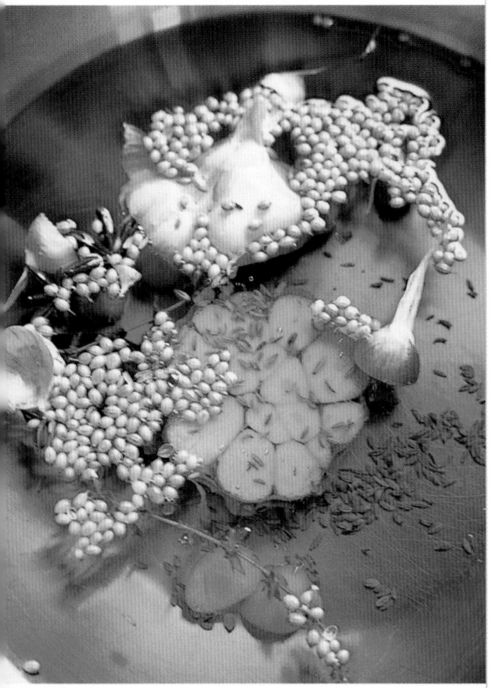

The recipes in this book fall into roughly three categories: luxury dishes from my established restaurant, Town; casual country- or family-style dishes from my new place, Country; and a few favorites that have nothing to do with my restaurants but that I couldn't resist including. Two of my biggest inspirations are my childhood and my pivotal experiences in France right after college. My dad's family is Armenian and my mom's is Polish, so I was exposed at an early age to the marvels of real food. My mother was a great intuitive cook; show her a recipe once and she got it forever. I also had three aunts who were almost as good in the kitchen as my mom. I learned a lot just by osmosis. After college, I got an urban-studies grant to go to France for a year and pursue a graduate degree in economics. I wound up falling in love with French culture and its near-mystical devotion to the total food experience. I spent most of my time and resources investigating the subject of good eating and fine dining. (There went the grant!) I realized this was my true passion and vocation, and I learned the classics of both Town- and Country-style French cuisine.

scallops

shrimp

skate

red snapper

spaghetti

strawberries

sweet potatoes

swiss chard

swordfish

tomatoes

truffles

tuna

veal

watermelon

yogurt

zucchini

My time in France also opened my eyes to the vast possibilities if you applied a little imagination and looked for modern twists on old standbys. That's pretty much my formula: learn the classics of French tradition, muster all the cultural influences that excite me, and come up with my own versions of these dishes. I try to alter traditional recipes by injecting an exciting new flavor or by cranking up the volume—that is, adding a brighter, stronger, more luxurious or exotic ingredient to render them extraordinary.

Almost all of the ingredients in the book, by the way, are readily available in any good supermarket or produce store; for the few that aren't, I supply Internet, phone, and mail-order sources. Some of the recipes consist of three or more component recipes and the assembly and presentation take the spotlight. I break them up so you can choose which parts you want to use; many of the components work well as stand-alones. Some recipes—Curried Shrimp Bisque, for example—have long and somewhat involved ingredient lists. In these cases, gathering all the ingredients is more than half the fun and the challenge. Consider the purchasing stage part of the entire process, just as the plating is; remember, preparing a dish is much more than just cooking a recipe. I don't believe in dumbing down everything, simplifying or streamlining recipes to the point where there's no nuance left. Most of the Country recipes in the book can be made either as an appetizer or, if you double the ingredients, a main course. I've tried to strike a balance between simple, easy-to-make recipes and more challenging ones, between meat and fish, entrées and side dishes, appetizers and desserts.

All the most important things in life happen either in the kitchen or around a table. We gather to celebrate, negotiate, discuss, fight, break up and make up, seal a deal, rekindle old friendships and discover new ones, and—most important of all—simply to enjoy the ancient ritual of breaking bread together. Which brings me to another important goal of this cookbook. I want to encourage people to spend more—and better-quality—time in the kitchen, and less time wired, plugged, or tuned in to the Internet and the TV. Of all the rooms in the house, you can arguably have the most fun and be the most productive in the kitchen. (Okay, I hear a few votes for the bedroom . . .) I believe people who spend time in the kitchen are happier and families who cook together stay together. I want you to take my recipes into the kitchen and experiment. It's a beautiful book but don't be afraid to get it dirty. And don't be afraid to make mistakes in the kitchen. Just get in there, have fun, and cook some good food.

GEOFFREY ZAKARIAN—NEW YORK CITY

A FEW BASIC INGREDIENT NOTES

COOKING FATS

Here is a summary of the various types of cooking fats I use and their best applications.

CLARIFIED BUTTER

A good choice for sautéeing or pan-frying if you want the extra richness and flavor, but it takes a little effort to prepare or obtain. It doesn't burn like regular butter because the milk solids have been extracted.

CANOLA OIL

Light and relatively neutral, with a high smoke point so you don't have to worry so much about it burning and introducing bitter flavors. Good for frying and sautéing.

GRAPESEED OIL

One of the lighter, more neutral oils, it works well as a finishing agent in raw preparations.

NUT OILS

Oils such as hazelnut, walnut, and pistachio are good for dressings in raw preparations such as salads, especially when there's a flavor compatibility—that is, when the nut's flavors find a favorable complement or contrast with one or more of the other ingredients.

OLIVE OIL

Olive oil is one of nature's greatest gifts to mankind. I almost always use some type of cold-pressed extra-virgin olive oil, as opposed to anything that's been filtered or refined. For cooking, I tend toward a lighter oil, while for finishing I'll pull out all the stops and use a heavy, green, fruity or peppery oil. The best oils have low acidity and are cold-pressed, with no filtering, refining, or chemical additives. Light olive oil, a relatively new product, is high-quality olive oil that's been carefully filtered to render it lighter in flavor and color, and also to give it a higher smoke point; it's appropriate for frying and other high-temperature cooking processes that could call for any number of vegetable oils.

In general, the lighter-colored extra-virgin olive oils such as Monini (a top brand from Umbria in central Italy) are best for vinaigrettes on uncooked foods. Some of the heavier first cold-pressed oils from small farms or top vineyards in Tuscany can be used to dress dishes alone, with no help from vinegar or other accompaniments. The big, fruity ones—used in moderation—can also make a good salad dressing. I'm always in search of the perfect olive oil, and I've found good ones from France, Italy, Greece, and California. Each has it own distinctions and subtleties. Some of the southern French ones are delightfully delicate and floral; some of the top Tuscans are rich, peppery, and unctuous; some of the Greeks are just massive and powerful. Each has its time and place. I encourage you to try as many as possible, and to experiment to find the best pairings with various ingredients.

PEANUT OIL

Like canola oil, it works well for frying and sautéing due to its high smoke point. It's a bit less flavor-neutral than canola, but this can be a plus, especially for Asian-accented recipes.

SALT

If there's a general, all-purpose, default salt in my cooking, it's the kosher variety. The large grains offer good definition and flavor; they also let you see what you're doing before the salt dissolves and disappears into the bubbling cauldron. I use it for all cooking and broiling.

Of the fancier salts, Maldon is one of my favorites; it's a medium-coarse sea salt from England with white, flat grains. I really like its flavor and texture. Maldon's French counterpart, *fleur de sel* (also a sea salt, or *sel de mer*), which is slightly gray in color, is expensive but great for rustic terrines and for finishing meat dishes. For raw foods, salads, or any other dishes of delicate texture or consistency that require an easily dissolved salt, use fine sea salt. Stay away from any of the mass-market iodine-enriched salts traditionally available in U.S. supermarkets; they're chemically altered and enhanced, and way too acidic.

As for quantities, my philosophy is always season to taste. Of all the principles of cooking, this is one of the most crucial: keep tasting and adjusting until you're satisfied. Try to err on the side of caution, which means undersalt a bit; your guests can always add more at the table. Also, be consistently aware that the degree of salting is a matter of preference; somewhat salty to you may be virtually inedible to the next person.

In my ingredient lists and recipe instructions through this book, I try to be as specific as possible with regard to all procedures, including salting. At times, you'll find a specific, defined amount ("1½ tablespoons"); feel free to adjust as you see fit. In other instances, you may find approximate measurements—"about 1 teaspoon," "a handful," or "a pinch"—or even a general guideline such as "lightly," "moderately," or "generously." None of this is meant to be precious, vague, disingenuous, or confusing; rather, it illustrates the point that in each instance and every respect, fine cooking is more art than science. And exact amounts are always determined by you, the chef, through regular tasting and adjusting.

TOWN

Country

ACORN SQUASH

TOWN

Acorn Squash, Serrano Ham, and Bufala Mozzarella

SERVES 4

2 tablespoons extra-virgin olive oil

1 medium acorn squash, halved, seeded, and cut into 8 wedges

Kosher salt and freshly ground black pepper

1 teaspoon (packed) dark brown sugar

½ teaspoon fresh thyme leaves

1 teaspoon honey

2 tablespoons unsalted butter

6 ounces thinly sliced serrano ham

½ pound fresh *mozzarella di bufala,* cut into 4 slices

With a nod to the famous Italian duo of prosciutto and melon, here's an eclectic multicultural trio of squash (sweet), ham (salty), and mozzarella (a hint of sour). The inspiration comes from one of my favorite dishes at the River Café in London, *ravioli nudi* (just the filling, no pasta) with roasted squash and pancetta. Serrano ham is similar to fine Italian prosciutto but more rustic, with a denser consistency and a gamier flavor. This makes it an even better foil for the smooth, rich cheese and the sweet, meaty roasted squash. You can use regular-size mozzarella or bite-size *bocconcini* ("little mouthfuls" in Italian).

INGREDIENT NOTE Genuine *mozzarella di bufala*—the Italian standard bearer of all fresh mozzarellas—is made from the milk of long-horned cattle (*bufala*) in two production zones, one just to the north of Naples and the other farther south, near Salerno. Bufala milk is creamier and richer, and yields a cheese that is sweeter and nuttier than your average mozzarella. Although it's often called "buffalo mozzarella" in the United States, it is not made from buffalo milk; *bufala* are actually more closely related to the water buffaloes found in parts of Africa and on the Indian subcontinent.

Preheat the oven to 400° F.

Lightly drizzle a baking sheet or pan with 1 tablespoon of the olive oil. Place the squash wedges on the baking sheet skin side down in one uncrowded layer. Season the squash lightly with salt and pepper; sprinkle it with the sugar and ¼ teaspoon of the thyme, then drizzle the honey on top. Break up the butter into small pieces and distribute them evenly on the squash. Place the baking sheet in the oven for 15 minutes. Lay the wedges on their sides and bake for another 15 minutes. Turn the wedges over to bake on their opposite sides and bake until they are soft and brown, about 15 minutes more.

Remove the squash from the oven and allow to cool until slightly warm to the touch. Using a small, sharp knife, carefully cut away the skin, taking care not to ruin the wedges' shape and integrity. Arrange two pieces of squash on each of four plates. Drape slices of serrano over the squash. Arrange a slice of mozzarella on top of the ham-draped squash, drizzle with the remaining tablespoon of olive oil, sprinkle with the remaining ¼ teaspoon of thyme leaves, season to taste with salt and pepper, and serve.

ACORN SQUASH

Country

Acorn Squash Pie with Anisette Cookie Crust

SERVES 6 TO 8 (ONE 9-INCH PIE)

FOR THE SQUASH

- 2 medium acorn squash
- 2 tablespoons canola or other neutral vegetable oil
- 1 tablespoon kosher salt

FOR THE COOKIE CRUST

- $1\frac{1}{2}$ cups finely ground anisette cookies (biscotti), from 10 to 12 cookies
- 8 tablespoons unsalted butter, melted

FOR THE FILLING

- $1\frac{1}{2}$ cups evaporated milk
- $\frac{1}{2}$ cup (packed) dark brown sugar
- $\frac{1}{4}$ cup granulated sugar
- 1 teaspoon ground cinnamon
- $\frac{1}{2}$ teaspoon ground ginger
- $\frac{1}{8}$ teaspoon ground cloves
- $\frac{1}{8}$ teaspoon ground nutmeg
- $\frac{1}{8}$ teaspoon ground star anise
- Grated zest of 1 orange
- 4 large eggs, lightly beaten
- 2 tablespoons dark rum
- Pinch of kosher salt
- 1 vanilla bean, split

TO SERVE

- 3 cups Whipped Cream (recipe follows)

Growing up, when all the other kids were out in the cold playing brutal sports like football, I was in the kitchen with my mom rolling pie crust. (Of course, the kids gave me a lot of grief.) This is a sophisticated variation on my mother's pumpkin pie, one of the first things I learned to make. It's a multipurpose pie, a little bit sweet and a little bit savory, that works equally well for dessert, lunch, or a late-night snack. Sometimes, I treat it like a great big turnover or Pop-Tart and eat it for breakfast alongside a cup of espresso. For dessert, you can serve it with crème fraîche or Whipped Cream (opposite). It's nice cold right out of the fridge (with that hot cup of coffee) or slightly warmed up (with chilled whipped cream or even ice cream).

INGREDIENT NOTE The anisette cookies (*biscotti*) can be purchased at an Italian food market or a gourmet specialty food store. Ten to 12 biscotti are enough to provide the $1\frac{1}{2}$ cups of ground-up cookies called for; biscotti can be flavored with anise, almonds, or hazelnuts.

PREPARE THE SQUASH PURÉE Preheat the oven to 400°F.

Cut the squash in half and scrape out and discard the seeds and stringy parts from their interiors. Drizzle each squash half with the oil, sprinkle them with the salt, place them on a baking sheet, and bake until tender, about 1 hour. Remove the squash from the oven and reduce the temperature to 350°F. Allow the squash to cool enough so they are easy to handle; scoop out the flesh and purée it in a food processor. You should have about 4 cups of purée.

PREPARE THE COOKIE CRUST In a large bowl, mix the cookie crumbs with the melted butter, working the butter into the crumbs with your hands until the mixture holds together. Press the crust mixture into a 9-inch pie pan. Cover with plastic wrap and chill for at least 30 minutes.

PREPARE THE FILLING In a large bowl, combine the squash purée with the evaporated milk, brown sugar, granulated sugar, cinnamon, ginger, cloves, nutmeg, star anise, orange zest, eggs, rum, and salt. Scrape the seeds from the vanilla bean into the bowl and mix thoroughly.

BAKE THE PIE Pour the filling into the pie pan. Place the pie in the oven to bake for about 35 minutes, or until the filling is fully set. When you jiggle the pan, the filling should no longer move; start checking after 25 minutes. Allow the pie to cool for about 20 minutes. Cut into wedges and serve warm with a generous dollop of Whipped Cream.

WHIPPED CREAM

MAKES ABOUT 3 CUPS

2 cups heavy cream

1½ teaspoons confectioners' sugar, or to taste

½ vanilla bean, split

In a well-chilled medium to large bowl, combine the heavy cream and confectioners' sugar. Scrape the seeds from the vanilla bean into the mixture. Whip vigorously with a whisk until soft peaks form.

ANCHOVIES

TOWN

Beignets of White Anchovies with Beans and Herbs

SERVES 8 TO 10 AS AN APPETIZER

- 1 large egg yolk
- 1 cup ice water
- 1 cup all-purpose flour, plus about ½ cup for dredging
- 1 cup shelled fresh cranberry beans (about ½ pound unshelled; see Ingredient Note)
- ¼ pound haricots verts, trimmed
- Vegetable oil for frying (about 3 quarts, depending on the size of your pot)
- ⅓ pound white anchovies (about 30), drained and patted dry
- Kosher salt
- ¼ cup basil leaves
- ¼ cup cilantro leaves
- ¼ cup tarragon leaves

NOTES ON DEEP-FRYING

Use canola, grapeseed, or some other neutral oil and heat it to 365°F.; don't let it smoke. (The smoke point for most frying oils is well over 400°F.) If you're not using a deep fryer or thermometer, test whether the oil is ready to fry by dropping a bit of batter or a leaf of one of the herbs in: if it sinks partially and then floats back to the top, sizzling, the oil is ready; if the test bit totally sinks, the oil is not hot enough; if it floats immediately and browns very quickly, the oil is too hot. Slide the food in carefully using tongs,

I first had grilled Mediterranean anchovies in the South of France in the early 1980s, and it completely changed my image of this little fish. When most people think of anchovies, they think of the standard preserved, canned variety—shriveled and really salty—found on supermarket shelves all over America. This recipe calls for white anchovies, which are much fresher, and are similar to the ones enjoyed all over the Mediterranean. They're cured in vinegar and deliver a delightful pickly burst of flavor. In this treatment, we fry them up, quick and easy, to create a really fun cocktail dish. Serve it in the summer, perhaps with a good glass of well-chilled Champagne. Ah, the bubbly . . .

INGREDIENT NOTE Fresh cranberry beans are available in summer; they have a very appealing, somewhat nutty flavor. If you can't find them at your market, or they're not in season, simply omit them and double the amount of haricots verts. It takes about 3 quarts of oil to fill a 10-inch diameter 4-quart heavy pot to a depth of 3 inches.

Combine the egg yolk with the ice water in a bowl and mix well. Add 1 cup of the flour and stir with a wooden spoon until the mixture is the consistency of pancake batter. Set the batter aside.

Bring a large pot of salted water to a boil over high heat. Prepare an ice-water bath. Add the cranberry beans to the boiling water and cook for 3 minutes. Add the haricots verts and cook for 2 minutes more. Drain the cranberry beans and haricots verts, then refresh them in the bath.

Fill a heavy, deep pot to a depth of 3 inches with oil and place it over medium-high heat until the oil is hot. The oil is ready for frying when a thermometer indicates a temperature of 365°F., or a small amount of batter immediately sizzles and puffs when dropped into the pot.

Place about ½ cup flour in a shallow bowl. Pat the anchovies dry with paper towels, dredge them in the flour, and coat them with the batter. Working in batches, deep-fry the anchovies until golden brown, 1 to 2 minutes, then transfer them to a plate or platter lined with paper towels to drain.

Dredge the haricots verts in flour, coat them with batter, deep-fry them for about 2 minutes, and transfer them to another paper-towel-lined plate to drain. Repeat the frying and draining procedure for the cranberry beans. (Alterna-

a slotted spoon, or a "spider." (Most deep fryers and electric frying pans have their own basket for this purpose.) Dry the food well before frying; otherwise it can splatter. Drain fried food well on paper towels to get rid of any excess oil, and season with salt while still hot.

tively, they may be fried without dredging in flour and coating with batter.) Season the haricots verts and beans with salt to taste.

Working in batches, drop the herbs into the oil and fry until crisp, about 2 minutes. Sprinkle the herbs with salt. Arrange the herbs, cranberry beans, haricots verts, and anchovies on a large platter and serve immediately.

ANCHOVIES

Country Bagna Cauda

SERVES 6 TO 8

$1/2$ cup salted butter

12 garlic cloves, sliced

20 white anchovy fillets

2 cups extra-virgin olive oil

Salt and pepper to taste

Grated zest and juice of 1 lemon, plus additional juice to taste

Raw or steamed vegetables, for serving

Bagna cauda is an old-fashioned Italian peasant concoction that trumps any other dip I can imagine. Legend has it that in Piedmont during the grape harvest, they would serve leftover bagna cauda with scrambled eggs as a hearty breakfast for workers who'd been up all night picking grapes. (By the way, whatever you did all night, it makes a great breakfast.) Bagna cauda is super-versatile and good for any occasion, year-round; I like to present it country-style on a big platter, with a display of raw vegetables and lettuces that might include fennel, radishes, celery, red and white endive, baby cos or bibb lettuce, ribs of nicely trimmed romaine, and scallions. Take care to thoroughly wash, dry, and neatly trim all the vegetables before arranging them. Another option: serve the bagna cauda with an assortment of lightly steamed baby vegetables.

Melt the butter in a high-sided skillet over low heat. Add the garlic and cook until it softens, about 5 minutes. Add the anchovies, stirring and mashing with a fork. Continue cooking until the flavors meld, about 3 minutes. Gradually whisk in the oil, and season with lemon zest and lemon juice. Transfer the bagna cauda to a ceramic pot, and serve warm with raw or lightly steamed vegetables and/or lettuces for dipping.

TOWN

Shinshū-Apple Purée

MAKES ABOUT 1½ CUPS

2 large or 3 medium Golden Delicious apples, peeled, cored, and sliced paper-thin

1 tablespoon light miso paste (shinshū)

I love purées, and this one is great because it consists of just two ingredients, which form a perfect yin-yang pairing. It's so good that it reminds me of scraping the cake batter out of the bowl and licking it off the spoon when I was a kid. I use it as an accompaniment for roasted veal, roasted or grilled chicken, and many types of seafood preparations. Or try this: create a parfait-type dessert with sweetened spiked whipped cream, vanilla ice cream, shaved chocolate, and this purée—all layered in a big coupe glass. The purée can also double as baby food (served at room temperature). For the serving size, you can figure on one-half to three-fourths cup of purée per person.

INGREDIENT NOTE Shinshū is a satisfyingly salty, lighter-colored variety of miso paste; it's available at Japanese specialty markets and health food stores. Golden Delicious apples work best for several reasons: they provide a good amount of sweetness to balance the salty miso; they have just the right water content—not too much, not too little; and they retain their color better than other types, without turning brown.

Place the apple slices in a small, heavy saucepan. Add 2 tablespoons of water and cook over medium-low heat, stirring frequently, until the apples are very soft and beginning to fall apart, about 8 minutes. Transfer to a food processor or blender, add the miso, and purée until smooth. (The purée should be slightly thicker than applesauce; add water if necessary to thin.) Return the purée to the pan, cover, and keep in a warm place until serving.

Country Apple Cider Soup

SERVES 4

1 medium butternut squash (about 1/2 pound)

4 tablespoons (packed) dark brown sugar

1 whole clove

1 piece star anise

1 cinnamon stick

3 allspice berries

4 tablespoons (1/2 stick) unsalted butter

2 cups sliced onions (1 medium onion)

1/4 cup minced fresh ginger (one 3- to 4-inch piece)

1/2 cup chopped turnips (1/2 small turnip)

1 vanilla bean, split

2 cups sliced Granny Smith apples (from 2 medium apples), peeled, cored, and sliced

Grated zest of 1 orange

3 cups sweet apple cider

1 cup hard apple cider

1/4 cup pumpkin seeds, for garnish (optional)

1/4 cup freshly squeezed lemon juice (1 large or 2 small lemons)

Kosher salt and freshly ground black pepper to taste

Rosemary Cream (recipe follows; optional)

To me, apples spell country comfort as much as any other food and remind me of all the treats in store when summer changes to fall. With the inclusion of hard (fermented) cider, this recipe is reminiscent of mulled cider, a very special treat. Just wait till you inhale the heady, spicy aromas filling your kitchen and wafting around the house; that alone is worth the price of admission. I first came up with this recipe when I was *chef de cuisine* at the famed 21 Club in the late 1980s. Our diners had had their fill of mulligatawny and split pea soup, and I wanted to offer something a little more lively. It was around that time they filmed the movie *Wall Street* in the area, and I remember the cast and crew really enjoyed this soup.

You can serve this soup hot on a chilly day, but it also works well at room temperature or even cold. Try it chilled in martini glasses as an appetizer, or drop about a teaspoon of it into a glass of Champagne for an apéritif. The Rosemary Cream is an optional fancy garnish.

Preheat the oven to 375°F.

Cut the butternut squash in half, scrape out and discard the seeds, and rub the flesh with brown sugar. Place the halves on a rack in the oven, cut side up. Roast the squash, uncovered, until very soft, about 1½ hours. Spoon the flesh and any juices into a bowl and reserve; discard the skin.

In a clean spice grinder or with a mortar and pestle, grind the clove, star anise, cinnamon, and allspice. Melt the butter in a medium pot over medium heat. Add the onions, stir in the ground spices, and cook, stirring frequently, until the onions are golden brown and soft, about 10 minutes. Stir in the ginger and cook until fragrant, about 3 minutes. Add the turnips, vanilla bean, apples, orange zest, the sweet and hard apple ciders, the reserved squash, and 1 cup of water. Bring the soup to a boil over high heat, then reduce the heat to low and simmer until the flavors are combined and the apples and turnips are soft, about 20 minutes.

Toast the pumpkin seeds (if using) either in a toaster oven or in a small skillet over medium heat until lightly browned, turning so they are evenly done on both sides.

Purée the soup in a blender. If you like, pass it through a fine strainer (chinois or china cap; this step is optional). Add the lemon juice, then season with salt and pepper to taste. Garnish with Rosemary Cream and toasted pumpkin seeds, if desired, and serve.

ROSEMARY CREAM

MAKES 1/2 CUP

1/4 cup fresh rosemary leaves
1/4 cup mascarpone cheese
1/4 cup heavy cream
Fine sea salt

Set up a double boiler by placing a small saucepan over a larger pan of barely simmering water. Combine the rosemary leaves, mascarpone, and cream in the top pan. Slowly melt the mascarpone, stirring frequently. Reduce the heat to low and allow the rosemary to infuse the cream, stirring occasionally, for about 15 minutes. Pass the rosemary cream through a strainer into a chilled bowl set over an ice bath; discard the rosemary leaves. Stir the cream frequently as it cools to room temperature. Season to taste with salt.

SERVING TEMPERATURES

One of my biggest concerns is to serve all foods—and particularly soups—at the proper temperature. At my restaurants, we serve soups warm but not piping hot. (Every once in a while, somebody sends a bowl back, in which case we make it *very hot* and hope nobody gets hurt!) Any food served too hot will just shut down your taste buds so you can't appreciate its flavors. Ideally, soup should be served at 140°F., which is a far cry from the boiling point of 212°F.

ARUGULA

TOWN

Arugula Cannelloni with Chanterelle Sauce

SERVES 4 AS A MAIN COURSE

FOR THE FILLING

- 5 tablespoons extra-virgin olive oil
- 1 pound ground veal (or about 1½ cups roughly chopped leftover braised veal)
- ½ teaspoon kosher salt, plus more to taste
- ½ teaspoon freshly ground black pepper, plus more to taste
- 1 cup diced carrot (2 medium carrots)
- 1 cup peeled, diced celery root (¼ pound, or half a small celery root) or 2 medium stalks celery, diced
- 1 cup diced onion (1 medium onion)
- 1 tablespoon minced garlic (1 large clove)
- ½ teaspoon ground allspice
- 1 teaspoon freshly ground nutmeg
- 3 tablespoons port wine
- 1½ cups Chicken Stock (page 262, or low-sodium canned)
- 2 tablespoons crème fraîche
- 2 tablespoons freshly grated Pecorino Romano
- 4 packed cups chopped arugula leaves

I worked a day in the kitchen of Alain Ducasse's Provençal country inn, La Bastide de Moustiers, and watched him make cannelloni. When it was time to fly home, I couldn't wait to get back in my kitchen to come up with my own recipe. I think of cannelloni as a bigger, better alternative to ravioli. Once you get the hang of making these cigar-shaped rolls of pasta, they're versatile and easy to prepare. They're baked rather than boiled, which makes them well suited to a multi-course meal: once you put them in the oven, you can finish up some other cooking or prepping while they're baking. This recipe combines French, American, and English influences; I've made about a ton of cannelloni in each country. The peppery arugula here helps focus the rich veal filling, and the sauce adds a note of positively sinful luxury. You can serve this as a main course, with four cannelloni per person, or an appetizer with two per person.

INGREDIENT NOTES For expediency, feel free to substitute store-bought egg roll or wonton wrappers for the homemade pasta. They're both available in the dairy case or freezer at supermarkets. Egg roll wrappers come in 1-pound packets of about twenty 6-inch squares (among other sizes); wonton wrappers are about half that size. Depending on the size of wrapper you get, you can roll them out with a rolling pin or trim them as necessary.

For a deluxe version of the filling, substitute about 1½ cups of roughly chopped leftover braised veal (see Poached Veal Shank, page 250) for the ground veal.

If you have a good pasta-rolling machine, our basic recipe for pasta dough should yield enough rolled-out dough to make 12 to 16 cannelloni. In fact, you should have extra, which gives you a comfortable margin for error. Whenever you make fresh pasta at home, I strongly recommend you make more than you'll need. It's good to be able to experiment and not worry about making a mistake and losing some of the dough.

FOR THE CANNELLONI

- ½ recipe Pasta Dough (page 265), or 16 egg roll or wonton wrappers
- 4 tablespoons (½ stick) unsalted butter, cut into ½-inch slices
- ½ cup freshly grated Parmigiano-Reggiano
- ½ cup Chicken Stock (page 262, or low-sodium canned)

FOR THE CHANTERELLE SAUCE

- 2 tablespoons extra-virgin olive oil
- 1 tablespoon unsalted butter
- 1 pound chanterelle, cremini, or other wild mushrooms, trimmed and sliced thin
- Kosher salt and freshly ground black pepper to taste
- ¼ cup chopped flat-leaf parsley

Since chanterelles can make a pretty serious dent in your savings, feel free to substitute cremini or some less expensive seasonal wild mushroom, such as pleurottes or oysters. One trick to economizing on mushrooms is to use a small amount of dried chanterelles, presoaked in water and chopped, adding them to less expensive fresh mushrooms to capture the chanterelles' flavor without the expense.

PREPARE THE FILLING Place 1 tablespoon of the oil in a large skillet over medium-high heat. When the oil is hot, add the veal, season with ¼ teaspoon of the salt and ¼ teaspoon of the pepper, and cook, stirring to break up the veal, until it is well browned, about 10 minutes. Drain the veal in a colander, and discard the fat. (If using leftover braised veal, skip this step.)

Add 2 tablespoons of the olive oil to the skillet. Reduce the heat to medium and add the carrots, celery root, onion, and garlic. Season with the remaining ¼ teaspoon of salt and ¼ teaspoon of pepper, and cook, stirring occasionally, until the vegetables are tender, about 15 minutes. Return the veal to the pan. Add the allspice, nutmeg, and port. Simmer for about 2 minutes, until the port is almost completely reduced. Add the stock and simmer until the pan is almost dry, about 12 minutes. Add the crème fraîche and cook, stirring, for 1 to 2 minutes. Remove the pan from the heat. Add the pecorino, and season to taste with salt and pepper. Transfer the veal mixture to a bowl and reserve.

Wipe out the skillet, place it over medium-high heat, and add the remaining 2 tablespoons of oil. Add the arugula, a handful at a time, and cook, stirring, until it wilts, about 4 minutes. Season the arugula to taste with salt and pepper, then drain thoroughly. Stir the arugula into the veal mixture, cover the bowl, and refrigerate until ready to use.

continued

PREPARE THE PASTA (IF USING DOUGH) Divide the pasta dough into 4 small balls. Using a pasta machine, roll the dough out through successively smaller settings until it is less than ⅛ inch thick and almost translucent; this should be at about the fifth setting. (The dough tends to become fragile and rip if rolled any thinner.) Cut the dough into a total of 16 rectangles, about 4 × 5 inches each.

Bring a large pot of salted water to a boil over high heat. Brush a thin coating of olive oil onto a large piece of parchment paper. Prepare a bath of ice water. Cook the rectangles of pasta, a few at a time, until they float, about 45 seconds. Transfer the pasta briefly to the ice-water bath to cool, then drain. Place the pasta rectangles on the oiled parchment paper, cover them with a damp cloth, and reserve at room temperature until ready to use. (Alternatively, the cooked pasta dough can be stored in layers of oiled parchment paper stacked on top of one another.)

If using 6-inch egg roll wrappers, trim to 4 × 5-inch rectangles; otherwise, adjust the size and number of cannelloni according to size of wrappers.

FORM THE CANNELLONI Preheat the oven to 350°F. Arrange a heaping tablespoon of veal-arugula filling along the shorter side of each rectangle of pasta dough. Roll the pasta around the filling as if you're rolling a cigar. Repeat the process until you have formed cannelloni with all the pasta rectangles.

Place the cannelloni in one layer in an ovenproof baking dish. Distribute the sliced butter evenly over the cannelloni, sprinkle with the Parmesan, then add the stock. Place the cannelloni in the oven to bake until the cheese is melted and beginning to brown, about 15 minutes.

SAUTÉ THE CHANTERELLES Combine the oil and butter in a large sauté pan over medium-high heat. When the butter begins to foam, add the chanterelles and lightly sauté them until softened, about 5 minutes. Season with salt and pepper to taste and add the parsley.

Spoon the baked cannelloni onto warm plates. Top each portion with chanterelle sauce, and serve.

ARUGULA

Country

Ziti with Arugula Pesto and Crispy Prosciutto

SERVES 6 TO 8

- **1/4 pound thinly sliced prosciutto**
- **1 pound arugula, thoroughly washed and trimmed of large stems and damaged or yellowed leaves**
- **1 cup extra-virgin olive oil**
- **1 small clove garlic**
- **2 tablespoons toasted pine nuts**
- **1 tablespoon unsalted butter**
- **1/2 cup freshly grated Parmigiano-Reggiano**
- **1 teaspoon kosher salt**
- **1 teaspoon freshly ground black pepper**
- **2 pounds ziti or other dry pasta (see Ingredient Note)**

When I was chef at Restaurant 44 at the chic Royalton Hotel, I used to eat lunch with my business partner, Brian McNally, on a regular basis. Being English, Brian has some funny ideas about politics, which led to some interesting arguments. But we both loved pesto.

Traditional Genoese-style pesto—made with basil, pine nuts, and Parmesan cheese—has garlic, a lot of garlic. In fact, most people add too much of it. In this variation, I use a relatively small dose to complement the arugula's spunky, peppery character. For storage, pesto is covered with a protective layer of olive oil, which will pool in the bottom of the container. Like too much garlic, this oil has a tendency to overwhelm the pesto's other flavors. This is why I highly recommend draining off the excess oil and replacing it with a judicious amount of whole butter just before using the pesto.

INGREDIENT NOTE This recipe calls for ziti, but spirals, shells, and any number of other multifaceted pasta shapes work well with pesto; the sauce lodges very nicely in all the little nooks and crannies, creating a scrumptious mix.

Preheat the oven to 200°F.

Line a baking sheet with parchment paper and place the prosciutto in a single layer on top. (Make another layer of paper topped with prosciutto if necessary.) Place the prosciutto in the oven until it is crisp, about 40 minutes. Remove from the oven and reserve, uncovered, in a cool, dry place.

Bring a large pot of salted water to a boil over high heat. Prepare an ice-water bath. Stir the arugula into the boiling water and blanch until it is bright green and tender, about 30 seconds. Drain the arugula, immediately refresh it in the ice water, and set aside, covered with a towel.

continued

In a blender, combine the oil, garlic, pine nuts, butter, Parmesan, salt, and pepper. Purée on high until all the ingredients are thoroughly combined. Turn off the blender and stir in the arugula with a spoon. Pulse the blender several times on high speed for intervals of about 10 seconds, until the arugula is fully incorporated into the oil mixture. (Take care not to leave the blender running so long that the pesto gets hot and melts the cheese.) In between pulses, stir the pesto to make sure it is puréed evenly.

Place the pesto in a bowl, cover tightly with plastic wrap to avoid discoloration, and reserve in the refrigerator; it will stay bright green for about an hour if properly covered. (If you plan to keep the pesto longer, pour a layer of olive oil on top, then seal the container; stored this way, the pesto will keep for more than a week.)

Bring a large pot of salted water to a boil over high heat. Add the pasta, adjust the heat so it maintains a steady boil, and cook, stirring occasionally, until it is done to your taste, 10 to 12 minutes. (The best doneness test for pasta is to taste a piece; when it begins to become tender but is still slightly chewy, it's done.) Drain the cooked pasta and transfer immediately to a large bowl. Add the arugula pesto and mix gently until the pasta is well coated. Crumble the slices of crispy prosciutto on top as a garnish, and serve immediately in warm bowls.

TOWN

Asparagus Soup with Morels

SERVES 6

- $2\frac{1}{2}$ pounds asparagus (preferably thin spears)
- 2 tablespoons salted butter
- 2 shallots, finely minced
- 2 cloves garlic, minced
- 3 cups Chicken Stock (page 262, or low-sodium canned)
- 1 dried bay leaf
- 3 sprigs thyme
- Kosher salt and freshly ground white pepper to taste
- 1 cup heavy cream
- 5 ounces small fresh morels, cleaned

With asparagus soup, there's one big red warning flag: overcooking, which results in dark color, mushy texture, and muddy flavors. Fresh asparagus just needs a little gentle coaxing to enhance its natural flavors. In this recipe, the asparagus is blanched in a bit of chicken stock, allowing its beautiful bright green chlorophyll to survive; the entire cooking process here takes a little more than 20 minutes.

INGREDIENT NOTE This recipe can be made with white or green asparagus; both go very well with the earthy yet subtle flavors of the mushrooms.

Snap off and discard the tough bottom ends of the asparagus. Cut off the tips and set aside. Cut the stalks into 1-inch segments.

Melt the butter in a medium saucepan over medium-low heat. Add the shallots and garlic and cook, stirring frequently, until they are tender, about 5 minutes. Spoon half the shallot-garlic mixture into a second medium saucepan and reserve.

Add the asparagus stalks (still reserving the tips) to the first saucepan along with the stock, bay leaf, 2 sprigs of the thyme, and salt and white pepper to taste. Simmer over medium heat until the asparagus is soft, about 12 minutes. Allow the soup to cool slightly, remove the bay leaf and thyme sprigs, then transfer it to a blender and purée until smooth. Add the heavy cream and pulse to combine. Taste and adjust the seasonings as needed. Return the soup to the pan and keep warm over low heat.

Bring a pot of salted water to a boil. Blanch the reserved asparagus tips by plunging them into the water for 2 minutes after the water returns to a boil; the tips should be tender but still bright green. Drain and set aside.

Put the morels in the pan with the reserved shallots and garlic. Add about $\frac{3}{4}$ cup of water and the remaining thyme sprig. Simmer over medium heat until the water is almost evaporated, about 7 minutes. Add the blanched asparagus tips, and season with salt and pepper to taste. Remove the thyme.

Ladle equal portions of warm soup into each of six bowls. Spoon a portion of the morel–asparagus tip mixture into each bowl and serve.

GREEN ASPARAGUS

Country

Asparagus Soup with Tomato-Asparagus Crostini

SERVES 6

ASPARAGUS SOUP

- **1½ pounds spinach, washed and drained**
- **Kosher salt and freshly ground black pepper to taste**
- **3 tablespoons extra-virgin olive oil**
- **1 small onion, chopped**
- **1 medium leek, white part only, thoroughly cleaned and chopped**
- **1 stalk celery, chopped**
- **1 small parsnip, peeled and chopped**
- **4 bunches of asparagus (about 3 pounds)**
- **2 cups Chicken Stock (page 262, or low-sodium canned)**
- **1 cup cilantro leaves**
- **1 cup flat-leaf parsley leaves**

At first glance, the instruction below to make asparagus juice may seem a little strange. But it really adds a lot to the soup, and in fact (weirdly enough) it tastes great on its own. If you have extra, pour yourself half a glass, squeeze in some lemon juice, and enjoy it straight up.

These two recipes—the soup and the crostini—work equally well separate or together. Feel free to make the soup or the crostini alone, but be assured they're a dynamic duo for a light lunch or an appetizer course. The crostini add a nice rustic touch, featuring an excellent, balanced trio of floral asparagus, mildly acidic tomatoes, and crumbly feta cheese.

PREPARE THE SOUP Place the spinach in a large skillet. Add salt and pepper and about 2 tablespoons of water. Cover tightly and steam over medium heat until the spinach wilts, about 5 minutes. Transfer the spinach to a bowl and reserve.

Place the oil in a large pot over medium-low heat. Add the onion, leek, celery, and parsnips, and sweat, stirring occasionally, until the vegetables are tender, about 20 minutes. Meanwhile, cut the tips from two bunches of the asparagus and reserve them to make the crostini (recipe follows). Chop the asparagus stalks, discarding the tough bottom ends. Add the chopped asparagus stalks to the pot and cook until tender, about 15 minutes. Add 2 cups of water and the stock and bring to a simmer. Season the soup with salt and pepper, and simmer over medium-low heat another 15 minutes. Allow the soup to cool for easier handling, then purée it in a blender in two batches, adding half the spinach, cilantro, and parsley to each batch. Allow the soup to cool to room temperature, then cover and refrigerate until ready to serve. (You can also serve the soup hot, in which case skip this step.)

PREPARE THE ASPARAGUS JUICE Trim the tough ends from the remaining 2 bunches of asparagus. Chop the stalks and tips, and purée them in a blender with 1¾ cups of water. Pass the puréed asparagus through a fine strainer and reserve the strained juice in the refrigerator until ready to serve.

FINISH AND SERVE Place the soup in a large saucepot over medium heat. Stir in the asparagus juice and bring the soup to a simmer. Ladle equal portions into each of six bowls and serve.

TOMATO-ASPARAGUS CROSTINI

MAKES 12 CROSTINI

- **1 cup reserved asparagus tips (set aside while making the soup)**
- **¼ cup crumbled feta cheese**
- **¼ cup chopped Tomato Confit (page 265)**
- **1½ cups torn basil leaves**
- **Cracked black pepper to taste**
- **1 baguette**
- **1 ripe Roma or plum tomato, halved and seeded**
- **¼ cup high-quality extra-virgin olive oil**

Preheat the oven to 350°F.

Bring a medium pot of salted water to a boil and prepare an ice-water bath with salted water. Drop the reserved asparagus tips in and cook until bright green and tender, about 1 minute. Remove the tips from the pot and plunge them into the salted ice water. Drain the asparagus and combine it in a mixing bowl with the feta, tomato confit, basil, and pepper.

Cut the baguette into 12 slices, each about ½ inch thick. Place the slices on a baking sheet and toast in the oven until lightly browned, 5 to 10 minutes per side. Rub each toasted slice of baguette with a tomato half and brush with olive oil before spreading a small amount of the topping on each. If serving the crostini with the soup, arrange two alongside each bowl.

WHITE ASPARAGUS

TOWN

Braised White Asparagus with Blood Orange Sauce

SERVES 6

- 3 pounds thick white asparagus spears
- 1 to 2 cups Chicken Stock (page 262, or low-sodium canned)
- 3½ tablespoons salted butter
- ½ teaspoon sea salt, plus more to taste
- ½ teaspoon freshly ground black pepper, plus more to taste
- 1 bay leaf, fresh or dried
- 1 cup fresh blood orange juice (4 to 8 oranges) plus 2 blood oranges for garnish
- 1 to 2 tablespoons extra-virgin olive oil

Diners at Town go gaga over this beautiful dish, and so will your dinner guests: it is the epitome of simplicity, elegance, and sophistication. Large white asparagus are generally available some time between February and June, depending on your location, climate, and seasonal weather. They have a tendency to be tough and stringy, which is why they respond so well to this braising treatment. Since they have no chlorophyll (the green stuff), they lack the grassy flavors of green asparagus, which for me is part of their charm. I love their earthy, slightly pungent flavor and mildly bitter aftertaste—qualities that go perfectly with the sweetness of the blood orange sauce in this recipe.

Cedric Tovar, who worked as one of my chefs at Town and is now at Django (also in New York City), showed me his technique for braising white asparagus in chicken stock. Whenever the first good fresh white asparagus arrived in February, they'd go straight into the pan, and our experiments led to this recipe.

Snap off the tough ends of the asparagus spears and peel the stalks with a vegetable peeler or paring knife. Trim off the tough triangular tip leaves. Place the spears in a single layer in a heavy skillet. Add enough stock to come about halfway up the sides of the spears. Add 2 tablespoons of the butter, season with the salt and pepper, and place the bay leaf on top. Cover the pan, bring to a simmer, and cook over medium heat until the spears are very tender, about 8 minutes.

Meanwhile, place the blood orange juice in a small, nonreactive saucepan and simmer over medium heat until reduced by half, about 4 minutes. Whisk in the remaining 1½ tablespoons butter. Season the sauce lightly with salt and pepper and set aside.

Peel the two oranges and remove all the pith. Divide the oranges into segments and reserve.

Drain the asparagus well and arrange equal portions of it on each of six plates. Spoon the blood orange sauce onto the plates around the spears. Drizzle the asparagus with oil, allowing some droplets to fall into the sauce. Season with salt and pepper to taste, arrange two or three orange segments on top of each portion of asparagus, and serve.

WHITE ASPARAGUS

Country

White Asparagus and Porcini Salad

SERVES 6

2 pounds medium-thick white asparagus

Fine sea salt

5 tablespoons extra-virgin olive oil

3 large fresh porcini or 6 large cremini mushrooms (6 to 8 ounces total weight)

1¼ cups loosely packed baby arugula or mâche lettuce, rinsed and dried

4½ tablespoons lemon juice (about 1½ lemons)

Freshly ground black pepper to taste

3 tablespoons hazelnut oil or porcini oil

Chunk of Parmigiano-Reggiano (about ½ pound), for garnish

If ever there was a happy couple blissfully enwrapped in a blanket of comforting earthy flavors, white asparagus and porcini are it. Fresh porcini are meaty and firm enough so you can slice them very thinly to serve raw in a salad like this. There's almost no cooking involved; in fact, I think this is my favorite don't-like-to-cook recipe, so if you're not in the mood tonight, this is a great solution. The slight bitterness of the baby arugula, the fruity complexity of a good extra-virgin olive oil, and the sea salt all work together to bring out the subtle taste of the porcini.

INGREDIENT NOTE Porcini can empty your wallet fast, so if you want to economize a bit, cremini are an excellent substitute; there isn't much lost in terms of flavor, although porcini are definitely more suave and sophisticated.

Snap off the tough ends of the white asparagus spears and peel them with a vegetable peeler or paring knife. Cut off the tough triangular tip leaves. Meanwhile, bring a large pot of salted water to a boil over high heat. Reduce the heat to medium, add the asparagus, and simmer until tender, about 7 minutes. Drain the asparagus and blot dry with paper towels. Arrange the asparagus on a plate, drizzle with about 3 tablespoons of the olive oil, and refrigerate until shortly before serving.

Just before serving, wipe the mushrooms clean with a damp paper towel. Peel the stems (omit this step if using cremini), trim the ends, and slice very thin lengthwise.

Place the arugula in a large bowl. Dress the salad with 2 tablespoons of the lemon juice and the remaining 3 tablespoons olive oil. Season with salt and pepper. Toss again.

Place equal portions of the asparagus spears on each of six plates. Arrange mushroom slices across the asparagus. Season the mushrooms and asparagus with salt and pepper to taste, then drizzle with hazelnut or porcini oil and the remaining 2½ tablespoons of lemon juice. Put a cluster of arugula or mâche on top of the mushrooms. Using a vegetable peeler, shave some Parmesan over each salad, and serve.

BLACK BEANS

TOWN

Black Bean Soup with Vin Jaune and Hazelnuts

SERVES 6 (MAKES 2½ QUARTS)

1 pound dried black beans

6 ounces serrano ham, in one piece

1 tablespoon extra-virgin olive oil

1½ cups sliced sweet onions, such as Vidalia (1 medium onion)

3 cloves garlic, minced

1 cup roughly chopped carrots (2 medium carrots)

1 cup roughly chopped celery (2 medium stalks)

2 tablespoons smoked or sweet paprika

1 teaspoon freshly ground black pepper

1 tablespoon kosher salt

1 large smoked ham hock (2 to 3 pounds)

2 teaspoons dried crumbled sage

2 teaspoons dried marjoram

1 fresh bay leaf

⅓ cup crème fraîche

2 tablespoons hazelnut oil

⅓ cup vin jaune or fino sherry

12 piquillo peppers, canned or dried (see instructions for skinning, opposite) finely diced

½ cup finely chopped toasted hazelnuts

¼ cup finely chopped flat-leaf parsley

My feeling is that if you want to measure up as a chef, you need a great recipe for black bean soup. I learned the rudiments when I was a student at the Culinary Institute of America, but I decided right then that I wanted to build a better black bean soup some day. Here it is.

INGREDIENT NOTES *Vin jaune* is a sherrylike wine from the Jura mountains of eastern France with a lovely, moderately sweet nuttiness. Fino sherry is an acceptable substitute.

Piquillos are Spanish red peppers, sweet and subtly smoky. It's easiest and best to use the canned ones, but you can prepare your own (see opposite).

Preheat the oven to 350°F.

Place the beans in a large pot with enough water to cover by several inches, about 6 cups. Bring the water to a boil over medium heat, then reduce the heat and simmer the beans until slightly soft, 15 minutes. Skim off any foam that rises to the surface. Drain the beans and reserve.

Meanwhile, cut the serrano ham into ¼-inch cubes. Place the olive oil in a large pot over medium heat. Add the ham and cook for about 5 minutes, rendering as much fat as possible. Add the onions and sweat, stirring occasionally, until they are translucent, about 15 minutes. Add the garlic, carrots, and celery, and cook, stirring frequently, until the garlic is tender and the rest of the vegetables begin to soften slightly, about 3 minutes more. Stir in the paprika and black pepper, cook for 1 minute, then add 2½ quarts (10 cups) of cold water. Raise the heat to high and bring the liquid to a boil. Add the reserved beans, salt to taste, the ham hock, sage, marjoram, and bay leaf.

Cover the pot and place it in the preheated oven (or simmer slowly on the stovetop) until the beans are very soft, the ham hock is pulling away from the bone, and the liquid is reduced by almost one third, about 4 hours.

Remove the ham hock, and reserve; remove the bay leaf. Purée the soup in a blender. (If it is too thick, thin it with a little water.) Season to taste with additional salt and pepper. Reheat the soup over medium flame. Dice the ham hock to use as a garnish. Finish the soup with crème fraîche, hazelnut oil, and vin jaune. Ladle hot into bowls, garnish with diced piquillo peppers and diced ham hock, sprinkle with finely chopped toasted hazelnuts and parsley, and serve.

BLACK BEANS

Country

Truffled Black Beans

SERVES 6 TO 8

2 slices bacon

1 medium carrot, halved

½ medium yellow onion

1 stalk celery

4 cloves garlic, crushed

1 pound dried black beans, soaked overnight in advance and thoroughly drained

2 dried bay leaves

1 sprig thyme

1 quart Chicken Stock (page 262, or low-sodium canned)

Kosher salt and freshly ground black pepper to taste

2½ teaspoons black truffle oil, or to taste

2 teaspoons Chardonnay (or other white wine) vinegar

I love black beans because they offer a big, bold, earthy flavor and a satisfying meaty texture. In this dish, I simmer them carefully to bring out the earthiness, purée them to enhance their richness, and then accent those qualities with a fine white wine vinegar and some black truffle oil. This is an intensely flavored, complete side dish. It goes equally well with poultry—roasted chicken or Cornish hens—and steamed or roasted fish, as in a nice thick fillet of cod or halibut presented on a bed of this purée.

Place the bacon in a 3- or 4-quart saucepot over medium heat and cook until the fat is rendered, about 7 minutes. Add the carrot, onion, celery, and garlic. Cook, stirring occasionally, until the vegetables are golden, about 10 minutes. Add the beans, bay leaves, thyme, stock, and 4 cups of water, and bring to a simmer over medium-high heat. Reduce the heat to medium-low and simmer until the beans are tender, about 40 minutes.

Drain the beans, reserving the cooking liquid. Remove and discard the bacon, herbs, and vegetables. Transfer 3 cups of the beans to a blender or food processor and put the rest of the beans back in the pot. Add ½ cup of the reserved cooking liquid to the blender or processor, and purée. Season the purée with salt and pepper to taste and stir it into the beans in the pot. Season with the truffle oil, vinegar, and additional salt and pepper to taste. Reheat over a low flame and serve warm with grilled or poached fish or meat.

INSTRUCTIONS FOR SKINNING DRIED PIQUILLO PEPPERS

Blanch and steep peppers in hot fat (350°F.) for 2 minutes, or until skin blisters. Remove from the fat and place in a bowl. Cover with plastic wrap and allow to cool for 20 to 30 minutes. Remove the plastic wrap. Slice the peppers open and lay peppers flat, skin side down, on your work surface. Remove seeds and pith, then turn peppers over and scrape off skin with a small sharp knife.

GREEN BEANS

TOWN

Green Bean Ragoût with Lamb and Basil

SERVES 4 TO 6 (MAKES 2 QUARTS)

- 1 tablespoon vegetable oil
- 1 pound lamb stew meat (breast or shoulder), on the bone
- 2 pounds green beans, tough ends trimmed off
- 1/4 pound smoked slab bacon, diced into 1/4-inch pieces
- 1 large white onion, finely chopped
- 2 cloves garlic, minced
- 1 cup verjus or unsweetened white grape juice
- 5 medium tomatoes, peeled, seeded, and chopped, or 2 16-ounce cans diced or crushed tomatoes
- 1 cinnamon stick
- About 3 cups Chicken Stock (page 262, or low-sodium canned, or water)
- Kosher salt and freshly ground black pepper to taste
- 4 tablespoons (1/2 stick) unsalted butter, at room temperature (optional)
- 1/2 cup roughly chopped fresh basil leaves
- 1/2 cup roughly chopped fresh cilantro leaves

If everybody has a memory of their grandma's cooking, this is mine. My father's mom, Azniv Zakarian, bless her soul, made a traditional Armenian peasant dish like this; she taught it to her daughters—my aunts—and they made it regularly for years, filling the kitchen with fabulous aromas of cinnamon and browning meat.

Ragoût is a French term applied to a wide range of stews featuring meats, fish, or vegetables. It comes from the verb *ragoûter,* which means to stimulate an appetite, so naturally ragoûts almost always appear as first courses or appetizers. Ragoûts often feature vegetables that are browned and then stewed in broth with herbs and tomatoes. This one deviates from the norm with a touch of "exotic" spice (the cinnamon) and with the fresh herbs added as a garnish. It also benefits from the hearty flavors of the meats—bacon and lamb—but without their heaviness in the final presentation. (If you like, you can prepare a rustic version by leaving the lamb meat and bacon in.)

INGREDIENT NOTES Standard green beans work well for this recipe. But even better are the less-common yellow wax beans, which react well to the braising treatment.

You can use any good unsweetened white grape juice but *verjus*—the French kind—is preferable.

TIMING NOTE The recipe is best when prepared a day in advance, allowed to cool, then refrigerated, so all the flavors have a chance to meld.

Preheat the oven to 375°F.

Place the oil in a large Dutch oven or ovenproof skillet over medium heat. When the oil is hot, add the lamb and beans, and cook, stirring frequently, until they are browned, about 10 minutes. Using a slotted spoon, transfer the beans and lamb to a bowl. Add the bacon to the pan and cook until the fat is rendered, about 5 minutes. Add the onion and cook, stirring occasionally, until soft and beginning to color, about 10 minutes. Add the garlic and cook until fragrant, about 2 minutes. Pour in the verjus and simmer until the pan is almost dry, about 5 minutes. Add the tomatoes and cinnamon, and cook for an additional 5 minutes.

Return the beans and lamb to the pan. Add enough stock to barely cover the beans, and season generously with salt and pepper. Bring the liquid to a simmer, cover the pan, and place it in the oven for 1 hour.

Remove the pan from the oven and allow the ragoût to rest at room temperature for 2 hours. When it is completely cooled, discard the cinnamon. Using a slotted spoon, transfer the beans, lamb, and bacon to a bowl or other storage container. Bring the braising liquid to a simmer and reduce by about half, 10 to 15 minutes. Pour the liquid over the beans, cover, and refrigerate overnight. (Alternatively, skip this step and simply proceed to the serving stage after cooling.)

Remove the lamb and bacon from the beans (optional). Bring the ragoût to a gentle simmer over medium-low heat. Swirl in the butter if using, spoon equal portions of the ragoût into shallow bowls, top each portion with a generous amount of basil and cilantro, and serve.

Country
Salad of Haricots Verts with Walnuts and Crème Fraîche

SERVES 6

1 pound haricots verts, trimmed

½ cup crème fraîche

1 tablespoon high-quality red wine vinegar

Juice of 1 lemon

Fine sea salt and freshly ground black pepper to taste

½ cup walnut halves, lightly toasted and roughly chopped

3 small Roma or plum tomatoes, peeled, seeded, and diced into ¼-inch cubes

4 cups cleaned and torn Bibb lettuce or mixed baby greens

1 tablespoon extra-virgin olive oil or black truffle oil

12 small purple or green basil leaves

¼ cup chopped chives, cut in ¾-inch pieces

1 cup freshly shaved Parmigiano-Reggiano

This recipe beautifully illustrates the notion that a simple preparation of a few fresh, seasonal ingredients, thoughtfully assembled and combined, can bring us pretty close to culinary nirvana. I first encountered a version of this salad when I worked in the kitchen of Chef Jacques Maximin at the Hôtel Negresco in Nice in the mid-1980s. Maximin was the first Michelin three-star chef I had the pleasure of working under; he would wear Hawaiian shorts with his chef's jacket and toque, and bark orders, a glass of Champagne in one hand and a cigarette dangling from his mouth. I thought, if all three-star chefs are like this guy, it's going to be a fun ride.

INGREDIENT NOTE Traditional crème fraîche is full-fat cream from unpasteurized milk that has fermented just slightly to give it a hint of tang and a thick, smooth texture; in modern dairy production, crème fraîche can be produced from pasteurized milk by introducing a specialized bacterial culture. In either case, it's somewhere between fresh cream and sour cream, and it demonstrates a marvelous ability to coat the beans, and balance and distribute all the other flavors in this salad.

Bring a large pot of salted water to a boil over high heat. Plunge the haricots verts into the boiling water and blanch until al dente, about 4 minutes, depending on how thick the beans are. (They should turn out somewhat tender but still chewy.) Drain the haricots verts in a colander, refresh them under cold, running water, and set aside.

In a small bowl, combine the crème fraîche, vinegar, and lemon juice and mix well. Season liberally with salt and pepper. (The dressing and the haricots verts can be prepared several hours in advance and refrigerated until ready to use.)

About 5 minutes before serving, combine the blanched haricots verts with the dressing. Add the walnuts and about three-fourths of the diced tomatoes, mix gently, and refrigerate.

Meanwhile, place the greens in a large mixing bowl with the oil. Season with salt and pepper to taste, and toss gently to combine. Place equal portions of greens on each of six salad plates. Mound the haricots verts on the greens. Garnish with basil leaves, chives, shaved Parmigiano-Reggiano, and the remaining diced tomatoes, and serve.

TOWN

Ribeye Steaks with Wilted Watercress and Romaine Marmalade

SERVES 6

FOR THE ROMAINE MARMALADE AND WATERCRESS (MAKES ABOUT 2 CUPS)

1 small clove garlic

¼ bunch of cilantro, trimmed

¼ bunch of flat-leaf parsley, trimmed

2 whole leaves romaine lettuce

2 tablespoons extra-virgin olive oil

Fine sea salt and freshly ground black pepper to taste

Fresh lemon juice to taste

4 bunches of organic watercress, stems removed (about 2 cups of leaves)

FOR THE STEAKS

4 8-ounce prime dry-aged bone-in ribeye steaks (each cut about ½ inch thick)

1 teaspoon kosher salt

½ teaspoon freshly ground black pepper

4 tablespoons extra-virgin olive oil

8 cloves garlic, lightly crushed

8 sprigs thyme

4 tablespoons salted butter

When I was developing the menu for Restaurant 44 at the Royalton Hotel in the late 1980s, I wanted a beef dish with a stimulating combination of two different flavors and textures in one dish. So I combined these steaks with Spiced Short Ribs (see page 50), serving both cuts side by side, arranged on the plate next to a large dollop of the "marmalade." For the combo, the ribs are made a day in advance, then spiced and browned while the steak is cooking. It's a dynamite one-two punch, appropriate for a festive occasion when you don't mind making the extra effort to put together a multistep meal.

INGREDIENT NOTE Ribeye is the ultimate steak: it has the fat and the flavor to outdo pretty much any other fine cut of beef. One whole steak is really too much for one person, though, so a good solution is to split it by serving slices. Pan-frying the steaks in two stages—first browning them over high heat, then basting them over reduced heat—is the best and easiest method to ensure they're cooked to your exact doneness preference. (Just make sure they're well browned in the first stage, then check carefully so as not to overcook them in the second. Remember to remove the steaks from the pan slightly underdone, since they'll cook a bit more when resting.) Regardless of the complexity of a recipe, it's always crucial to start with the best cuts of beef available; I recommend dry-aged steaks from a top producer such as Niman Ranch.

PREPARE THE ROMAINE MARMALADE AND WATERCRESS Preheat the oven to 350°F.

In a blender or food processor, combine the garlic, cilantro, parsley, and romaine. Add the oil, and purée until smooth. Season with salt, pepper, and lemon juice to taste, and set aside.

Place the watercress leaves in a large ovenproof skillet. Dress them with about half the romaine purée (the remainder can be refrigerated and used later to garnish other meat dishes or spread on toasts to make bruschetta). Season with additional salt and pepper to taste and place the pan in the oven, stirring once or twice, until the watercress begins to wilt, about 8 minutes. Remove from the oven, cover, and reserve in a warm place.

COOK THE STEAKS Season the steaks with the salt and pepper. Heat two large skillets over a high flame (alternatively cook the steaks in batches). Place 1 to 2 tablespoons of oil in each pan, so the pans are just filmed with oil. Sear the steaks until well browned, about 3 minutes per side. Reduce the heat to medium-low. Divide the garlic, thyme, and butter among the pans and cook, basting the steaks with the browning butter, until done to your liking (about 3 minutes for medium-rare). Transfer the steaks to a plate, cover loosely with aluminum foil, and set aside to rest for at least 7 minutes. Keep the garlic and thyme in browned butter warm at the back of the stove.

Slice each steak into three thick, equal-size portions. Spoon equal portions of the wilted watercress–romaine purée mixture onto each of six warm plates. Arrange the sliced steak on each plate. Strain the steak pan juices and pour them on top of the meat. Garnish each plate with the garlic and thyme from the steak pan, and serve.

Country
Grilled Flank Steak with Smoked Barbecue Sauce

SERVES 8

2 cloves garlic, minced

1 tablespoon chopped flat-leaf parsley

1 teaspoon celery salt

2 tablespoons extra-virgin olive oil, plus additional for oiling the rack and drizzling

1 teaspoon cracked black pepper

1 teaspoon sugar

1 teaspoon cayenne pepper

4 pounds flank steak (2 steaks)

Smoked Barbecue Sauce (recipe follows)

6 large tomatoes, peeled, seeded, and cut into ½-inch chunks

Kosher salt

6 slices crusty peasant bread

Flank steak is an inexpensive cut from the underside of the animal, below the loin, traditionally used for London broil. Growing up in a working-class family that didn't have a lot of money for fancy cuts, I learned to eat—and love—the tougher, fattier ones. The flank is firm-textured, layered, and lean, so it calls for some marinating and a relatively gentle cooking process—not the kind of blasting with heat or flame-grilling you'll find it often receives. In this recipe, both the marinade and the barbecue sauce are vehicles for getting the most out of this cut. The sauce is made with a nod to Chef Bobby Flay, who makes a kicking barbecue sauce. It's best if prepared the night before, and can be frozen and used later to brush on any number of grilled meats, including burgers; I also use it with grilled corn on the cob.

MARINATE THE STEAKS, 6 HOURS IN ADVANCE In a small mixing bowl, combine the garlic, parsley, celery salt, 2 tablespoons oil, black pepper, sugar, and cayenne. Rub the mixture all over the flank steaks. Place the steaks in a nonreactive dish and cover with plastic wrap, or in a large resealable plastic bag, and refrigerate for 6 hours.

COOK THE STEAKS Remove the flank steaks and the barbecue sauce from the fridge and allow them to come to room temperature. Prepare a charcoal fire in an outdoor grill. The fire is ready when the coals have burned down so they are grayish white on the outside and glowing hot on the inside; you should be able to hold your hand flat 5 inches above the grill for no more than 5 seconds. If you can hold it there longer, the fire isn't hot enough. (Alternatively, set the burners on a gas grill to medium-high, or use a large cast-iron skillet or griddle pan over medium-high heat, and proceed with grilling instructions.)

Place the tomato chunks in a mixing bowl, drizzle with olive oil, season generously with salt, and toss gently to combine, then set aside. Lightly oil the grill rack. Grill the flank steak until medium-rare, about 5 minutes per side, brushing the steak with the barbecue sauce when it is turned. Transfer the steak to a large platter, brush it generously with more barbecue sauce, and allow it to rest for 5 minutes.

While the steak is resting, lightly brush the slices of bread with oil and grill them until toasted. Slice the steak into ¼-inch-thick pieces across the grain on an angle and serve with the grilled country bread, tomato chunks, and extra barbecue sauce on the side.

SMOKED BARBECUE SAUCE

MAKES ABOUT 3 CUPS

2½ teaspoons dark molasses

2 tablespoons soy sauce

¼ cup Worcestershire sauce

½ cup red wine vinegar

½ cup rice wine vinegar

1½ teaspoons smoked paprika

1 quart orange juice (preferably fresh)

1 cup White Beef Stock (page 261, or low-sodium canned)

1 cup ketchup

In a large nonreactive saucepot, combine the molasses, soy sauce, Worcestershire sauce, red wine vinegar, rice wine vinegar, paprika, and orange juice. Bring to a slow, steady boil over medium-high heat, and cook until reduced by at least half or until slightly syrupy, about 20 minutes. Add the stock and ketchup, and reduce by half again, about 15 minutes. Pass the sauce through a strainer into a storage container. Allow to cool to room temperature, cover, and refrigerate until ready to use.

TOWN

Spiced Short Ribs with Mashed Potatoes

SERVES 6

- 4 tablespoons extra-virgin olive oil
- 3 white onions, cut into eighths
- 4 medium carrots, cut into thick slices
- 2 large leeks, washed thoroughly and cut into thick slices
- 2½ teaspoons kosher salt
- 4 heads of garlic, halved crosswise
- 3½ tablespoons coriander seeds
- 2 tablespoons black peppercorns
- 1 bunch of thyme (about 12 sprigs)
- 8 sprigs rosemary
- 2 fresh bay leaves
- 6 thick center-cut short ribs, bone-in, each about ¾ pound
- 3 tablespoons celery salt
- 3 tablespoons Aleppo pepper flakes, or other hot red pepper
- 4 allspice berries
- 4½ tablespoons cumin seed
- 4 tablespoons unsalted butter

Ribs are one of those traditional inexpensive cuts that have been "discovered" by restaurant chefs over the past decade. But no matter how you dress them up, they're just a wonderful, fundamental comfort food. Short ribs take a little more time and effort to coax to their peak flavor and texture, but once you do they're luxurious and meltingly tender. In this recipe, I gussy up the braised ribs by spicing, slicing, and browning them. Feel free to take the shortcut, however, and serve them with nothing more than a sauce of their braising liquid, reduced to your liking, and some mashed potatoes on the side.

INGREDIENT NOTE Dried Aleppo peppers are a naturally sun-dried red pepper from the area around the town of the same name in Syria; they're available from Kalustyan's (see "Sources and Resources," page 266).

PREPARE THE SHORT RIBS, 1 DAY IN ADVANCE Preheat the oven to 375°F.

Place 2 tablespoons of the olive oil in an ovenproof skillet or Dutch oven large enough to hold the ribs in a single layer over medium heat. When the oil is hot but not smoking, add the onions, carrots, leeks, and 1 teaspoon of the salt. Cook, stirring occasionally, until the vegetables are soft, about 15 minutes. Add the garlic, 2 tablespoons of the coriander seeds, the peppercorns, thyme, rosemary, and bay leaves.

Season the short ribs with 1 teaspoon of the salt and add them to the pan. Pour in enough water to just cover the ribs (about 2 quarts) and bring to a simmer. Transfer the pan to the oven. Simmer the ribs, turning them every 30 minutes, until they are very tender, about 2 hours. (You can take a shortcut from here and serve the ribs plain, on or off the bone, skipping the steps that follow. Simply allow the braising liquid to cool so the grease floats to the top; skim and discard the grease with a large spoon or ladle; place the degreased braising liquid in a saucepan over medium-high heat; bring it to a boil; and cook until it is reduced to your liking. Use the reduced braising liquid as a sauce for the ribs and potatoes.) Remove the pan from the oven and allow the ribs to cool in the braising liquid, strain to remove the vegetables, then cover and refrigerate, still in the braising liquid, overnight.

The next day, prepare the seasoning spice by grinding the remaining 1½ tablespoons coriander seeds with the celery salt, hot red pepper flakes, all-

spice, and cumin in a spice grinder or mortar. Place this spice mixture in a shallow bowl, wide dish, or large plate.

Skim and discard the congealed fat from on top of the braising liquid. Remove the short ribs from the liquid. Bring the liquid to a boil in a medium-sized saucepot over medium-high heat and cook until the liquid is reduced by half, about 10 minutes, to make a thickish sauce for the ribs.

Cut the meat from the bones. Pat the meat dry with a paper towel, then trim any excess fat or cartilage. Slice the ribs across the grain into 3/8-inch-thick medallions. Dredge each rib slice in the spice mix. Place the remaining 2 tablespoons of oil in a large skillet over medium-high heat. Season the spiced rib medallions with about 1/2 teaspoon salt. When the oil is hot but not smoking, add the ribs to the pan. Brown the meat for 1 to 2 minutes, then flip each piece and add the butter. Brown the other sides of the medallions, basting regularly. Transfer the medallions to a plate lined with paper towels to drain of excess oil and fat, then arrange them on warm dinner plates, and serve with mashed potatoes and 1 or 2 tablespoons of the reduced braising liquid.

MASHED POTATOES

Using the proper equipment and techniques is important—especially with basic dishes like this one. The best way to make a smooth purée of potatoes is by using a ricer. A potato masher works, too, but your potatoes will still have lumps. Electric food processors or food mills don't work because they develop the gluten too much, resulting in a gooey, sticky consistency. You can get away with using your electric mixer (on medium speed with the whisk attachment), but it's risky.

SERVES 6

2 pounds russet or Idaho (baking) potatoes

1/2 cup whole milk, plus more to taste

4 tablespoons (1/2 stick) unsalted butter, plus more to taste

Kosher salt and freshly ground black pepper to taste

Peel the potatoes and dice them into 1/2-inch cubes. Place them in a vegetable steamer over medium-high heat and steam until soft and tender, 15 to 20 minutes.

Meanwhile, warm the milk in a small saucepan over medium-low heat. When the potatoes are cooked, drain them and pass them through a ricer back into the steamer pot. Using a wooden spoon, gently stir in the butter and the warm milk until well incorporated. Season generously with salt and pepper, taste, and adjust seasoning. Add more milk if you want to dilute the purée; add more butter if you want to make it richer. Serve warm.

Country Burgers and Chips

SERVES 6

FOR THE BUTTERED CHIPS

- **3 medium russet, Idaho (baking) potatoes**
- **3 to 4 cups canola oil**
- **3 to 4 cups Clarified Butter (page 264)**
- **Fine sea salt**

FOR THE BURGERS

- **3 pounds organic prime ground beef chuck (preferably grass-fed)**
- **1 teaspoon kosher salt**
- **½ teaspoon freshly ground black pepper**
- **3 tablespoons salted butter**
- **1½ tablespoons chopped flat-leaf parsley**
- **6 English muffins (preferably Wolferman's)**
- **1 large beefsteak tomato, cut into 6 slices**
- **Gingered Coleslaw (page 67), for serving**

The beauty of a good hamburger is its simplicity and its powerful ability to satisfy our most primal cravings. I love burgers and I eat a lot of them. Quite a few of the chefs I've worked with scratch their heads and wonder why this guy, who fancies himself a gourmet chef and likes to update all these classic French dishes, is obsessed with the humble hamburger. Because I firmly believe that if a cook can make a good burger—if he or she can master this most elemental preparation—then all the rest will fall into place. (Roasting a chicken and making a vinaigrette are in the same category.)

A few keys to cooking a flawless burger: Be sure the meat is somewhat coarsely ground. Make the patties firm but don't squeeze them too hard—and certainly don't ever press them down on the grill. Make sure your grill rack is clean and lightly oiled. Never season the inside of a burger; at best, place a dab of parsley butter or garlic butter on top as it rests after cooking, then season it to taste with salt and pepper once it's on your plate. Use real charcoal—not briquettes—and let your fire burn down so all the coals are glowing very hot; there should never be any flames licking the grill. The fire is ready when you can bear to hold your hand flat 5 inches above the grill for just under 5 seconds; any longer and the fire isn't hot enough.

INGREDIENT NOTES I like a thin, crisp, toasted English muffin with my burger; it accentuates the flavor and texture of a thick, juicy burger. I highly recommend Wolferman's brand.

There are some pretty good chips—potato and other types—available in the markets; however, I invite you to embrace the pleasure and challenge of making your own buttered potato chips.

PREPARE THE BUTTERED CHIPS Peel the potatoes, then slice them paper thin (this is most easily done with a mandoline). Hold them in a large bowl of cold water to avoid discoloration. In a large, deep stockpot, combine the oil and clarified butter, and heat to 350°F. Check the temperature with a thermometer or drop a slice of potato into the oil; if it sizzles immediately, the oil is hot enough. (The chips can also be fried in an electric deep fryer.) Drain the potato slices well and pat them dry. (It is very important they are completely dry; otherwise, they can become soggy or mushy when cooked.) Working in batches and stirring frequently, fry the chips in the hot oil until crisp and golden brown. Drain the chips on a baking sheet lined with paper towels; season with the sea salt while still warm.

COOK THE BURGERS Prepare a charcoal grill and position the rack 4 inches above medium-high heat. Lightly oil the grill. Form the beef into 6 patties, and season on both sides with the salt and pepper. Cook the burgers, charring well on both sides, until almost but not quite done as desired, 3 to 4 minutes per side for medium-rare. (Gas grills may require 1 to 2 minutes more total cooking.) Transfer the burgers to a rack to rest for 5 minutes. Top each burger with about ½ tablespoon of butter and a sprinkling of chopped parsley. Meanwhile toast the English muffins on the grill.

Reheat the burgers on the grill for about 1 minute. Serve them on the toasted English muffins, topped with tomato slices, with the chips and coleslaw on the side.

BEEF

TOWN

Beef Mignonettes with Curried Peppercorn Cream

SERVES 4

- ¼ cup four-peppercorn mix
- 1 tablespoon kosher salt
- 8 1-inch-thick slices filet mignon (3½ to 4 ounces each), trimmed of excess fat
- 6 tablespoons extra-virgin olive oil
- 2 small shallots, minced
- 1 teaspoon Madras curry powder
- 1 cup full-bodied red wine (Bordeaux or zinfandel)
- 2 cups stock (preferably beef, but vegetable or chicken can be substituted)
- 1 tablespoon unsalted butter
- 2 tablespoons crème fraîche
- Fine sea salt and freshly ground black pepper
- 2 tablespoons julienned fresh mint leaves (cut into thin strips)

This one-pan recipe is the ideal solution for a quick Friday night dinner. It's a great way to introduce a level of sophistication and elegance into a meal with minimal complications. And whoever came up with the idea of combining beef, cream, peppercorns, and brandy—essentially a flourish on the classic *steak au poivre*—was a kitchen Einstein. The thin slices of filet mignon—*mignonettes*—don't require a great deal of cooking or seasoning. Serve this with a big Bordeaux or some other assertive red wine and perhaps some lightly buttered, steamed haricots verts (thin French-style green beans). For an extra flavor kick, try adding sautéed mushrooms to the sauce.

INGREDIENT NOTE Four-peppercorn mix (black, white, green, and pink) can be bought at most gourmet grocery stores. Or you can put together your own mix. Regarding the peppercorn types, the more the merrier.

Crack the peppercorns (this is most easily done by putting them in a plastic bag and crushing them with a rolling pin). Combine them with the salt in a shallow bowl. Roll the filets in the mixture to lightly coat them. Place 2 tablespoons of the oil in a large sauté pan over medium-high heat. When the oil is hot, add four of the filets and cook them for 2 minutes per side. Transfer the filets to a large plate and reserve in a warm place. Wipe out the pan and repeat the process, cooking the remaining filets in 2 more tablespoons of oil.

Wipe out the pan. Add the remaining 2 tablespoons of oil to the pan over medium heat. Add the shallots and cook until they soften slightly, 1 to 2 minutes. Add the curry powder. Cook, stirring, until the shallots are tender and the curry aromatic, about 1 minute more. Add the wine, raise the heat to medium-high, and cook until syrupy, about 4 minutes. Add the stock and cook until reduced by half, about 10 minutes. Remove the pan from the heat and swirl in the butter and crème fraîche. Reduce the heat to low, and return the filets to the pan until just heated through. Season to taste with salt and pepper. Place two filets on each of four warm dinner plates, pour equal portions of sauce on top, and serve with generous sprinklings of fresh mint as a garnish.

Country

Beef Tenderloin with Bacon and Creamed Leeks

SERVES 4

- **6 slices thick-cut bacon (6 ounces)**
- **3 tablespoons unsalted butter**
- **6 large leeks, white and light green parts, halved lengthwise, thoroughly rinsed, and cut crosswise into 1-inch sections**
- **1/4 cup crème fraîche or sour cream**
- **Kosher salt and freshly ground black pepper**
- **1 2-pound center-cut beef tenderloin (7 to 10 inches long), trimmed and tied**
- **3 tablespoons extra-virgin olive oil**
- **16 cloves garlic**
- **8 sprigs thyme**
- **1 cup Chicken Stock (page 262, or low-sodium canned)**

Americans are hooked on meat that's fork-tender, so with a cut called "tenderloin" that's naturally what they expect. But in fact the tenderloin—unlike the fattier cuts such as ribeye or sirloin—is a relatively dense, lean piece of meat. Therefore, it benefits greatly from the "fattening up" treatment in this recipe. I first encountered a version of this dish way back in 1982 on one of my European adventures. I went to visit a Belgian girl I had met in her hometown of Brussels; she took me out to dinner and I fell in love with this dish. The girl is ancient history, but the dish is still with me. When you sweat the leeks in a covered pan, they release all their delicious sugars and liquids, and attain a luxuriously smooth consistency, ideal for soaking up the cream and bacon. (The leeks, prepared separately, also make an excellent side for grilled steaks or lamb chops, or a roasted chicken.) I suggest you uncork a bottle of a big, toothsome California cabernet to highlight the hearty, earthy flavors of this roast.

INGREDIENT NOTE For this recipe, try to use the middle section of the tenderloin. The "head" of the tenderloin, called a *châteaubriand,* is much wider and thicker. From there, the tenderloin tapers down to a much thinner tail. Since the thickness of the meat largely determines doneness, it's much better to use the center section, which is a more uniform shape and size. Have your butcher trim and tie the cut.

PREPARE THE CREAMED LEEKS Place the bacon in a large skillet over medium-high heat and cook until it is brown and crisp, about 3 minutes per side. Transfer the bacon to paper towels to drain off excess fat. Cut the drained bacon into 1-inch sections.

Pour off all but 2 tablespoons of the bacon fat and place the skillet over medium heat. Add the butter and stir in the leeks. Cover the skillet with a sheet of wax paper and a tight-fitting lid and cook the leeks, stirring once or twice, until they are tender, about 8 minutes. Uncover the skillet, raise the heat to medium-high, and cook the leeks until they are lightly browned, about 2 minutes. Add the crème fraîche, season with salt and pepper to taste, and cook over low heat until the leaks are creamy and their sauce is thickened, 5 to 6 minutes more. Stir in the reserved bacon and set aside in a warm place until ready to serve.

ROAST THE TENDERLOIN Preheat the oven to 425°F.

Rub the tenderloin all over with 1 tablespoon of the oil, and season generously with salt and pepper. Place the remaining 2 tablespoons of oil in a medium roasting pan or ovenproof skillet over medium-high heat. When the oil begins to shimmer, place the tenderloin in the pan and cook until browned all over, about 7 minutes. Add the garlic and thyme, and cook for 1 minute more. Add ½ cup of the stock to the pan, stir with a wooden spoon to dislodge any brown bits stuck to the bottom, and transfer the pan to the oven. Roast the tenderloin for 5 minutes, then turn it over and add the remaining ½ cup of chicken stock. Roast the tenderloin for about 3 minutes more, then check for doneness; an instant-read thermometer inserted in the center should register 125°F. for medium-rare.

FINISH AND SERVE When the roast is done to your liking, transfer it to a cutting board, cover loosely with aluminum foil, and allow it to rest for 10 minutes. Then remove the strings and cut the roast into thick slices. Serve with the garlic and thyme sprigs from the pan as garnishes, and the creamed leeks on the side.

TOWN

Beet and Strawberry Risotto

SERVES 6 AS AN APPETIZER

2 medium beets, whole (skin on)

Kosher salt

¾ cup sherry vinegar

3½ tablespoons honey

3 shallots, minced

3 cups hulled and coarsely chopped strawberries (just under 1 pound)

2 tablespoons extra-virgin olive oil

½ small yellow onion, diced

1½ cups risotto rice, preferably carnaroli

1 cup dry white wine

1½ cups Chicken Stock (page 262, or low-sodium canned)

3 tablespoons unsalted butter

2 tablespoons crème fraîche

A very long time ago, in the enchanted countryside of northern Italy, I had a strawberry-beet risotto. In fact, it was so long ago the details escape me. But the flavor-memory never went away. So I did some research in old Italian cookbooks and eventually came up with this version, which has wowed many diners. Roasting the beets brings out their inherent sweetness; cooking the strawberries tones down some of their sweet fruitiness; and the twain meet somewhere in the middle to find balance and harmony. The honey-vinegar combination of the *gastrique* supports this harmony, contributing to the sweet-sour equilibrium. (*Gastrique* is a term from classic French cuisine for a vinegar-sugar solution that has been reduced, and is used for fruit-based sauces in dishes such as duck à l'orange.) This risotto can be served as a side dish to darker, gamier poultry meats—duck and grilled squab come to mind. But I prefer to eat it on its own.

INGREDIENT NOTE Of the three types of risotto rice—arborio, vialone nano, and carnaroli—the carnaroli is my favorite. Risotto rices are short-grained and starchy but firm enough to hold up to long, slow cooking in well-flavored broths and stocks. With proper cooking, they soak up the aromatics and present them in a succulent yet toothsome package. Carnaroli, a hybrid created in the mid–twentieth century, was designed to highlight these properties. If you can't find carnaroli, either of the other two varieties does a good job.

Preheat the oven to 375°F.

Cover a small roasting pan (a cake pan will work) with kosher salt to a depth of about ¼ inch. Place the beets on the salt and roast them in the oven until a paring knife stuck into one of them encounters no resistance, at least 1 hour. Remove the beets from the oven, allow them to cool, then peel and dice them.

PREPARE THE GASTRIQUE Place the vinegar, honey, and shallots in a small nonreactive saucepot over medium heat and simmer, stirring occasionally, until the mixture reduces by three quarters, about 7 minutes. Remove the pot from the heat and allow to cool.

Purée 2 cups of the strawberries in a blender, then set aside.

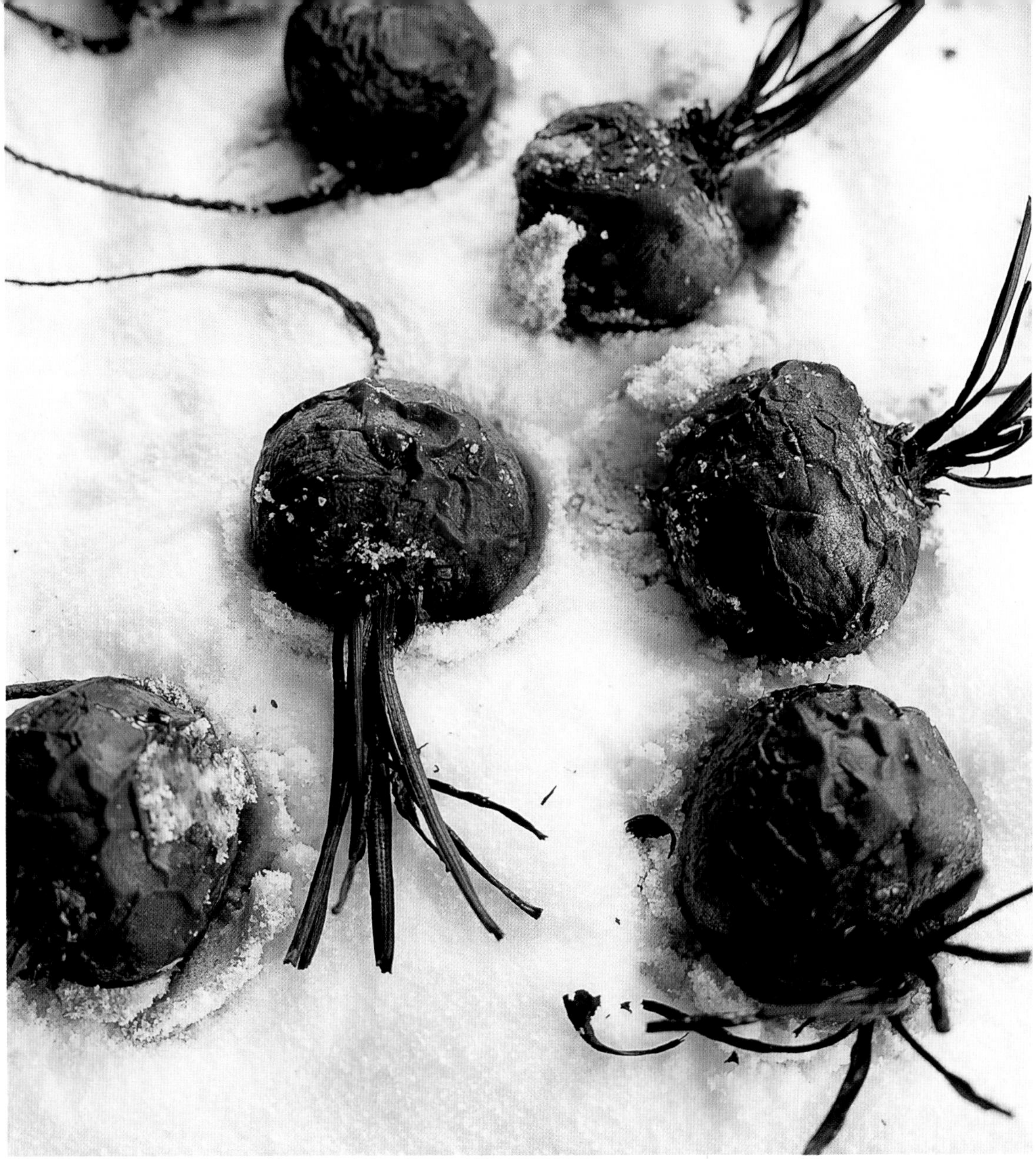

Place the oil in a medium skillet over medium heat. Add the onion and sweat until translucent, about 5 minutes. Add the rice and cook, stirring frequently with a wooden spoon, until it no longer appears chalky on the outside, about 3 minutes. Add the wine and simmer, stirring frequently and scraping the bottom of the pot with the spoon, until the rice has absorbed most of the wine, about 5 minutes. Add the stock and simmer, stirring, until the stock has largely been absorbed, about 7 minutes more. Stir in the reserved gastrique and the strawberry purée. Continue simmering and stirring until the rice is fluffy but still firm to the taste, about 3 minutes more. Add the remaining 1 cup of strawberries and the beets. Stir in the butter and crème fraîche and serve immediately.

BEETS

Country

Baked Beets over Salt

SERVES 8 AS A SIDE DISH

- **8 medium beets, washed but unpeeled**
- **1 pound kosher or coarse sea salt**
- **½ cup extra-virgin olive oil**
- **Leaves of 4 sprigs tarragon, chopped**
- **Juice of ½ lemon**
- **1 tablespoon cracked black pepper**

Since my mom's family was Polish, we ate a ton of beets. She roasted beets at least once a week and served them sliced or diced with a creamy vinaigrette, often on a bed of lettuce. I much prefer roasting the beets to the more traditional notion of boiling them. The boiled ones lose a lot of their color and vitamin content to the cooking water, while baking them on a bed of salt provides a stable temperature for thorough, even cooking. Once they've cooled enough to handle, you can peel them without much mess, then serve with steamed or roasted whole fish or chicken. Just a touch of lemon juice helps offset their emerging sweetness.

Beets are great family food because they possess two traits guaranteed to attract kids: bright color and sugar. They're healthy, but they practically taste like dessert. If you're in a hurry, you can microwave them: Simply peel and slice them thick, stack them in a microwaveable dish in overlapping pattern, add a little salt, pepper, and olive oil, and zap them on high for 4 to 5 minutes. Then give them the same treatment suggested here, or just add butter.

Preheat the oven to 375°F.

Cover a medium sheet pan with kosher salt to a depth of about ¼ inch. Place the beets on the salt, evenly spaced, and lightly drizzle with some of the oil. Place in the oven to bake for 30 minutes, or until done (check by inserting the tip of a sharp knife or a metal skewer into a beet; if you encounter no resistance, the beets are done).

Remove the beets from the oven, transfer to a platter, and allow to cool. Peel the beets by hand while still warm but easy to handle. Cut them in large chunks, place them in a bowl, sprinkle with tarragon, lemon juice, and olive oil to taste. Add a generous portion of cracked black pepper. Toss lightly and serve.

BROCCOLI

TOWN

Chilled Broccoli Soup

SERVES 4 TO 6

- 5 tablespoons salted butter
- 1 leek, white part only, washed thoroughly and sliced thin
- 3 heads of broccoli
- ½ teaspoon sea salt
- ½ teaspoon freshly ground black pepper
- 6 cups Chicken Stock (page 262, or low-sodium canned), warmed
- 1 cup coarsely chopped flat-leaf parsley (about ½ bunch)
- ¼ cup heavy cream
- 4 slices bacon, cut into lardons (thin crosswise lengths)
- 1 lemon

President George H. W. Bush used to say, "Luckily, the store ran out of broccoli," and in this view he faithfully represented many of his countrymen. Here's a recipe that might change even the former president's mind.

I think broccoli—in any form—tastes better served around room temperature or somewhat chilled, but certainly not piping hot. Serve this soup about 30 minutes after you take it out of the fridge; it should be noticeably below room temperature but climbing well above refrigerator temperature. Excess cold and hot have the same deadening effect on the taste buds.

Melt 3 tablespoons of the butter over medium-low heat in a large pot. Add the leek and cook, stirring occasionally, until soft, about 20 minutes.

Meanwhile, separate the florets from 2 of the heads of broccoli, reserving them for garnish. Chop the remaining broccoli florets and stems into small pieces. Add the chopped broccoli to the leeks. Season the vegetables with salt and pepper, then add the warm stock. Bring to a boil over medium-high heat, and simmer until the broccoli is tender, about 5 minutes. Add the parsley, remove the soup from the heat, and purée it in a blender or food processor. Stir in the cream, season with salt and pepper to taste, and pass the soup through a fine strainer. Allow to cool to room temperature, then refrigerate until shortly before serving.

Bring a medium pot of salted water to a boil. Prepare an ice bath. Blanch the reserved broccoli florets by plunging them into the boiling water for 1 to 2 minutes. Refresh the blanched florets in the ice bath. Melt the remaining 2 tablespoons of butter in a small skillet over medium heat. Allow the butter to brown slightly, then add the broccoli florets. Cook the broccoli in the browned butter for about 1 minute, then transfer to a container and refrigerate until ready to serve.

Render the bacon in a skillet over medium heat. When the bacon is crisp, after 5 to 7 minutes, remove it from the pan with a slotted spoon and transfer it to a plate lined with a paper towel to drain.

To serve, place equal portions of blanched broccoli florets in each of six chilled bowls. Ladle the soup into the bowls, sprinkle crispy bacon onto each serving, and squeeze a few drops of lemon juice into each bowl.

Country

Char-Grilled Broccoli with Pear-Curry Vinaigrette

SERVES 4

1 large head of broccoli

1 tablespoon extra-virgin olive oil

1 teaspoon kosher salt

1 teaspoon freshly ground black pepper

Freshly shaved Pecorino Romano, for garnish (optional)

FOR THE VINAIGRETTE (MAKES 1½ CUPS)

½ plus 1 tablespoon cup extra-virgin olive oil

¼ medium white onion, sliced thin

½ of a ripe skin-on pear, cored and sliced thin

1 teaspoon Madras curry powder

2 teaspoons kosher salt

1 teaspoon freshly ground black pepper, plus more to taste

2 tablespoons sherry vinegar

¼ cup dry white wine

½ cup unsweetened apple cider, plus additional as needed

Broccoli suffers greatly from the perception that it's "good for you" and not much else. This simple recipe transforms it into a delicious, sensually appealing dish that's great as an appetizer, salad, or side dish. Charring the florets brings the broccoli's flavors and aromas dramatically into focus. The florets should turn darkish brown in parts, but not black.

PREPARE THE BROCCOLI Bring a large pot of salted water to a boil over high heat. Cut off the stem of broccoli so as not to detach or separate the florets. Discard the stem. Plunge the head of broccoli into the boiling water and cook for about 30 seconds after the water returns to a boil. Drain the broccoli, then shock it under cold running water. Pat the broccoli dry with paper towels. Cut the head lengthwise into four equal-sized portions and set aside.

PREPARE THE VINAIGRETTE Heat 1 tablespoon of the oil in a medium saucepan over a medium flame. Add the onion, pear, and curry powder; season with the salt and pepper. Cook, stirring occasionally, until the onion is soft and translucent, about 10 minutes. Add the vinegar and white wine, and cook, still over medium heat, reducing the liquid until the pan is almost dry, about 10 minutes. Add the apple cider and simmer over low heat until the flavors blend, 5 minutes more. Place the contents of the pan in a blender and purée on medium speed for 1 minute. With the blender still running, add the ½ cup oil in a slow stream. The vinaigrette should be smooth and creamy; if necessary, thin it with additional apple cider. Season the vinaigrette with salt and pepper to taste, pass it through a fine strainer, and reserve at room temperature until ready to use.

FINISH AND ASSEMBLE Prepare a charcoal grill and position the rack 4 to 6 inches above medium-high heat. Place the quarters of broccoli head in a large mixing bowl along with 1 tablespoon of oil, the salt, and pepper; toss gently to coat the broccoli. Grill the broccoli for about 8 minutes, turning the pieces so they are lightly charred on all sides.

Pool about 3 tablespoons of the vinaigrette on each of four plates; place one portion of broccoli on each plate, and serve warm. As an optional garnish, shave some Pecorino Romano on top of each portion at the table.

CABBAGE

TOWN

Savoy Cabbage in Brodo Val D'Aosta

SERVES 4

- **1 savoy cabbage, halved and cored**
- **¼ pound pancetta or slab bacon, diced**
- **2 tablespoons extra-virgin olive oil**
- **2 teaspoons kosher salt**
- **1 teaspoon freshly ground black pepper**
- **8 slices crusty country bread, about ¾ inch thick**
- **1 large clove garlic, halved**
- **5½ cups Beef Consommé (page 261) or light beef stock or chicken stock**
- **¼ pound thinly sliced prosciutto**
- **Pinch of ground cinnamon**
- **Pinch of freshly ground nutmeg**
- **1 black truffle (optional)**
- **⅔ pound fontina, cut into 16 thin slices**
- **3 tablespoons julienned celery leaves (cut into thin strips)**
- **3 tablespoons finely diced, peeled, and seeded tomato**

Val D'Aosta is a spectacular area of the western Alps in northern Italy where cabbage-and-bread soup is a traditional dish. This is a jazzed-up version consisting of crostini made from cabbage, prosciutto, and the local fontina cheese resting in a bowl of delicate consommé—a sophisticated and elegant yet relatively uncomplicated presentation. You'll have fun constructing the crostini; once that's done, the dish is easy to put together. It's perfect for lunch or supper on a fall or winter afternoon. Serve it with a good bottle of lighter red wine, such as pinot noir or gamay (Beaujolais). The black truffle is an optional fancy garnish.

INGREDIENT NOTES Savoy is a lighter, milder cabbage variety, with subtle flavor and a nice ribbed texture, widely acknowledged as the "class act" of the cabbage family.

For the consommé, there are plenty of good options: I have no problem taking a shortcut with store-bought broths or consommés because there are so many good ones available these days—canned, frozen, and in cartons. Our Town recipe for White Beef Stock (page 261) works well for the broth here, but you can also take the extra step and make a clarified consommé (see page 261), adding further delicacy and sophistication to the preparation.

Wash the cabbage thoroughly, then dry. Remove the tough ribs, then tear the leaves into thirds. Place the pancetta and oil in a large skillet over medium heat. Cook, stirring occasionally, until the pancetta renders and begins to brown, about 5 minutes. Add the cabbage leaves and season with about 1 teaspoon salt and ½ teaspoon pepper. Reduce the heat to medium-low and cook, stirring frequently, until the cabbage is wilted and tender, about 7 minutes. Set aside.

Preheat the oven to 375°F.

Place the bread slices on a large sheet pan and toast in the oven until lightly browned on both sides, about 3 minutes. Place the toasted slices in a baking pan. Drizzle each slice with 1 to 2 tablespoons of consommé. Spoon a little of the cabbage and pancetta mixture onto each piece (you will ultimately be making two layers, so divide the mixture accordingly). Lay a piece of prosciutto on each mound of cabbage, then season with dustings of black pepper, cinnamon, and nutmeg. Using a very sharp knife, shave 16 very thin slices from the truffle (if using). Put one slice on top of each crouton, then top with a slice of cheese. Repeat the layers once more beginning with cabbage and ending with cheese.

Cover the baking pan loosely with aluminum foil. Bake the crostini until the cheese is melted and the cabbage is warmed through, about 30 minutes. Bring the remaining consommé to a boil over medium-high heat. Season with about 1 teaspoon salt and ½ teaspoon pepper, or to taste. Using a spatula, carefully place two crostini in each bowl. Julienne the remaining truffle (slice it into thin slivers) and drop a generous pinch in each bowl. Add equal portions of celery leaves and diced tomatoes to each bowl. Ladle equal portions of consommé into each bowl and serve immediately.

Country

Gingered Coleslaw with Golden Raisins

SERVES 6

1 small head of savoy cabbage, cored

1 large carrot

1 tablespoon finely minced ginger (1 1-inch piece)

1½ teaspoons finely minced garlic (1 small clove)

3 tablespoons Mayonnaise (page 264, or store-bought, preferably Hellman's)

1 tablespoon unsalted butter

¼ cup yellow raisins

1 tablespoon sherry vinegar

Fine sea salt, freshly ground black pepper, and sugar to taste

In the spirit of offering sophisticated variations on the classics, here is my favorite coleslaw—a recipe I'm sure you'll agree is as irresistibly delicious as it is simple to prepare. Due to my Polish roots, I had no choice but to learn to love cabbage at a young age; the trick is to find some flavors to counteract some of its sulfurous taste, which can wipe out your palate. In this case, it's the ginger.

This slaw goes best with a good burger (see page 52), but I also love it in a sandwich with sliced roasted turkey or leftover meat loaf, or as a side dish for scrambled eggs at brunch. It calls for savoy cabbage, which has more delicate leaves than your standard white or green cabbage yet is still plenty crisp. One of the great pitfalls of coleslaw is "soupiness," which is why it's important to use small amounts of vinegar and mayonnaise; and I also recommend making the slaw no more than 1 to 2 hours in advance—just long enough to chill it before serving.

INGREDIENT NOTE I'm a big fan of Hellman's mayonnaise—I think it's one of the best commonly available commercial prepared-food products. So feel free to make your own mayo or go ahead and buy a jar of Hellman's.

Shred the cabbage and julienne the carrot (cut it into thin slivers). Combine the cabbage and carrots in a bowl. Add the ginger, garlic, and mayonnaise, and mix well.

Heat the butter in a medium skillet over a medium flame. Add the raisins and cook until soft and golden brown, about 2 minutes. Add the warm raisins to the slaw, mix well, then season with the vinegar and salt, pepper, and sugar to taste. Cover and refrigerate until ready to serve.

CHEESE

TOWN

Aged Gouda with Maple-Apple Strudel

SERVES 6

FOR THE FILLING

2 tablespoons unsalted butter

2 cups diced Granny Smith apples (2 apples)

½ vanilla bean, split lengthwise

¼ teaspoon ground cinnamon

⅓ cup maple syrup

FOR THE PHYLLO WRAPPING

⅓ cup Clarified Butter (page 264), melted and cooled, or regular melted butter, plus additional for brushing the strudel

⅓ cup maple syrup

3 sheets phyllo dough

¾ tablespoon sugar

FOR THE CANDIED NUTS (OPTIONAL)

⅔ cup maple syrup

1 teaspoon pure vanilla extract

¼ cup brandy

1 teaspoon unsalted butter

1 cup roughly chopped toasted walnuts

FOR THE SAUCE

½ cup maple syrup

3 large egg yolks

Juice of 1 lemon

¾ pound aged Gouda

Cheese is one of the great marvels of the culinary universe, so why not give it an important role in your kitchen repertoire? At Town, we offer after-dinner cheeses and highlight each selection with a complementary recipe. For a home dinner party, you can get a lot of mileage from this approach. This marriage of strudel and aged Gouda—with its deep, caramel flavors—is a take-off on the classic apple pie–Cheddar pairing. I remember my mom served apple pie with melted Cheddar, which I thought was pretty weird when I was ten years old. (Like most kids, I wanted my pie with vanilla ice cream.) But I learned to love it, and this recipe recalls that dish fondly. The strudel should be served slightly warm and the cheese should be at room temperature. (Whatever you do, avoid serving any cheese too cold.)

INGREDIENT NOTE Frozen phyllo dough is readily available in the freezer sections of most grocery stores.

PREPARE THE FILLING Place the butter in a large sauté pan over medium heat until it browns. Add the apples, vanilla bean, and cinnamon and cook, stirring occasionally, until the apples soften and brown slightly, about 5 minutes. Add the maple syrup and simmer until it reduces and starts to caramelize, about 3 minutes. Remove the pan from the heat, discard the vanilla bean, and set aside the apple filling.

PREPARE THE PHYLLO WRAPPING Preheat the oven to 350°F.

Whisk the clarified butter with the syrup in a medium bowl (or emulsify with a blender). Lay out one sheet of phyllo dough on a clean, dry work surface. Brush the dough with the syrup mixture, then place a second phyllo sheet on top. Brush the second sheet with syrup mixture, then cover it with the final phyllo sheet. Brush the top sheet with syrup.

The phyllo is now ready for filling and rolling. Spread the apple filling on the phyllo in an even layer, leaving a margin of 2 to 3 inches to the edges of the dough. Fold over one of the long sides of the dough (most phyllo comes in rectangular sheets), tucking the short edges over the filling. Tightly roll the phyllo around the filling into a cylinder, taking care to press out any air bubbles that may develop. Transfer the strudel to a parchment-lined baking sheet, with the loose edge tucked underneath. Brush the top of the strudel with some additional clarified butter. Using a sharp knife, cut small angled slits in the top of the strudel at 1-inch intervals. Bake the strudel for 10 minutes, then remove it from the oven and sprinkle it with the sugar. Return the strudel to the oven and continue baking until it is brown and crisp, about 10 minutes more. The strudel can be served directly from the oven or reheated.

PREPARE THE CANDIED NUTS WHILE THE STRUDEL IS BAKING (IF USING) Combine the syrup, vanilla, brandy, and butter in a large saucepan over medium heat. Reduce the mixture by half, about 7 minutes. Add the nuts and cook, stirring frequently with a wooden spoon, until the syrup crystallizes and coats the nuts, 3 to 5 minutes more. Keep the nuts warm at the back of the stove or spoon the hot walnuts onto a parchment-lined baking sheet and allow to cool completely. (When cooled down, the walnuts turn into a delicious maple brittle.)

PREPARE THE SAUCE Place the maple syrup, egg yolks, and lemon juice in a stainless-steel bowl. Position the bowl on top of a saucepan containing simmering water, making sure the water doesn't touch the bottom of the bowl. Whisk continuously as the yolk mixture froths and then thickens, about 2 minutes. Remove the sauce from the heat.

Cut the warm strudel into 6 equal portions. Spoon sauce over each portion, then garnish with candied walnuts, if using. Using a sharp knife, cut very thin slices of cheese. Arrange several slices of cheese on top of each portion of strudel and serve.

Country

Brin d'Amour and Tomato Bagna Cauda

SERVES 6 TO 8

6 medium tomatoes

2 cloves garlic, minced

½ cup plus 2 tablespoons extra-virgin olive oil

1 teaspoon kosher salt

½ teaspoon freshly ground black pepper

½ tablespoon black peppercorns

6 sprigs rosemary

18 thin slices baguette, lightly toasted

3 heads of endive, washed, dried, and separated into leaves

1 pound Brin d'Amour cheese

When I was about twelve, I would run home from school at lunchtime almost every day to watch *The Galloping Gourmet* while eating a grilled cheese-and-tomato sandwich in front of the TV. Hosting that show one day is still my dream job, and those sandwiches are still one of my favorite foods. I'm still making them, too, in this fancy form with sheep's-milk cheese and toasted baguette slices.

Brin d'Amour is a rustic, herb-coated cheese from the island of Corsica. (It means "breath of love" in the local dialect—one of the all-time great food names.) The cheese is fairly soft yet firm enough to be easily sliced. I love how its smooth, mouthwatering chalkiness contrasts with the tomato-garlic–olive oil combination in the bagna cauda. Basically, we're taking the old cheese-tomato combination and massaging it into something special.

INGREDIENT NOTES The Brin d'Amour is definitely not a pedestrian grocery-store cheese; on the other hand, it's usually available at gourmet shops and fine supermarkets. A whole Brin d'Amour weighs between 1½ and 2 pounds, so you won't need to use an entire cheese for this recipe.

The tomatoes are oven-roasted, then left in the oven to dry for at least 2 hours, and subsequently marinated for at least another 2 hours, but preferably overnight—a very effective way to concentrate and focus their flavors.

Preheat the oven to 350°F.

Core and quarter the tomatoes, and scoop out the seeds. Place the tomatoes in a bowl. Add the garlic, 2 tablespoons of the oil, the salt, and pepper, and mix well. Place the tomatoes directly on a baking sheet and roast them in the oven until fairly dry-looking, about 40 minutes. If using a gas oven, turn it off and leave the tomatoes to dry for 4 hours. If using an electric oven, turn it to the lowest setting and continue to roast for 2 more hours.

Allow the tomatoes to cool, then place them in a bowl with the remaining ½ cup of oil, the peppercorns, and the rosemary. Set aside, covered, in a cool place, for at least 2 hours but preferably overnight.

To serve, arrange the toasted baguette slices and endive leaves, alternating, around the edge of a deep platter. Drain the tomato quarters, reserving the oil and rosemary. Lean the tomatoes against the endive leaves. Put the reserved oil and rosemary in a small saucepan and warm over low heat. Cut the cheese into ¼-inch-thick slices. Lean a slice against each piece of toast. Pour the warm oil into the center of the platter (or into a small bowl set in the center) and serve, placing the platter in the center of the table for guests to help themselves using fingers or forks.

CHERRIES

TOWN

Pickled Cherries with Mushrooms à la Grecque

SERVES 4 TO 6 (MAKES 1 QUART)

4 tablespoons unsalted butter

1 pound bluefoot mushrooms, brushed clean, trimmed, and sliced thick

Kosher salt and freshly ground black pepper to taste

1 cup fresh lemon juice (3 to 4 lemons)

1 cup dry white wine

2 dry bay leaves

2 tablespoons black peppercorns

1 tablespoon Madras curry powder

2 cups dried sweet cherries

½ cup extra-virgin olive oil

The inspirational image I attach to this recipe is the scene in *The Witches of Eastwick* where Jack Nicholson is devilishly gorging himself on cherries. When they're ripe, in June and July, I'm just like that: I can't stop eating them—sometimes I even get carried away and eat the pits.

In classic cuisine, a dish *à la Grecque* ("in the Greek style") is cooked with oil, wine, lemon juice, and herbs. This recipe mimics that approach, incorporating the concentrated sweetness and tartness of the dried cherries into a delicious pickle. The mushrooms—fairly neutral-tasting and spongelike—absorb all the other flavors and distribute them nicely. I recommend serving this with some of the richer, fattier cuts of meat—steak or lamb chops, or perhaps drizzled on some tender, meaty braised lamb shanks.

INGREDIENT NOTE Bluefoot (or blue leg) mushrooms are the cultivated version of a wild mushroom called Blewitt (aka bluette). They have a beautiful signature blue stem and are fairly meaty and very mild. If none are available, substitute regular cultivated large button or white mushrooms.

Place 2 tablespoons of the butter in a large skillet over medium heat. Add half the mushrooms and sauté until lightly browned, 3 to 5 minutes. Turn the mushrooms over and cook about 5 minutes more. Transfer the mushrooms to a bowl. Wipe out the pan and repeat the cooking procedure for the remaining mushrooms in the remaining butter. Season the sautéed mushrooms with salt and pepper to taste, and set aside.

In a small nonreactive saucepot, combine the lemon juice, wine, bay leaves, peppercorns, and curry powder. Bring the mixture to a boil over medium-high heat, then reduce the heat to low and simmer for 15 minutes. Meanwhile, make a sachet of the dried cherries by gathering them up in a piece of cheesecloth and tying it with twine. Place the sachet in the pot and add about 1 cup of water (enough so the sachet is about three quarters covered). Simmer the cherries in the sauce for another 15 minutes. Remove the cherry sachet and set aside.

Strain the sauce through a fine sieve, discard the solids, and return it to the pot. Bring the sauce to a simmer over medium heat and reduce, if needed, to about 1 cup. If you have less than 1 cup of sauce, add a little water. Add the mushrooms to the sauce and simmer until tender and flavorful, about 10 minutes. Season to taste with salt and pepper. Transfer the mushrooms and their sauce to a bowl. Remove the cherries from the sachet and add them to the mushrooms. Add the oil and set aside to cool. Cover and refrigerate until ready to use. The dish can be served cold or warm.

CHERRIES

Country

Cherries with Red Wine Granita

SERVES 6

FOR THE GRANITA

1 cup Beaujolais or other gamay wine

1 cup sugar

1⅓ cups white grape juice

FOR THE CHERRIES

3 hibiscus tea bags

¼ cup sugar

1 stalk lemongrass, tough outer layer peeled

Grated zest of 1 orange

Grated zest of 1 lemon

2 pounds sweet cherries, pitted

I leave most of my summer fruit at room temperature because it helps keep it juicy, ripe, and deliciously perfumed. Cherries, which are one of my favorites, are an exception. I like them quite cold; there's something about their flavor and sweetness that just works better at lower temperatures. Marinating the cherries—in this case, in a fragrant, floral-scented herbal tea—is a great way to extract more of their irresistible essence.

The key to making a good granita—one that has the consistency of Italian ice rather than a solid frozen block—is to chop or scrape it at least twice during the freezing period. You can serve this dish as a summer dessert with some butter cookies or shortbread cookies (see Lemon and Yogurt Trifle, page 146) on the side. Or even, for a surprise effect, serve it as a premeal eye-opener, before the first course.

INGREDIENT NOTE Kalustyan's (see "Sources and Resources," page 266) offers hibiscus tea. If you can't find it in your local market, you can substitute any berry or pomegranate tea. This recipe calls for an herbal tea that is bright colored and has a good acid/sweet balance; Celestial Seasonings Red Zinger is a good choice.

PREPARE THE GRANITA, 4 HOURS OR MORE IN ADVANCE Combine the wine, sugar, and grape juice in a nonreactive saucepan over medium heat. Simmer the mixture just until the sugar dissolves, then set aside to cool. Pour the wine mixture into an 8-inch-square metal baking pan, cover with plastic wrap, and place in the freezer for about 2 hours. Remove the granita from the freezer and chop it well with a knife. (Or shave it with an ice cream scoop.) Cover the pan again and return the granita to the freezer for about 1½ more hours, then remove and repeat the chopping procedure. Transfer to a covered 1-quart container and keep frozen until ready to serve.

PREPARE THE MARINATED CHERRIES, AT LEAST 4 HOURS IN ADVANCE Bring 3 cups of water to a boil in a medium saucepan. Add the tea bags, remove the pan from the heat, and allow the tea to steep for about 5 minutes.

Cut the lemongrass into 2-inch sections for easier handling. Add the sugar, lemongrass, orange zest, and lemon zest to the tea. Bring it to a simmer over medium heat and stir until the sugar dissolves. Remove from the heat and discard the tea bags. Place the cherries in a bowl and pour the marinade over them. Cover and refrigerate until cold, at least 4 hours.

To serve, spoon the cherries with some of their liquid into stemmed glasses, discarding the solids. Spoon a generous oval-shaped spoonful of granita on top of each portion of cherries, and serve.

CHESTNUTS

SERVES 6

2 tablespoons unsalted butter

$4\frac{1}{2}$ cups Roasted Chestnuts (recipe follows)

4 stalks celery, sliced

2 dried bay leaves

$\frac{1}{2}$ bunch of thyme (about 6 sprigs)

2 tablespoons maple syrup

$1\frac{1}{2}$ cups Chicken Stock (page 262, or low-sodium canned)

1 tablespoon cracked black pepper

ROASTED CHESTNUTS

You'll need $2\frac{1}{4}$ pounds of fresh chestnuts to yield $4\frac{1}{2}$ cups of roasted nuts. Select chestnuts that are smooth, heavy, shiny, and firm. Make a long slit or cross-shaped cut in the flat part of each nut to allow the steam to escape when roasting.

Preheat the oven to 400°F. Place the chestnuts in a single layer on a large baking sheet (or 2 sheets) and roast them for 15 to 20 minutes, turning them over halfway through. Chestnuts are easier to peel while still hot. Wrap the roasted nuts in a towel, remove them one by one, and peel carefully so as not to burn your hands. Remove the hard outer shells and the inner brown skins.

TOWN

Peppered Chestnut Stew

I'd like to say I have cozy childhood memories of roasting chestnuts on an open fire. But I don't. My first encounter with this incredible cold-weather treat was when I was in my twenties, somewhere in northern Paris; they were cooked outdoors over coals in a big, black barrel. From that moment on, I vowed chestnuts would stay in my life. They're evocative of everything I love about the arrival of cold weather. In my mind's eye, I see the hills of Tuscany and Umbria, and the fields and forests of Brittany, where they're a favorite comfort food. Roast a chestnut and crack through its outer layers and you reveal a thick, dense, meaty, soft, subtly perfumed, and immensely satisfying inner essence of nut. Serve this dish with grilled or roasted meat or poultry.

INGREDIENT NOTE Fresh chestnuts are available in fall and early winter. With this recipe I'm providing a standard method of roasting chestnuts in the oven. There are several other ways to cook them, all of which can work well as a preamble to this recipe. If you like your chestnuts with a toasty, smoky accent, just wrap them in foil, throw them on a wood or charcoal fire, and roast them that way. (Yes, Nat, there's nothing quite as good as chestnuts roasting on an open fire. . . .) Peel them, sprinkle with salt, and enjoy. Another fun way to prep your chestnuts is to deep-fry them: simply score them and fry in light vegetable oil at 375°F. for 2 to 3 minutes; they'll start to open up on their own, so all you have to do is drain the excess oil on paper towels and peel. If you prefer to start with preroasted chestnuts—no fuss, no mess—they can be obtained either canned or jarred (usually imported from France or Spain) at gourmet markets or online from outfits such as ChefShop.com (see "Sources and Resources," page 266).

Preheat the oven to 375°F.

Melt the butter in a large ovenproof skillet over medium heat. Add the chestnuts, celery, bay leaves, and thyme, and stir well. Once the chestnuts start caramelizing, 5 to 7 minutes, add the maple syrup, stock, and pepper. Bring to a boil, cover the pan with parchment paper or aluminum foil, and place it in the oven for 15 minutes to braise the chestnuts. Remove the pan from the oven and allow the chestnuts to cool. Serve the chestnuts in their braising liquid (which will have reduced considerably) at room temperature or slightly warm.

CHESTNUTS

Country Chestnut Chips

SERVES 4 TO 6

2 pounds fresh chestnuts

1 quart Clarified Butter (page 264) or vegetable oil

Fine sea salt

It's not hard for me to write a paean to the mighty chestnut, which is not only the quintessential Old World comfort food but a powerful icon of family togetherness and the warmth of hearth and home on a fall or winter evening. I love the chestnut's subtle flavors, its distinct fragrance, its meaty texture, and its natural sugars, which emerge with just a little coaxing. (Chestnuts are also low in fat and high in fiber.) Serve these chips in a small bowl instead of nuts, with a Champagne apéritif; they look like little potato chips but they deliver a rich, peppery, smoky surprise.

INGREDIENT NOTES Peanut or sunflower oil can be substituted for the clarified butter, but the butter yields a much better flavor.

There are a number of ways to shell chestnuts. I'm not going to recommend you crack them open with a hammer (it's possible, but I'd prefer you don't hurt yourself or anybody else, and I generally try to avoid lawsuits arising from my recipe instructions). The oven-roasting method of opening chestnuts explained below is well worth the effort.

Preheat the oven to 400°F.

Score the chestnuts with an X-shape cut about 1/16 inch deep on the flat side. Place them in the oven for about 15 minutes, until they begin to open up. When they're cool enough to handle, remove the shells and inner peels.

Slice the peeled, shelled chestnuts about 1/8 inch thick with a very sharp mandoline (slicer), or the shaving section of a four-sided cheese grater. (It can also be done with a very sharp chef's knife, but this can be dangerous, so take extra care.)

Place the clarified butter in a sauce- or stew pot over medium heat. The pot should be about 6 inches deep, and the butter or oil should be at least 2 inches deep. (Alternatively, you can use an electric deep fryer.) Use a candy or deep-frying thermometer to gauge the temperature of the butter; when it reaches 350°F., it is ready for frying. Place the chestnut slices in the hot clarified butter and cook them until golden brown, about 2 minutes. Remove the chestnut chips with a spider or slotted spoon, and place them on a plate lined with paper towels to drain. Season with salt to taste and serve.

CHICKEN

TOWN

Chicken Confit Salad

SERVES 6

FOR THE CHICKEN CONFIT

- 2 tablespoons kosher salt
- 1 teaspoon freshly ground black pepper
- 1 shallot, sliced thin
- 3 cloves garlic, sliced
- 2 dried bay leaves
- 4 sprigs thyme
- 6 chicken thigh quarters (legs attached)
- About 4 cups extra-virgin olive oil, goose fat, or chicken fat

FOR THE SALAD AND GARNISH

- ¼ pound slab bacon, diced
- 12 thin slices baguette
- 6 tablespoons extra-virgin olive oil, plus additional for brushing the croutons
- 1 clove garlic
- Sea salt and freshly ground black pepper
- 5 tablespoons red wine vinegar
- 2 heads of frisée lettuce, rinsed, dried, cored, and torn into pieces
- 1 bunch of arugula or watercress, rinsed, dried, and thick stems removed
- 1 tablespoon finely minced flat-leaf parsley

One of the biggest dilemmas in roasting a whole chicken—or even grilling a cut-up one—is how to cook both the thighs and the breasts to the appropriate doneness at the same time. If the thighs are done, the breasts are dried out; if the breasts are still moist, the thighs aren't done yet. Here's a clever solution, one that yields at least two excellent meals from each chicken. Buy your 4-pound chicken (or chickens), have it cut up into eighths, sauté the breasts for one meal, use the wings for an appetizer, and make the legs into a confit—the ancient, time-tested method for preparing and preserving any kind of dark meat such as rabbit, duck, pork, or chicken legs. They come out irresistibly moist and flavorful and are complemented beautifully by the greens in this salad. Serve it for lunch, as an opening course, or for a light supper.

TIMING NOTE This recipe calls for the chicken thighs to be marinated and refrigerated for one day prior to cooking, and then refrigerated overnight again after cooking. In fact, the confit can be refrigerated for up to ten days after it is prepared.

PREPARE THE CONFIT Sprinkle 1 tablespoon of the salt and ½ teaspoon of the pepper over the bottom of a shallow dish large enough to hold the chicken in a snug single layer. Add half the shallot and half the garlic. Crumble one of the bay leaves and pick the leaves from two of the thyme sprigs; add the herbs to the salt mixture. Arrange the chicken on top, skin side up. Sprinkle the chicken with the remaining 1 tablespoon of salt and ½ teaspoon of pepper, the shallots, and garlic. Crumble the remaining bay leaf and pick the leaves off the remaining thyme, and scatter the herbs over the chicken. Cover the dish with plastic wrap and refrigerate for 24 hours.

Place the cold chicken in a pot at least 4 inches deep and large enough to hold the chicken thighs in a single layer without crowding. Pour in enough oil to cover the chicken completely (3 to 4 cups). Bring the oil to a simmer over medium heat, skimming any impurities that rise to the surface with a spoon. Adjust the heat as necessary to maintain a gentle simmer. Cook the chicken until it is very tender and the meat begins to pull from the bone, about 1 hour and 45 minutes. Allow the confit to cool, then cover the pan and refrigerate the chicken in the oil overnight.

PREPARE THE SALAD Preheat the oven to 350°F.

Place the bacon in a small skillet over medium heat and sauté until it is rendered and lightly browned, about 8 minutes. Drain the bacon on a plate covered with paper towels. Discard all but 2 teaspoons of the bacon fat.

Brush the bread with a little fresh oil, lay it on a baking sheet, and place in the oven to toast until golden, about 15 minutes. Rub the warm toast with garlic, season it with salt and pepper, and set aside.

Remove the chicken thighs from the refrigerator, take them out of the pan, and blot them dry with paper towels. Warm a nonstick skillet over medium heat. Add the chicken, skin side down, and sauté until the skin is browned, 2 to 3 minutes. Turn the chicken and sauté the other side for 2 to 3 minutes.

Meanwhile, place 6 tablespoons of the fresh oil in a small nonreactive dish. Whisk together with the vinegar and the reserved bacon fat. Season to taste with salt and pepper. Place the frisée and arugula in a salad bowl. Add enough dressing to coat the greens and toss gently. Season to taste with salt and pepper.

Drain the chicken on a plate lined with paper towels, then debone using a small knife. Slice the warm chicken into bite-size pieces and add it to the salad. To serve, place two slices of toast on the side of each plate. Mound salad in the center, then garnish with the reserved bacon and the parsley.

CHICKEN

Country

Peri-Peri Chicken

SERVES 4

- **1 chicken, about 4 pounds, washed, patted dry, back removed, trimmed of excess fat and skin, and cut into 8 pieces**
- **¾ cup store-bought peri-peri sauce**
- **8 cloves garlic**
- **1 teaspooon coarse sea salt**
- **1 teaspoon freshly ground black pepper**
- **1 Preserved Lemon (see opposite, or store-bought)**
- **12 green olives, pitted**
- **2 fresh lemons**

This is a recipe I originally learned from my good friend Colin Cowie, the charming and irrepressibly dynamic lifestyle guru and party planner who also happens to be one hell of a chef. It comes from the Cape Malay cuisine of his native southern Africa. I added a couple of twists, but it remains a marvelously simple and delicious concoction. I think of it as one of my best emergency pantry dinners: you can whip it up in a flash for an impromptu dinner and impress your guests with a real blast of flavor. It's also one of these dishes that's good on the first day, better on the second, and even better on the third. (So make it over the weekend and enjoy it reheated during the week.) You can dress it up with any number of fun garnishes: scallions, cilantro, red pepper, parsley, or a green leafy vegetable such as spinach or kale. Serve it with plain white or jasmine rice on the side.

INGREDIENT NOTES Although the recipe for preserved lemons is fun and satisfying to produce at home, it does take about a month, so you can save a lot of time by buying them. They're available at many gourmet food shops and Middle Eastern specialty stores as well as through Kalustyan's online (see "Sources and Resources," page 266). The recipe is tasty without the preserved lemons, but they add a nice touch.

Peri-peri is the preferred sauce for this recipe, but you can substitute any similar, good-quality prepared hot pepper sauce. Peri-peri, billed as Africa's hottest chile pepper, was brought to the continent in the sixteenth or seventeenth century by Portuguese and Spanish spice traders. My favorite brand of prepared peri-peri sauce is Perks (African Heat); according to their company line, peri-peri sauce is as popular in Africa as ketchup or barbecue sauce is in the United States. The sauce is also available through Nando's, a worldwide franchise of chicken restaurants and peri-peri–based sauces of Afro-Portuguese origin (see "Sources and Resources," page 266).

Combine the chicken and peri-peri sauce in a bowl or resealable plastic bag. Wrap the bowl or seal the bag and put the chicken into the refrigerator to marinate for at least 2 hours. (The longer the chicken marinates, the spicier it will turn out.)

Preheat the oven to 450°F.

Bring a small saucepan of water to a boil over high heat. Add the garlic cloves, reduce the heat to medium, and simmer until the garlic is almost tender, about 10 minutes. Drain and place the garlic in a baking dish just large enough to hold the chicken pieces in a single layer. Lay the chicken, skin side up, over the garlic, and season with the salt and pepper. Roast the chicken for 20 minutes. Flip each piece and roast for 20 minutes more. Turn the chicken pieces again and check for doneness (their juices should run clear and a thermometer inserted into the center of each piece should register 160°F.). Continue cooking if necessary, checking for doneness every 10 minutes or so.

Scrape the pulp from inside the preserved lemon and discard; rinse the lemon to remove excess salt. Bring a small pot of water to a boil and blanch the preserved lemon by plunging it in the water for 30 seconds to 1 minute. Drain the lemon and coarsely chop or julienne (cut into fine strips).

Remove the chicken from the oven and preheat the broiler. Baste the chicken with the pan juices, then brown the skin under the broiler, rotating the pan every 2 or 3 minutes, until the skin is crisp and golden, about 7 minutes total. Remove the pan from the broiler and add the olives and the blanched preserved lemon. Cover the chicken loosely with foil and let it rest in a warm spot for up to 15 minutes. (The chicken can also be cooled, then refrigerated; reheat it in the oven at 375°F. for about 15 minutes.)

To serve, transfer the chicken to a platter. Squeeze the juice from the two fresh lemons over the chicken to help balance the flavors and cut the bite of the hot marinade.

PRESERVED LEMONS

Wash 6 lemons under cold running water, then pat them dry. Cut a small slice crosswise out of the bottom of each lemon so it can stand upright. With the lemon standing upright, make two cuts at a 90-degree angle to each other about two thirds of the way down through the lemon as if you were going to cut it into quarters; don't cut all the way through. Squeeze the cuts open and fill each lemon with about 1 tablespoon of kosher salt. Pack the lemons tightly into a jar. Fill the jar completely with vegetable oil, close tightly, and refrigerate for 1 month. Before using the lemons in recipes, simply scoop out the remaining flesh and rinse in cold running water.

CHICKEN

SERVES 2 TO 4

FOR THE BRINING SOLUTION AND CHICKEN

- ½ cup sugar
- ½ cup kosher salt
- 2 dried bay leaves
- 1 cinnamon stick
- 1 tablespoon black peppercorns
- 1 tablespoon coriander seeds
- 1 piece star anise
- 1 tablespoon dried dill seeds
- 1 tablespoon dried tarragon
- 1 3½-pound chicken

TO ROAST

- 1 teaspoon celery salt
- Kosher salt and freshly ground black pepper
- 2 sprigs thyme
- 2 sprigs rosemary
- 4 cloves garlic, lightly crushed
- 1 lemon, cut into eighths
- 4 tablespoons unsalted butter, at room temperature
- 1 teaspoon sweet paprika
- 1 tablespoon extra-virgin olive oil
- 2 tablespoons dry white wine

TOWN

Butter-Basted Roasted Chicken

Everybody wants to know how to roast a chicken flawlessly; it's one of the holy grails of cooking. This is one of my favorite methods. It may not work perfectly for you on the first try—nine times out of ten, people overcook their first chicken—but don't worry, you'll succeed. This recipe involves a two-step process: browning the chicken on top of the stove, then oven-roasting it with several bastings. This creates an extraordinary *jus* (collection of pan juices) from the combination of butter, wine, lemon, and seasonings, and guarantees the moistness of the chicken. Baste carefully: take the pan out of the oven; close the oven door to maintain its interior temperature; thoroughly baste on top of the stove; then return the pan to the oven.

INGREDIENT NOTE I recommend an organic, free-range, grain-fed chicken; my favorite brand is Giannone, from Canada. The key difference with Giannone chickens is that they're processed for shipment by an air-chilling method instead of the more traditional ice water, which allows them to remain juicier when cooked. Giannone chickens are available through D'Artagnan; Murray's kosher chickens are also very good (see "Sources and Resources," page 266).

BRINE THE CHICKEN OVERNIGHT Dissolve the sugar and salt in 3½ quarts of warm water in a very large pot; leave plenty of room to spare for the chicken. Add the bay leaves, cinnamon, peppercorns, coriander, star anise, dill, and tarragon, and the chicken. Place the pot in the refrigerator overnight.

ROAST THE CHICKEN Preheat the oven to 375°F.

Remove the chicken from the brine and pat dry inside and out with paper towels. Season the chicken cavity moderately with celery salt, kosher salt, and pepper. Stuff the cavity with the thyme, rosemary, garlic, and lemon. Separate the skin from the breast with your fingers and place about 1 tablespoon of the butter under the skin on each side. Truss the chicken (see sidebar instructions; this step is optional), and season it generously with the paprika, salt, and pepper.

Place the oil in a large ovenproof sauté pan over medium heat. When the oil is hot, place the chicken in the pan (one thigh should be resting on the bottom of the pan) and cook until one side is brown, about 5 minutes. Turn the chicken over and brown it on the other side, about 5 minutes more. Reposition the chicken in the pan, breast side up. Dot the chicken with the remaining 2 tablespoons of butter and place it in the oven. After 15 minutes, remove it from the oven, pour the wine over the chicken, and baste it with its pan juices. Baste the chicken every 15 minutes until done, removing it from the oven and keeping the oven door closed to maintain the oven's interior temperature. When done, after about 1 hour, a meat thermometer inserted into the thickest part of the thigh will indicate 160°F. (Alternatively, you can prick the thigh with a metal skewer; if the juices run clear, the chicken is done.) Allow the chicken to rest for 10 minutes before carving. Serve with the *jus* from the pan and a piece of crusty peasant bread.

TO TRUSS A CHICKEN

Use a piece of cooking or butcher's twine 2½ to 3 feet long. Bring the twine up under the tail of the chicken and wrap it around the two ends of the drumsticks so they stay together. Pull both ends of the string up toward the wings, then wrap them around the respective wings, then around the chicken. Turn the chicken over and, where the two ends of the string meet, tie them together snugly so both the wings and drumsticks stay close to the body of the chicken.

If you prefer, take a shortcut and just tie the chicken loosely with some string to hold the drumsticks and wings close to the body.

CHICKEN

Country

Roasted Chicken with Herb Salad

SERVES 4

FOR THE ROASTED CHICKENS

- 1/2 cup mascarpone
- 1 1/2 teaspoons minced flat-leaf parsley
- 1 1/2 teaspoons minced fresh thyme
- 1 1/2 teaspoons minced fresh tarragon
- Grated zest of 1/2 lemon
- 1 small clove garlic, minced
- 1/2 teaspoon kosher salt
- 1/4 teaspoon freshly ground black pepper
- 1 3 1/2-pound chicken

FOR THE HERB SALAD

- 3 tablespoons hazelnut oil
- 2 tablespoons fresh orange juice
- 2 teaspoons snipped chives (about 1/4 of a small bunch)
- 2 teaspoons minced shallot (1 medium shallot)
- Kosher salt and freshly ground black pepper to taste
- 1 1/2 cups mâche lettuce or watercress
- 1/2 cup basil leaves
- 1/4 cup celery leaves
- 1/2 cup flat-leaf parsley leaves
- 2 tablespoons chervil leaves or extra flat-leaf parsley

One of the great chicken-roasting challenges is to keep it moist and interesting without getting too fancy or complicated. This recipe is my way of throwing a chicken changeup: rather than stuffing the cavity with some combination of savory ingredients, I create a paste with herbs, lemon, and mascarpone cheese (to hold things together) and work it under the skin. This adds flavor and helps guarantee that the meat stays moist. Another key to the process is the resting time of 20 minutes, which keeps the juices from running out when you carve the chicken.

ROAST THE CHICKENS Preheat the oven to 400°F.

Place the mascarpone, minced parsley, thyme, tarragon, lemon zest, and garlic in a small mixing bowl; stir to combine. Season generously with salt and pepper. Using your fingers and starting at the back end of the chicken, loosen the skin from the breast, leaving the skin nearest the neck opening attached. Spread the mascarpone filling under the skin. Season the cavity lightly with salt and pepper.

Place the chicken in a large roasting pan, and season it on the outside lightly with salt and pepper. Place the chicken in the oven to roast for 15 minutes. Reduce the temperature to 350°F. and continue to roast until an instant-read thermometer inserted in a thigh registers 160°F. or the thigh juices run clear, 45 to 55 minutes. Allow the chicken to rest in a warm place for 20 minutes.

PREPARE THE HERB SALAD In a small bowl, whisk the hazelnut oil together with the orange juice, chives, and shallot. Season to taste with salt and pepper.

Place the mâche, basil, celery leaves, parsley, and chervil in a salad bowl. Toss the herbs and greens with half the vinaigrette; place the remainder of the dressing in a serving vessel to be passed around at the table.

FINISH AND SERVE Carve the chicken and transfer the meat to a large platter. Serve the herb salad on the side. (Alternatively, place equal portions of the herb salad on each plate, then top each portion with slices of chicken.)

TOWN

Liquid Gold Chocolate Tart

SERVES 8 (MAKES ONE 10-INCH TART)

FOR THE SWEET TART DOUGH

3/4 cup (1 1/2 sticks) unsalted butter, at room temperature

1/3 cup confectioners' sugar

1 large egg yolk

1 1/2 cups all-purpose flour

1 tablespoon heavy cream

FOR THE FILLING

7 ounces dark chocolate

1/2 cup whole milk

1/3 cup heavy cream

1 large egg

FOR THE GARNISH

Caramel Ice Cream (recipe follows)

Caramel Sauce (recipe follows)

Edible gold leaf (optional)

Some desserts are just down-home, sweet comfort food evocative of warm childhood memories. Others are pure celebration. This is most definitely of the latter category. It was inspired by a taste epiphany I had at a small inn in the south of France in 2000. For dessert, we were served lightly toasted baguette slices with just a pinch of salt, a drizzle of olive oil, and a delicious spread of smooth chocolate at room temperature—simplicity, elegance, and the essence of chocolate. This tart, by way of that inspiration, is one of our signatures at Town, where we present it in individual 6-inch servings; here I've converted it to a simpler, more convivial format—a single large pie. What could be better than a warm chocolate tart topped with oozing caramel sauce and doubled up with a luscious caramel ice cream? This is a dessert that fulfills some of our strongest taste cravings—sweet, salty, chocolate, chocolate, and chocolate . . . and did I mention chocolate? You may not think of ice cream as salty, but this particular version supplies just enough of that taste to counterbalance the unctuous sweetness of the caramel.

INGREDIENT NOTES Ideally, the dark chocolate should be 60 percent cocoa solids; Valrhona is a recommended brand.

If you don't want to go to the trouble of making the ice cream yourself, Häagen-Dazs Dulce de Leche is a perfectly acceptable substitute.

PREPARE THE DOUGH, APPROXIMATELY 4 HOURS IN ADVANCE Place the butter and confectioners' sugar in the bowl of an electric mixer. Using the paddle attachment on low speed, mix until just combined, taking care not to overmix. (The mixture should not turn creamy.) Add the egg yolk and gradually mix until just combined. Add the flour all at once and combine until the flour is incorporated three fourths of the way. Turn off the mixer and add the cream. Restart the mixer on low and continue to mix the dough until it just comes together. Remove the dough from the mixer. Flatten it into a disk, wrap in plastic wrap; and chill in the refrigerator for several hours.

PREPARE THE TART Preheat the oven to 375°F. Bring the dough to room temperature.

Roll out the tart dough to approximately 1/8 inch. Place the dough in a 10-inch tart pan. Trim the edges and use any excess dough to patch tears. Chill the unbaked tart shell in the freezer for 15 minutes, then line it with parchment paper or aluminum foil. Weight the dough with dried beans or pie weights and bake in the oven until the edges no longer look raw, approximately 10 minutes. Remove the beans and lining paper and bake the crust until light golden, about 10 minutes more. Remove from the oven and reserve at room temperature. Reduce the oven temperature to 300°F.

PREPARE THE FILLING Chop the chocolate and set it aside in a medium bowl. Combine the milk and cream in a medium saucepan and bring to a boil over medium-high heat. Pour the milk mixture over the chocolate and allow to stand until the chocolate softens, 2 to 5 minutes. Place the egg in another mixing bowl and whisk lightly. Whisk the chocolate and cream together until smooth; continue to whisk the chocolate, and pour this mixture over the egg. Strain the chocolate mixture through a chinois or china cap (fine strainer), then pour it into the prebaked tart shell. Bake the tart until the filling is almost set, about 25 minutes. Remove from the oven and allow the tart to set for at least 5 minutes more before unmolding and serving.

Serve the tart warm or at room temperature, topped with warm caramel sauce and accompanied by a scoop of caramel ice cream. For an extra touch, garnish the tart with edible gold leaf.

continued

CARAMEL ICE CREAM

MAKES ABOUT 1 QUART

- 2 cups whole milk
- 7 large egg yolks
- 1 cup sugar
- 1 cup heavy cream
- 1 tablespoon pure vanilla extract
- 1 teaspoon kosher salt

PREPARE THE ICE CREAM, 1 DAY IN ADVANCE Bring the milk to a simmer in a large, heavy saucepan over medium heat. Meanwhile, place the egg yolks and ½ cup of the sugar in a large bowl and whisk until thoroughly combined. When the milk reaches a simmer, gradually whisk it into the egg yolks, adding no more than ¼ cup at a time. Pour the mixture back into the saucepan and cook over medium-low heat, stirring constantly with a wooden spoon, until it thickens enough to coat the spoon, about 5 minutes. Pour the ice cream base through a fine sieve into a bowl set over ice and stir to cool.

Combine the remaining ½ cup sugar and 2 tablespoons of water in another heavy saucepan. Cook over medium-high heat, without stirring, until the sugar caramelizes and reaches a deep amber color, about 5 minutes. Remove the caramel from the heat and whisk in the heavy cream a couple of tablespoons at a time. Allow the caramel to cool for 30 minutes, then whisk it into the ice cream base. Add the vanilla and salt and mix thoroughly. Chill overnight and process in an ice cream machine according to manufacturer's instructions.

CARAMEL SAUCE

MAKES ABOUT ½ CUP

- ½ cup sugar
- ½ cup heavy cream
- ½ vanilla bean, split and scraped

Combine the sugar and 2 tablespoons of water in a small, heavy saucepan over medium heat. Cook, stirring occasionally, until the mixture is a deep caramel color, about 5 minutes. Remove the caramel from the heat and gradually whisk in the cream. Add the vanilla bean and simmer the sauce over medium-high heat until it reduces by about one-quarter, approximately 2 minutes. Carefully remove the vanilla bean and serve warm.

Country

Deep Dark Chocolate Pudding

SERVES 4

5 egg yolks

2 cups heavy cream

6 ounces bittersweet chocolate, chopped, plus an additional 2 ounces shaved, for garnish (preferably 58 to 61 percent chocolate content)

1 tablespoon coffee liqueur

About 1/2 cup Whipped Cream (page 19), for garnish

I believe the impulse to have a chocolate dessert is a profound, fundamental desire—something stronger than a mere taste craving. After a meal, I think of three basic options: chocolately, lemony, or puddinglike. More often than not, chocolate is my first choice. This pudding is about as satisfying as it gets when it comes to chocolate desserts. Ruth Rogers and Rose Gray, chefs at the wonderful River Café in London, make the best chocolate pudding with crème fraîche; whenever I make a chocolate dessert, I thank them for setting the bar so high. I recommend you sit on your couch, watch an episode of your favorite TV show with your favorite person (or pet) nearby, and have a bowl of this pudding. Guaranteed you'll go to bed a happy person.

Place the egg yolks in a mixing bowl and lightly whisk to break them up. Place the cream and chocolate in a medium saucepan over low heat and melt, whisking constantly. Gradually whisk the cream-chocolate mixture into the egg yolks, initially adding no more than 1/4 cup at a time. Pour the pudding mixture back into the saucepan. Cook over low heat, stirring constantly, until the mixture coats a spoon, about 5 minutes. (Lift the spoon out of the pudding and draw your finger across the back; if the line drawn by your finger remains, the pudding is ready.) Add the coffee liqueur. Pour the pudding through a fine sieve into a medium serving bowl. Allow to cool slightly, then cover with plastic wrap and chill (or leave plastic wrap off to form a skin). Once chilled, serve with lightly whipped cream and lots of shaved chocolate.

COD

TOWN

Cod Pot Roast with Winter Vegetables

SERVES 6

- 6 large savoy cabbage leaves
- 6 6-ounce fillets boneless, skinless cod
- 6 small shallots, finely minced
- 1½ teaspoons sea salt, plus more to taste
- 1 teaspoon freshly ground black pepper, plus more to taste
- 6 tablespoons salted butter
- 2 medium bulbs fennel
- 9 small fingerling potatoes, scrubbed and halved
- 18 pearl onions (optional)
- 2 tablespoons extra-virgin olive oil
- 2 medium carrots chopped into ¼-inch pieces
- 1 large butternut or hubbard squash (2 to 3 pounds), peeled and chopped into ¼-inch pieces
- 2½ cups Chicken Stock (page 262, or low-sodium canned)
- 1 cup dry white wine
- 1 teaspoon honey
- Grated zest and juice of 3 lemons
- Leaves of 1 bunch of flat-leaf parsley, chopped

Just about every recipe I've ever designed is connected to a special vision of time and place. With this one, the time is winter and the place is New England. Forget about corned beef and cabbage; here's a seafood dish to trump that traditional New England meal. Growing up in that part of the country, ironically, did not leave me with many positive seafood experiences. What a shame: all those beautiful fresh catches, and they killed them twice by either overcooking them in the restaurants or processing them into frozen fish sticks. (About the only good seafood you could hope to get on a night out was a boiled lobster.) Even my mother—a great cook—used to overdo her cod and scrod. I never had the heart to tell her while she was still alive. Mom's cod had the two telltale signs of overcooking—milky white liquid underneath and overly flaky flesh. I suppose dishes like this one are my way of compensating for the lost meals of my youth. It accentuates the fresh, moist essence of the fish by wrapping it in a delicate savoy cabbage leaf and oven-braising it just long enough to cook through.

PREPARE THE CABBAGE AND COD Bring a medium pot of salted water to a boil. Blanch the cabbage leaves by plunging them briefly into the water—no more than 30 seconds. Transfer the leaves to a colander and refresh under cold running water. Pat the leaves dry; carefully cut out and discard the tough ribs.

Lay the cabbage leaves out on a clean work surface. Place a cod fillet on each leaf. Sprinkle the fish with the shallots, season with the salt and pepper, and top each fillet with about 1 tablespoon of butter. Wrap the cabbage leaves around the cod and refrigerate.

PREPARE THE FENNEL Trim and discard (or reserve for another use) the tough outer layers, core, and stalks of the fennel bulbs. Chop the trimmed fennel into ¼-inch pieces and set aside.

PREPARE THE POTATOES Place the potatoes in a medium pot and cover them with cold water. Season with salt and bring to a boil over medium-high heat. Reduce the heat to medium and simmer for 10 minutes. Remove from the heat but allow the potatoes to cool in the cooking water. Peel the potatoes and reserve.

PREPARE THE ONIONS, IF USING Bring a medium pot of water to a boil. Plunge the onions into the water for 30 seconds to 1 minute. Transfer them to a colander and, when they're cool enough to handle, slide off their outer skins. Trim the stem and root ends and set aside.

BRAISE THE VEGETABLES AND COD Remove the cabbage-wrapped cod fillets from the refrigerator and allow them to come to room temperature.

Place the oil in a large high-sided ovenproof skillet over medium-low heat. When the oil is hot, add the carrots, onions (if using), and fennel. Cook, stirring occasionally, until the vegetables begin to soften, about 15 minutes. Add the squash and cook for about 1 minute. Add 1½ cups of the stock, and bring to a simmer over medium heat. Cook until the vegetables are tender, about 15 minutes. Add the wine and simmer until it has reduced by three-fourths, about 15 minutes more. Preheat the oven to 400°F. Add the reserved potatoes and the remaining 1 cup of stock, and simmer until the stock reduces by one third, about 10 minutes. Stir in the honey, then carefully arrange the cabbage-wrapped cod fillets in the pan. (The liquid should come halfway up the side of the fillets; if it doesn't, add a little water.) Cover the pan and transfer it to the oven. Braise the fish in the oven until it is just opaque, 8 to 10 minutes (unwrap a cabbage bundle to check).

Remove the pan from the oven, uncover, and simmer over medium heat, 3 to 5 minutes. Baste the cod bundles with the simmering liquid. Add the lemon juice and zest. Adjust the seasoning if necessary with additional salt and pepper. Place one cod bundle and an equal portion of vegetables and braising liquid in each of 6 warm bowls (or deep plates). Garnish with parsley, and serve.

COD

Country
Escabeche

SERVES 6

- **½ cup extra-virgin olive oil, plus additional for sautéing the fish and onions**
- **3 pounds skin-on cod fillet, cut into 6 equal-sized pieces**
- **1½ teaspoons kosher salt**
- **¾ teaspoon freshly ground black pepper**
- **2 medium yellow onions, diced**
- **1 bunch of cilantro, chopped**
- **½ bunch of parsley, chopped**
- **½ cup chopped pitted green olives**
- **1 tablespoon drained capers**
- **1 tablespoon juice from the caper jar**
- **1 cup rice wine vinegar**

Escabeche is originally a Spanish dish of poached or fried fish enhanced with a pickly marinade. It's popular all around the Mediterranean and also, in variations, in the Caribbean; in Jamaica, they call it *escovitch* (pronounced "ess-co-VEECH"). This version was largely inspired by one of my former chefs, Fernando Zapata, who's from Colombia. The recipe calls for marinating the sautéed cod overnight; I recommend you make a large batch because it's even better on the second day. It's also tremendously versatile: you can serve it underneath some tuna tartare or on grilled toasts as a bruschetta; toss it into warm potatoes and add a squeeze of fresh lemon; fry it up with a little olive oil and break some eggs on top; or present it on a bed of Boston or butter lettuce as an appetizer or a salad course.

Place 2 tablespoons of the oil in a large skillet over medium heat. Season the cod fillets with 1 teaspoon of the salt and ½ teaspoon of the pepper. When the oil is hot, add two fillets to the pan, skin side down. (Work in batches so the fillets have plenty of room in the pan.) Cook the fish without moving it until the first side is crisp, about 5 minutes. Using a spatula, carefully turn the fillets over. Try to keep them whole, but don't worry if they break up a bit. Brown the fillets until just cooked through, about 1 minute more. Transfer the fillets to a glass or nonreactive ceramic container large enough to hold all of them in a single layer. Wipe out the pan in between batches if necessary, add more oil, and repeat the procedure, browning all the fillets.

When all the fillets are browned, reduce the heat to medium-low and add the onions. Season with the remaining ½ teaspoon of salt and ¼ teaspoon of pepper and cook, stirring frequently, until the onions are soft and translucent, about 10 minutes. Spoon the onions over the fish. Scatter the cilantro, parsley, olives, and capers on top. Add the caper pickling juice and the vinegar. Pour ½ cup oil on top, making sure all the marinade ingredients are evenly distributed, cover the container, and refrigerate for at least 24 hours before serving.

TOWN

Raspberry and Lavender Macaroons

MAKES ABOUT 16 COOKIES

- ½ cup plus 3 tablespoons sliced almonds
- 1½ tablespoons granulated sugar
- 1 cup plus 2 tablespoons confectioners' sugar
- 4 large egg whites, at room temperature
- 1 or 2 drops of red food coloring
- 1½ teaspoons dried or edible fresh lavender flowers, for dusting
- 1 to 2 tablespoons raspberry jam, for filling

If the measure of a great cookie recipe is how hard it is to stop eating them, then this one rates very high. It's also foolproof and fun to make. Try these with a good, strong cup of espresso after your meal or as a midmorning pick-me-up. For some reason, coconut worked its way into macaroons in America; in a classic France macaroon, there isn't any. Not that I have anything against coconut, but I prefer the elegant simplicity of the French version. The lavender in this variation not only provides lovely color but it also helps bring out the best in the raspberries.

INGREDIENT NOTES Dried lavender flowers are available from various mail-order services including GourmetSleuth, San Francisco Herb Co., and Flower DepotStore (see "Sources and Resources," page 266). You can substitute 1½ cups almond flour for the almonds; simply skip the grinding procedure and sift the flour and sugars together.

Preheat the oven to 275°F.

Combine the almonds and sugar in a food processor and pulse until the almonds are finely ground. Add the confectioners' sugar and pulse to combine. Sift the mixture to remove any large bits of almond. Set aside.

Place the egg whites in the bowl of an electric mixer fitted with the whisk attachment and begin to whip them on medium speed. Once the whites are very foamy, add one or two drops of food coloring (enough to turn the whites pink). Continue to whip the whites until they form stiff glossy peaks, about 4 minutes total. (Be careful to not overwhip or they will reliquefy.) Remove from the mixer and fold the ground almond mixture into the whites in three equal portions. On the third addition, be sure to fold until the batter smooths out.

Fill a pastry bag (disposable works best) with the batter. Line one or two large baking sheets with parchment paper. Using a small hole, pipe out nickel-sized drops of batter onto the parchment-lined sheets until the batter is finished. They should be spaced ½ an inch to ¾ of an inch apart. (Alternatively, this can be done by hand using a small spoon.) Sprinkle half the uncooked macaroons with the lavender flowers. Allow the uncooked macaroons to dry at room temperature for 15 minutes, then place them in the oven to bake until firm and barely golden at the edges, about 12 minutes. Rotate the baking sheet 90 degrees after about 6 minutes. The macaroons should be puffed and pink—not brown. Turn off the oven and remove the macaroons, allowing them to cool for about 10 minutes. If the macaroons are still sticky after cooling, simply return them to the shut-off oven to dry for about 30 minutes.

Peel the dried macaroons from the parchment paper. Make sandwiches by using one plain macaroon for the bottom, topped with a dab of jam, and one lavender-dusted macaroon for the top.

COOKIES

Country
Chocolate and Coconut Macaroons

MAKES 12 COOKIES

3/4 cup sugar

2 1/2 cups sweetened shredded coconut

3 large egg whites

1 tablespoon pure vanilla extract

Pinch of kosher salt

1/2 cup mini chocolate chips

This is the American country cousin of the lavender macaroons (opposite)—with the inclusion of coconut, which does not go in the French version—and I think it rivals a really good chocolate chip cookie recipe for its delicious addictiveness. These are simultaneously gooey and firm, and truly impossible to put down. Chocolate and coconut are the salt and pepper of the dessert realm, a fascinating pair with intriguing contrasts of flavors and textures.

Preheat the oven to 350°F.

In a bowl, combine the sugar, coconut, egg whites, vanilla, and salt, and mix thoroughly (this is best done with your hands). Stir in the chocolate chips.

Line a regular baking sheet with parchment or use a nonstick silicone baking sheet. Using a tablespoon, scoop up portions of the coconut mixture, then use your hands to form each into a packed ball about 1 inch in diameter. Set the macaroons 1 1/2 inches apart on the baking sheet and bake until golden brown, about 20 minutes. Allow to cool for 10 minutes, then transfer to a plate or rack to cool completely.

CORN

TOWN

Chilled Corn Soup with Fresh Nutmeg

SERVES 4

3 ears fresh summer corn, husked

2 tablespoons unsalted butter

1 medium sweet onion, such as Vidalia, chopped

1 small shallot, chopped

1 cup heavy cream

1 teaspoon freshly grated nutmeg

Kosher salt and freshly ground black pepper to taste

Red Pepper Coulis (recipe follows; optional)

4 sprigs mint, for garnish

During its late-summer harvest, corn is everywhere. Therefore, like basil and a few other seasonal favorites, it suffers from a fair amount of abuse (the old "too-much-of-a-good-thing" syndrome). Here's a little something different—a soup that emphasizes the corn's natural sweetness. The red pepper coulis is an optional garnish that adds another touch of natural sweetness to the ensemble. For an extra-fancy garnish, top with toasted walnuts.

Cut the kernels off the corn cobs and reserve them. Place the cobs in a large pot with 6 cups of water. Bring the water to a boil over high heat, then reduce the heat and simmer for 30 minutes. Pass this corn broth through a strainer and reserve.

Place the butter in a saucepot over medium heat; add the onion and shallot and cook, stirring occasionally, until the shallot is tender but not yet beginning to brown, about 10 minutes. Add the corn kernels, stir for 1 to 2 minutes, then add the corn broth. Gently simmer until the corn is tender, about 30 minutes; the time will vary widely depending upon the age and variety of the corn.

Using a slotted spoon, transfer the vegetables to a blender. Add about 1½ cups of the cooking liquid (reserve any remaining liquid to thin the soup if necessary). Purée the corn with the broth for 5 minutes. Stir in the cream. Press the mixture through a fine strainer, thinning if necessary with reserved corn broth or water. Stir in the nutmeg, then season with salt and pepper to taste. Allow the soup to cool to room temperature, then chill in the refrigerator.

Place the cold soup in chilled cups. Garnish with a decorative drizzle of red pepper coulis, if using, and sprigs of fresh mint. Serve immediately.

MAKES ABOUT 1 CUP

1½ tablespoons unsalted butter

1 red bell pepper, cored, seeded, and roughly chopped

1 shallot, sliced

1 clove garlic, coarsely chopped

2 sprigs oregano

Juice of 2 limes

½ of a chipotle pepper in adobo

RED PEPPER COULIS

Place the butter, red pepper, shallot, garlic, and oregano in a saucepan over medium-low heat. Sweat until the vegetables are very soft, about 15 minutes. Remove the vegetables from the heat, place them in a blender along with the lime juice and chipotle, and purée. Pass the mixture through a fine strainer into a bowl and allow it to cool to room temperature.

Extra coulis can be refrigerated for up to a week. The coulis is delicious with eggs or on sandwiches.

CORN

Country
Corn Risotto

SERVES 6

3 ears sweet white summer corn, kernels removed from cobs, and cobs reserved

1 quart Chicken Stock (page 262, or low-sodium canned)

6 tablespoons unsalted butter

1 small bulb fennel, trimmed and diced

Kosher salt and freshly ground black pepper

3 tablespoons extra-virgin olive oil

½ medium yellow onion, diced

1½ cups risotto rice (preferably carnaroli)

1 cup dry white wine

½ cup freshly grated Parmigiano-Reggiano, or to taste

In Italy, the cradle of risotto, they don't eat much corn. With the notable exception of polenta, a form of cornmeal, the Italians feed their cobs to the livestock. But rice and corn, two grains of very different sizes and origins, share quite a few traits: they both pair well with butter and cheese, and they both beg for a little salt to bring out their best sweet-starchy traits. So here I'm combining the New World with the Old, corn with rice. Purists might say it's a bastardization of an Italian national dish. I prefer to think of it as the modern echo of an old American comfort-food staple—creamed corn.

Break the reserved corn cobs in half and place them in a large pot with the stock. Bring the stock to a simmer over medium-high heat. Turn off the heat and steep the cobs in the stock for 30 minutes.

Melt 2 tablespoons of the butter in a sauté pan over medium heat. Add the fennel and sweat until soft, about 10 minutes. Remove the fennel from the pan and set aside. Add another 2 tablespoons of the butter to the pan and sweat the corn kernels until soft and velvety, 10 to 15 minutes. Season the corn with salt and pepper to taste, and set it aside.

Pass the corn stock through a strainer and discard the cobs. Place the oil in a skillet over medium heat. Add the onion and sweat, stirring occasionally, until the onion starts to soften, about 3 minutes. Add the rice and cook, stirring frequently with a wooden spoon, until it no longer appears chalky on the outside, 4 to 5 minutes. Add the wine and simmer, stirring frequently, until the wine is absorbed, about 5 minutes. Add 1½ cups of the chicken-corn stock and simmer, stirring frequently, until the liquid is absorbed, about 7 minutes. Add another 1½ cups of stock and simmer, still stirring frequently, until the liquid is largely absorbed and the rice appears fluffy but is still slightly firm to the taste. (If the rice is still hard or chewy, add the remaining stock. The total cooking time for the risotto should be about 20 minutes.) Stir in the reserved fennel and corn kernels, the remaining 2 tablespoons of butter, and the Parmesan. Season to taste with salt and pepper, and serve.

BLUE CRABS

TOWN

Hot Crab Tea and Tomato-Caper Raviolini

SERVES 6

FOR THE CRAB TEA

- **1½ pounds tomatoes (4 to 5 medium or 3 large), halved**
- **1 large bulb fennel (about 1 pound), trimmed and halved**
- **1 3-inch piece fresh ginger, peeled**
- **4 sprigs tarragon**
- **12 live medium blue crabs**
- **Kosher salt**

FOR THE CRAB SALAD

- **1 heaping cup (about ½ pound) cleaned fresh lump crabmeat**
- **2½ tablespoons cilantro leaves**
- **Kosher salt**

Tomato-Caper Raviolini (recipe follows, optional)

Crabs are another lifestyle food of my native New England, but they fall into the special-treat category since they were always a little too pricey for our family budget. I remember we'd have them maybe once or twice a year on a summer trip to Cape Cod or Martha's Vineyard. This simple, elegant dish, based on crabs, has two distinct and contrasting components. First, there's the tea, a quick, simple preparation that highlights the delightfully briny flavor of the crabs. It's a light broth, like a clear seafood consommé, the antithesis of traditional creamy seafood bisques. Second, you have the raviolini, which are compact, carefully composed little power-packs of flavor adding zest to the broth. Feel free to skip the raviolini and make the crab tea on its own. Serve it warm, as described below, or chilled as a jellied consommé.

PREPARE THE TEA Place the tomatoes, fennel, ginger, tarragon, and 2 gallons of cold water in a large pot, and bring to a simmer over medium-high heat. Using a pair of long tongs, add the crabs. Cover and cook until the crab shells are bright red, about 5 minutes. Remove the lid and reduce the heat to medium-low. Pull the crabs from the pot and put them into a large bowl or roasting pan. Allow the crabs to cool a little. Cut them in halves or quarters using kitchen shears, a meat cleaver, or a large knife; be sure to capture the escaping crab juice in the bowl or pan. Return the crabs and juices to the pot. Adjust the heat so the tea is barely simmering and cook until it is flavorful, about 2 hours. Allow the tea to cool for about 20 minutes, then strain it through a sieve lined with cheesecloth (or a large coffee filter), into a large saucepot, discarding the solids.

Bring the tea to a boil over medium-high heat. Skim any foam that rises to the surface. Allow the tea to cool to room temperature, then refrigerate until shortly before serving.

FINISH AND ASSEMBLE THE DISH Just before serving, mix the lump crab with the cilantro leaves and season with salt to taste. Mound equal portions of this crab salad in the center of each of six bowls. Meanwhile, bring the crab tea to a simmer and season to taste with salt. If using the raviolini, drop them into the pot (approximately 6 per serving), for 30 seconds. Ladle equal portions of crab tea and raviolini into each bowl and serve.

TOMATO-CAPER RAVIOLINI

MAKES 36 RAVIOLINI

- 1 tablespoon finely chopped fresh tarragon
- 1 tablespoon finely chopped fresh chervil
- 1 tablespoon finely chopped flat-leaf parsley
- 2 tablespoons finely chopped capers
- 3 tablespoons Mayonnaise (page 264, or store-bought, preferably Hellman's)
- ½ anchovy fillet, minced
- 1 small basil leaf, minced
- 3 halves oven-dried tomatoes, chopped (recipe follows)
- Kosher salt and freshly ground black pepper
- 9 egg roll wrappers
- Flour, for dusting

Place the tarragon, chervil, parsley, capers, mayonnaise, anchovy, basil, and tomatoes in a bowl. Season moderately with salt and pepper, and mix well.

On a clean, floured work surface, trim or roll out a wonton or egg roll wrapper (depending on its size) to about 4 inches square. Cut the wrapper into four 2-inch squares. Transfer these squares to a plate. Put about ¼ teaspoon filling in the center of each square. Brush the edges of each wrapper with a trace of water, then fold one corner of each to meet the opposing corner, forming 4 triangular raviolini. Repeat the procedure with the remaining wonton wrappers. Store the raviolini on a baking sheet lined with parchment paper about an inch apart; sprinkle with a light dusting of flour. (The raviolini can be kept this way in the refrigerator for a few days; if they're wrapped in plastic, placed in freezer bags, and frozen, they can be kept up to two months. You will have excess filling so, if you like, make extra raviolini and freeze them for future use.)

OVEN-DRIED TOMATOES

MAKES 12 PIECES

- 3 medium tomatoes, cored, seeded, and quartered
- 1 clove garlic, minced
- 3 tablespoons extra-virgin olive oil
- 1 teaspoon salt
- ½ teaspoon freshly ground black pepper

INGREDIENT NOTE As a shortcut, you can substitute 3 or 4 sun-dried tomatoes, soaked in warm water for about 20 minutes, then diced.

Preheat oven to 350°F.

Place the tomatoes, minced garlic, and oil in a mixing bowl. Season to taste with salt and pepper. Toss well, then spread the ingredients directly on a baking sheet and place in the oven to bake until fairly dry-looking, about 40 minutes. If using a gas oven, turn off the heat and leave tomatoes until concentrated looking, about 4 hours. (In an electric oven, turn to the lowest setting and cook for about 2 more hours.)

Country Potato-Crab Tartlets

In today's seafood culture, good crabs are easy to find. Decent recipes are pretty common for stone crabs, king crab legs, and even blue crabs. But finding a really great recipe for crab cakes can be a rare life-enhancing moment. This is my variation. It has no bread or flour; it features the essence of earth (potato) and sea (crab); and it delivers a fancy little package—delightful in appearance and presentation—in exchange for relatively little effort. Quite a few dishes are best served with a chilled glass of good Sancerre wine; this is certainly one of them.

SERVES 4

- **½ pound fresh jumbo lump crabmeat, picked through to remove any shell fragments and cartilage**
- **½ cup peeled, roughly grated celery root**
- **1 tablespoon minced fresh chives**
- **½ cup julienned leek, white part only (1 large leek)**
- **⅓ cup Mayonnaise (page 264, or store-bought, preferably Hellman's)**
- **3 tablespoons Dijon mustard**
- **Kosher salt and freshly ground black pepper**
- **2 medium russet or Idaho (baking) potatoes, peeled**
- **½ cup Clarified Butter (page 264), light vegetable oil, or a mix of regular butter with vegetable oil, for frying**
- **2 tablespoons chopped fresh chives, for garnish**

Place the crab meat, celery root, chives, leek, mayonnaise, mustard, ½ teaspoon salt, and ¼ teaspoon pepper in a bowl. Gently mix all the ingredients until they are well combined. Cover the bowl with plastic wrap and reserve in the refrigerator while preparing the potato tarts.

Grate the potatoes into a large bowl, then cover them tightly with plastic wrap so they won't discolor; reserve the grated potatoes at room temperature until ready to cook.

Turn on the oven to its lowest setting.

Place 2 tablespoons of the clarified butter in a medium nonstick sauté pan or skillet over medium heat. When the pan is hot, place a mounded tablespoon of the grated potato in the pan. Flatten the potato into a small pancake with the back of a spoon. Season the potato lightly with salt and pepper, then place about 1 tablespoon of the crab filling in the center of the cake, pressing down lightly so the filling spreads almost to the edges of the cake. Cover the filling with another portion of potato, again pressing down lightly to form a tartlet about ½ inch high. Repeat the process to form 4 tartlets. Cook each tartlet without moving it until its underside is golden brown, about 4 minutes. Turn the tartlets over and cook until their other sides are golden brown, 2 to 3 minutes more. Season lightly with salt and pepper. Remove to a plate lined with paper towels and blot off any excess oil. Transfer to a baking sheet in the oven to keep warm. Repeat the process to create 8 tartlets (2 per person). Garnish the tartlets with chopped chives and serve warm.

SOFT-SHELL CRABS

TOWN

Tempura Soft-Shell Crabs

SERVES 4

FOR THE TEMPURA BATTER

6 tablespoons cornstarch, plus additional for dusting the crabs

6 tablespoons cake or pastry flour

Pinch of cayenne pepper

Pinch of kosher salt

½ teaspoon baking powder

1 cup seltzer water

FOR THE CRABS

8 soft-shell crabs, cleaned (have your fishmonger do this or see instructions, page 102)

1 quart whole milk

Vegetable oil for frying (preferably peanut oil)

FOR THE SALAD AND GARNISH

½ cup crème fraîche (optional)

Juice of 2 limes (optional)

1 sheet nori (dry seaweed), toasted and crumbled (optional)

2 small or 1 medium head of frisée or Bibb lettuce, broken into bite-size pieces (about 1 cup tightly packed per serving) or Cucumber-Kimchee Salad (recipe follows)

3 tablespoons extra-virgin olive oil or sesame oil

1½ tablespoons red wine vinegar or rice wine vinegar

Fine sea salt and freshly ground black pepper to taste

Soft-shell crabs are like white truffles and a few other seasonal specialties: when they're around, it's time to seize the moment and make sure they find a way to your table. When I was about sixteen, my dad helped me discover soft shells when he took me to dinner at the famous No Name Restaurant in Boston. Ever since, I've looked forward eagerly to the arrival of the soft-shells every spring.

I generally avoid frying seafood because there's a tendency to blunt its delicate flavors and textures. Tempura, which is much subtler than any other frying method, is an exception. A good tempura involves relatively thin batter; light, neutral-tasting oil; and a hot frying temperature. Soft-shell crabs are about the right size to benefit from this type of treatment. When you pull the cooked crabs out of the oil, the batter should be white, not brown or golden, and somewhat transparent—another advantage when you're presenting a visually appealing item such as soft-shells. I recommend peanut oil for most deep-frying, including tempuras; it's light and neutral and has a high smoke point. I'm offering two options for serving the crabs: a streamlined version with a simple salad, or a fancier version with Cucumber-Kimchee Salad (page 103). The point is to offer a base with some refreshing crunch and acidity to highlight all that's good about this seafood treat.

INGREDIENT NOTES You can have your fishmonger clean the soft-shell crabs, which involves removing the eyes and gills, in which case they should be brought home, refrigerated, and cooked the same day. Otherwise, you can bring them home live and clean them yourself. Soft-shell crabs are regular blue crabs that have lost their hard outer shells as part of the springtime molting process; they will live a couple of days in the fridge.

Nori is the thin, dried seaweed used to wrap the rice in a sushi preparation. It's usually toasted before it's used. You can buy the sheets and simply crumble them up after lightly toasting them in the toaster oven for about 1 minute.

For an extra Asian twist, try substituting sesame oil and rice wine vinegar for the olive oil and red wine vinegar in the salad.

continued

PREPARE THE TEMPURA BATTER Sift the cornstarch with the flour, cayenne, salt, and baking powder into a mixing bowl. Gradually whisk in the seltzer until the mixture attains the consistency of thin pancake batter; it should coat a spoon without being too clumpy or runny. If the batter is too thick, add a little more seltzer; if too thin, add some flour. Allow the batter to rest at room temperature for about 10 minutes.

COOK THE SOFT-SHELL CRABS Rinse the crabs well in cold water, pat them dry, then place them in a large bowl or dish with enough milk to just cover them. Have the bowl with the tempura batter ready next to the stove. Fill a large heavy pot with vegetable oil to a depth of at least 3 inches. (The pot should be at least 6 inches deep to prevent overflow and to minimize spattering.) Heat the oil over a medium-high flame until a thermometer indicates a temperature of 350°F., or a drop of water in the pot sizzles immediately. Working in small batches, dip the crabs in batter to coat them, dust with additional cornstarch, then fry in the oil until very crispy, 3 to 4 minutes each. Remove the crabs to a plate lined with paper towels to drain off excess oil. Season the crabs with fine sea salt while still hot and reserve in a warm place; they should be served warm but not hot.

ASSEMBLE AND FINISH THE DISH For the optional garnish, place the crème fraîche in a small mixing bowl and whisk in the lime juice. Set aside. Place the lettuce in a large bowl. In a small bowl, make a vinaigrette by whisking together the oil and vinegar. Season to taste with fine sea salt and black pepper. Add the vinaigrette to the lettuce and toss well to combine.

Arrange equal portions of green salad or Cucumber-Kimchee Salad on each of four dinner plates. Position two soft-shell crabs on top of each salad. (The crabs can be left whole or cut in half.) Drizzle thin ribbons of the crème fraîche–lime garnish (if using) around the plates and onto the salads. Drizzle a small amount of kimchee marinade (if using) around each plate. Sprinkle each portion with a pinch of nori flakes (if using) and serve immediately.

TO CLEAN LIVE SOFT-SHELL CRABS

Wash them thoroughly in cold water and pat dry. Use a pair of kitchen shears or sharp scissors to trim the head along the full width of the crab, just behind the eyes. Be careful not to snip off legs or pincers. Lay the crab on its back and carefully pull off the triangular tail or apron. Lift up the points of the top shell to reveal the gills; they are featherlike and opaque in color. Snip these off at their base or pull them out carefully with your fingers.

CUCUMBER-KIMCHEE SALAD

- $1\frac{3}{4}$ cups rice wine vinegar
- 2 tablespoons fish sauce
- 6 cloves garlic, sliced very thin
- 1 $2\frac{1}{2}$- to 3-inch (thumb-sized) piece ginger, peeled and juliennned
- $\frac{1}{4}$ teaspoon ground coriander
- Pinch of cayenne pepper
- Pinch of red pepper flakes
- 1 cup (tightly packed) whole ramps, thoroughly rinsed and drained, or 5 scallions, white part only, cut on the bias into 1-inch pieces
- $1\frac{1}{2}$ cups peeled, quartered, thinly sliced watermelon radish, white radish, daikon, or jicama
- 1 medium turnip, peeled, quartered, and thinly sliced
- 1 large English (hothouse) cucumber, peeled
- $\frac{1}{2}$ cup grapeseed oil
- 1 teaspoon mustard seeds or $\frac{1}{2}$ teaspoon Dijon mustard

INGREDIENT NOTE Ramps, also known as wild leeks, are a member of the onion family that look something like a scallion but with wider, flatter leaves and a more assertive flavor, which is why you should blanch them before incorporating them into the kimchee. They're available in farmer's markets and produce stores from late winter into early summer. Ramps are great when in season, but since they can be difficult to locate, feel free to substitute scallions anytime.

PREPARE THE KIMCHEE, AT LEAST 6 HOURS ADVANCE Place the vinegar, fish sauce, garlic, ginger, coriander, cayenne, and pepper flakes in a medium saucepot and bring to a boil over high heat. Meanwhile, bring a medium pot of salted water to a boil. Add the ramps to the water and blanch for 1 minute. Transfer to a colander, refresh under cold running water, then drain thoroughly. Combine the ramps, radishes, and turnip in a large bowl. Pour the contents of the saucepot into the bowl to cover the vegetables. Allow the contents of the bowl to cool to room temperature. Cover, and refrigerate for at least 6 hours or overnight.

PREPARE THE SALAD Cut the cucumber in half crosswise, then julienne into long, thin, spaghettilike strands; discard the seedy core. Drain the kimchee vegetables, reserving the marinade. Combine the cucumber and kimchee vegetables in a mixing bowl. In a separate bowl, whisk the oil together with $\frac{1}{4}$ cup of the reserved pickling liquid and the mustard seeds. Pour the dressing over the salad and toss gently to combine.

SOFT-SHELL CRABS

Country

Soft-Shell Crabs with Red Onion, Fennel, and Orange Salad

SERVES 6

12 small to medium soft-shell crabs, cleaned (have your fishmonger do this, or see the instructions on page 102)

1 teaspoon kosher salt, plus more to taste

1 teaspoon freshly ground black pepper, plus more to taste

¼ cup Wondra flour, or fine cornmeal

About ½ cup Clarified Butter (page 264) or vegetable oil

1 firm medium red onion

1 medium bulb fennel, sliced crosswise about ¼ inch thick

3 whole oranges, peeled and cut into segments

1 tablespoon chopped fresh dill, plus additional for garnish

2 tablespoons sherry vinegar (preferably imported from Spain)

4 tablespoons extra-virgin olive oil

One of the risks of deep-frying or quick-sautéing soft-shell crabs is that they're liable to pop open in your mouth with an explosion of gritty juice when you bite down. This can be a tad inconvenient. And it's one reason why I prefer to cook soft-shells much more slowly over lower heat, allowing them to come to a delectable crispy crunchiness in their own good time. Here, I'm suggesting a traditional Sicilian-style salad of red onion, fennel, and orange to highlight the crabs' wonderful, delicate sea flavors.

INGREDIENT NOTE Crabs should be cooked the same day they are purchased and cleaned. Because it doesn't smoke or burn easily, clarified butter is preferable for sautéing the crabs.

Season the crabs with 1 teaspoon salt and 1 teaspoon pepper, and sprinkle them with flour. Melt 2 to 3 tablespoons of the clarified butter in a large skillet over low heat. (All 12 crabs will not fit into one skillet, so you can either work in batches or use three skillets.) Add only as many crabs as can easily fit into the pan without crowding, belly side down. Sauté the crabs without disturbing them (they should just barely sizzle) until they are golden brown and crisp, about 15 minutes. Turn the crabs over and continue sautéing until crisp on the other side, another 10 to 15 minutes. Once the crabs are browned, set them aside in a warm place. They should be served warm, not hot.

Slice the onions very thin with a sharp knife. Soak the slices in ice water for 10 minutes to take away some of the strong flavor. Drain them in a colander, then dry them with a kitchen towel. Place the onion slices in a mixing bowl. Add the fennel, orange segments, dill, vinegar, and oil. Season with salt and pepper to taste, and toss gently to combine.

Mound equal portions of the salad in the middle of each of six plates. Cut the soft-shell crabs in half from head to tail down the middle of the back. Arrange four halves on each plate, legs up, around the salad. (In order to make nice round mounds of salad at the restaurant, we use a ring mold. If you don't have one of those at home, you can simply shape a mound with your hands. Or lightly pack it into a coffee cup, then invert the cup onto the plate.) Finally, drizzle some of the dressing left in the salad bowl around each plate, garnish with fresh dill, and serve.

CUCUMBERS

MAKES 4 COCKTAILS

12 ounces Hendrick's gin

4 teaspoons white vermouth (optional)

12 to 16 slices skin-on English (hothouse) cucumber, about 1/8 inch thick

Sea salt

TOWN

Hendrick's Gin Martini

Permit me to rant: martinis are made with gin, not vodka. Period, amen. Forget about that James Bond shaken-not-stirred bravado. Vodka martinis are, in my not-so-humble opinion, an insult to the art and science of fine bartending. First of all, vodka has no flavor. (If you're looking for an efficient way to ingest alcohol, why not just take a pill?!) With gin, you get flavor—intriguing, complex, multilayered flavor based on the juniper berry and a carefully controlled mix of grains. With the Hendrick's brand, you get a bonus: the hint of cucumber—light, subtle, and really the ideal complement to gin's juniper flavors. Toss out those nasty little cocktail olives and try serving your martinis with fresh, crunchy slices of cucumber. I think you'll be converted.

FROM THE LABEL OF HENDRICK'S GIN This handcrafted gin is distilled from a proprietary recipe which includes traditional botanicals such as juniper, coriander and citrus peel. The "unexpected" infusion of cucumber and rose petals results in a most iconoclastic gin. It is not for everyone.

INGREDIENT NOTE Noilly Prat is my preferred brand of white vermouth. As martini drinkers know, however, to make a truly dry martini the vermouth is often added in minuscule quantities or even left out entirely. So suit yourself in that respect. But in any case, be sure to shake your cocktail very well so it turns icy cold.

Pour the gin over ice in a cocktail shaker. Add the vermouth and shake very well. Strain the martinis into chilled glasses. Serve slices of cucumber sprinkled with sea salt as an accompaniment.

CUCUMBERS

Country

Cool Water Cucumber Sorbet

MAKES ABOUT 3½ CUPS

2 large English (hothouse) cucumbers (2 pounds)

1 cup sugar

Simple pleasures are the best. I always get excited when a recipe can be this good with just two ingredients. Although it contains sugar, this simple sorbet is not meant as a dessert, but rather as a "savory." Like the cucumber slices in the martini recipe, this is also a great accompaniment for cocktails. Try putting a generous scoop in a coupe glass and topping it off with some Champagne. It's cool and refreshing, which makes it a good side dish for hors d'oeuvres of smoked salmon or caviar. You can also use it to make a cucumber salad of contrasting textures: chop some fresh cucumbers, season and dress them very lightly, top them with some of the sorbet, and garnish with chopped fresh cilantro and chives.

Peel the cucumbers and reserve the peels. Place the sugar in a medium saucepan with 1 cup of water and bring to a boil over medium heat. When the sugar has dissolved, add the cucumber peels and remove from the heat. Set the syrup aside to steep for 10 minutes. Strain the syrup and reserve; you should have about 1¼ cups.

Roughly chop the cucumbers and place them in a blender or food processor. Purée the cucumbers, then pass the purée through a fine strainer. Add ¾ cup of the syrup to the strained purée. Mix well, then taste, adding more syrup if necessary.

Transfer the cucumber mixture to a covered container and chill for at least 1 hour. When the mixture is thoroughly chilled, process it in an ice cream maker according to manufacturer's directions. Store the sorbet in a covered glass or plastic container in the freezer until ready to serve.

CURRY

TOWN

Curried Shrimp Bisque

SERVES 8

FOR THE BISQUE

3 tablespoons extra-virgin olive oil

1 cup chopped onion (1/2 medium onion)

1/2 cup chopped fennel (1/2 small bulb)

3 tablespoons chopped garlic (3 large cloves)

1 cup chopped carrots (2 medium carrots)

2 red bell peppers, seeds and skin removed, chopped

1 or 2 fresh small hot red peppers, minced

6 stalks lemongrass, inner parts only, chopped

1/2 cup peeled, finely chopped ginger

1 tablespoon mixed peppercorns

1 dried bay leaf

3 kaffir lime leaves (optional)

2 ripe medium tomatoes, peeled, seeded, and roughly chopped

1 large mango, peeled and chopped, pit reserved

1/2 cup fresh lime juice

1 2/3 cups (1 13 1/2-ounce can) coconut milk

6 cups Chicken Stock (page 262, or low-sodium canned)

16 medium fresh shrimp, peeled and deveined, shells reserved

1/2 cup coriander seeds, toasted

Fine sea salt and freshly ground black pepper to taste

Given the remarkable explosion in the popularity and availability of Asian ingredients over the past decade, the shopping list for this bisque—albeit rather extensive—should represent an enjoyable adventure at your local market. Once you've assembled everything, the prep and cooking are a breeze. And the result is a stimulating, exotic potpourri that elevates the curry-shrimp partnership to a new level and shows how just the right amount of curry is really a great thing. I particularly enjoy the way the sweet, fresh combination of shrimp and mango calls out for peppery spice, a call that's answered beautifully by a multifaceted mix of vegetables and seasonings. If you like, add a cup of chopped pineapple to the simmering broth for an extra boost of fruity sweetness. And for a fancy garnish, add about six big pieces of popcorn to each bowl before ladling in the soup.

INGREDIENT NOTE Kaffir lime leaves are available at most Asian markets and also through Kalustyan's online or by phone (see "Sources and Resources," page 266).

PREPARE THE BISQUE Warm the oil in a large pot over medium heat; add the onion and fennel and cook, stirring occasionally, until the vegetables are soft and golden, 20 to 30 minutes. Add the garlic and cook for about 2 minutes. Add the carrots, bell peppers, hot peppers, lemongrass, ginger, peppercorns, bay leaf, and kaffir lime leaves (if using). Continue to cook until the vegetables soften, about 10 minutes. Add the tomatoes, mango and mango pit, and lime juice. Simmer, stirring occasionally, until the juices reduce by about half, 15 to 20 minutes. Add the coconut milk, stock, and reserved shrimp shells. Raise the heat to medium-high and bring the soup to a boil. Skim off any foam that forms, add the coriander seeds, and reduce the heat to medium-low. Simmer, skimming from time to time, until the broth is flavorful, about 30 minutes. Season the broth, with salt and pepper to taste. Remove the mango pit. Pass it through a fine strainer (chinois or china cap), discarding any solids. Purée the soup in a blender (this step is optional). Season to taste with additional salt and pepper, if necessary. Refrigerate the soup until ready to use or keep warm over low heat.

FOR THE SHRIMP MARINADE

1½ tablespoons peanut oil

Flesh of 3 limes, no pith, chopped

1½ tablespoons fish sauce

¼ cup thinly sliced Thai basil leaves

¼ cup finely diced pineapple

1½ cloves garlic minced with 1 teaspoon sea salt

Fine sea salt

MARINATE THE SHRIMP Place the peanut oil, lime, fish sauce, basil, pineapple, and garlic in a small bowl along with 1 cup of water. Mix well to combine all ingredients. Slice each shrimp in half, add to the marinade, and mix well. Marinate the shrimp for 20 to 30 minutes (but no longer), then drain them and reserve, discarding the marinade.

TO SERVE Gently reheat the bisque, if necessary. Place 4 marinated shrimp halves in the bottom of each of 8 soup bowls. Ladle warm bisque into each bowl and serve.

CURRY

Country Curry-Spiced Nuts

SERVES 6 TO 8 (OR MORE FOR COCKTAILS)

1 large egg white

2 tablespoons sugar

2 tablespoons Madras curry powder

1 teaspoon kosher salt

½ teaspoon cayenne pepper

1 pound raw whole mixed nuts, peeled

Juice of 1 lemon

Here's a simple snack recipe that manages to incorporate elements of sweetness, salt, and spice to jazz up your cocktail nuts.

INGREDIENT NOTE I like the extra kick of Madras curry powder, which is a little hotter than regular old curry powder.

Preheat the oven to 350°F.

Place the egg whites and sugar in a large bowl, and whisk to combine. Place the curry powder, salt, and cayenne in a separate bowl, and mix thoroughly. Coat the nuts first with the egg white–sugar mixture, then with the spices. Drizzle the nuts with the lemon juice.

Arrange the nuts in a single layer on a parchment-lined baking sheet. Bake until they are crisp and the spice is toasted but not burned, about 20 minutes. Remove from the oven and allow the nuts to cool for at least 10 minutes before serving. They are good warm or at room temperature, and can be stored in an airtight container in a cool place for about a week.

DUCK

TOWN

Duck à l'Orange "Town"

SERVES 4

FOR THE DUCK AND SPICE MIX

- 1 tablespoon juniper berries
- 1 tablespoon coriander seeds
- 1 tablespoon fennel seeds
- 4 pieces star anise
- 1 tablespoon cardamom seeds
- 1 tablespoon kosher salt
- 4 duck leg quarters (preferably Long Island)
- 6 cups duck fat, oil, clarified butter, or a mix of fats (enough to cover the legs)

FOR THE GLAZE

- 3 cups fresh orange juice
- 2½ tablespoons honey

FOR THE SPINACH SALAD AND SERVING

- 1½ pounds spinach, stemmed and washed
- 2 tablespoons extra-virgin olive oil
- ¼ cup freshly squeezed lemon juice (1 large or 2 small lemons)
- Fine sea salt and freshly ground black pepper to taste
- Onion and Shiitake Garnish (recipe follows; optional)

When I ran around France for a year starting in 1980, I checked out all the little restaurants and inns I could find. Duck was on just about every menu, and that's how I learned to appreciate how to cook (and sometimes how *not* to cook) this bird. There are two basic ways of doing it—the yin and yang of duck, so to speak: one is to confit the legs, which I think of as "properly overcooking"; the other is to pan-roast the breast, which involves "properly undercooking." This recipe, which I developed in the late 1980s for Restaurant 44 at the Royalton Hotel, is my take on the former approach. (The Duck Breast with Buckwheat Pilaf, page 113, is my adaptation of the latter.) Rather than a classic *canard à l'orange,* where the bird is either oven- or pan-roasted and then an orange-based sauce is made from the pan drippings, this is actually an orange-glazed duck leg confit. You can't beat a confit for convenience and versatility; it's just a great way to capture the succulent flavor of dark meat such as duck legs. Whether you serve this rich preparation for an opening course, a main dish or lunch, one leg per person is plenty.

INGREDIENT NOTES Almost any type of fat—olive oil, various other types of vegetable oil, clarified butter—can be used to prepare a confit; the more viscous, the better because it cooks more slowly. Once the confit is made and stored, you can also use the fat itself, with its deliciously infused spices, to fry up some eggs, a veal chop or two, or perhaps some chicken legs and thighs.

I encourage you to double the following recipe for spice mix and make a confit of 8 (rather than 4) duck legs. The 4 you don't use can be preserved by the traditional method (in the fat) and used later. All you've got to do with the leftover legs is remove them from their fat, brown them nicely on either side, and serve.

TIMING NOTE This recipe is designed to be prepared in several discrete steps. The confit can be made days in advance. The glaze can also be prepared well in advance. The optional onion and shiitake garnish can be made ahead of time. The finishing and assembly can be completed in 20 to 25 minutes before serving.

MARINATE THE DUCK, AT LEAST 12 HOURS IN ADVANCE In a clean coffee or spice grinder or mortar, combine the juniper, coriander, fennel, star anise, and cardamom, and grind together to a coarse powder. Set 2 tablespoons of this spice mix aside for use in the glaze.

Season the duck legs with the salt then rub them with the spice mix. Lay them skin side down in a pie plate or other shallow container, cover with plastic wrap, and refrigerate for at least 12 but up to 48 hours.

PREPARE THE CONFIT Place the duck legs, with the spice mixture still adhering, in a large saucepot big enough to hold the legs snugly with just a little overlap, and deep enough to allow them to be submerged completely in liquid. Add enough duck fat to cover the legs and bring to a simmer over medium-low heat. Gently simmer the duck legs (the fat should bubble ever so slightly; turn it down if it is too active), skimming occasionally, until a paring knife easily penetrates the meat and the meat begins to pull from the bone. Start checking for doneness after about 1½ hours; they may need another hour.

Allow the duck to cool in the fat, then lift the legs into a clean container and ladle the fat over them (discard the spices that have settled to the bottom). The confit may be stored in the refrigerator, covered, for up to 2 months.

PREPARE THE GLAZE Bring the orange juice to a boil in a small nonreactive saucepan over medium-high heat. Reduce the heat to medium and simmer until the juice is viscous and only ½ cup remains, about 30 minutes. Stir in the honey and simmer for 1 minute, then remove from the heat. Add the reserved 2 tablespoons of spice mixture and set aside, covered, in a cool place.

FINISHING AND ASSEMBLY Preheat the oven to 350°F.

Heat an ovenproof skillet over medium-high flame. Add the four duck legs, skin side down, and a little less than 1 tablespoon of the duck fat. Allow the skin on the duck legs to brown thoroughly, 3 to 5 minutes. Turn the legs over carefully and transfer the pan to the oven. Warm the duck legs through, about 5 minutes. Meanwhile, place the onion and shiitake garnish in the oven (if using) to warm.

continued

PREPARE THE SPINACH SALAD Place the spinach in a stainless-steel bowl or ovenproof saucepan. Dress the spinach with the olive oil and lemon juice, and season with the salt and pepper (about 1 teaspoon each, or to taste). Put the bowl or pan in the oven and allow the spinach to begin to wilt while the duck warms, 3 to 5 minutes. Remove the spinach from the oven and toss it gently. Remove the onion and shiitake garnish from the oven (if using.)

When the duck is warm, remove it from the oven and heat the broiler. Brush the duck with a light coating of the glaze and set under the broiler until the glaze is bubbly, 1 to 2 minutes. Remove the duck from the oven.

Arrange onions and shiitakes around the outside of each plate (if using). Mound the spinach in the center of the plates. Top each salad with a leg of duck confit and serve.

ONION AND SHIITAKE GARNISH

SERVES 4

- **24 pearl onions, peeled and soaked in hot water for 10 minutes**
- **2 tablespoons unsalted butter**
- **1 tablespoon sugar**
- **2 tablespoons white wine vinegar**
- **1 teaspoon kosher salt**
- **1 teaspoon freshly ground black pepper**
- **1 tablespoon extra-virgin olive oil**
- **½ pound shiitake mushrooms, stemmed and julienned**
- **1 large shallot, minced**

Place the onions, in a single layer, in a deep, heavy skillet. Add 1 tablespoon of the butter, the sugar, vinegar, salt, and pepper. Add enough water to come about halfway up the onions, about ¾ cup. Simmer the onions over medium heat, turning them occasionally, until they are tender and the water has all but evaporated, about 20 minutes (if most of the liquid is gone but the onions are still undercooked add a little more water). When the pan is almost dry, glaze the onions, rolling them in the caramelized butter from the bottom of the pan. Transfer the glazed onions to a bowl and reserve.

Heat the oil and 1 tablespoon of the butter in a large skillet over medium heat. Add the shiitakes and cook until they begin to soften and brown, about 3 minutes. Turn the shiitakes and add the minced shallot. Cook, stirring occasionally, until the mushrooms are soft, about 4 minutes more. Add the shiitakes to the glazed onions. Set aside until ready to assemble the dish.

DUCK

Country

Duck Breast with Buckwheat Pilaf

SERVES 6

FOR THE SPICE RUB

- **½ teaspoon cumin seeds**
- **½ teaspoon allspice berries**
- **½ teaspoon fennel seeds**
- **½ teaspoon coriander seeds**
- **10 whole cloves**
- **5 cardamom pods**
- **2 pieces star anise**
- **3 dried bay leaves**
- **½ teaspoon ground turmeric**
- **½ teaspoon Madras curry powder**

FOR THE DUCK

- **3 duck breasts (magret; 1 pound each)**
- **2 tablespoons duck fat or Clarified Butter (page 264)**
- **Kosher salt and freshly ground black pepper to taste**
- **½ cup port wine**
- **1½ tablespoons unsalted butter, diced**

Buckwheat Pilaf (recipe follows)

My mom was a great cook and although she was Polish, she figured out the cuisine of my dad's Armenian heritage very early on. She was like a sponge in the kitchen: show her a recipe once and she would pick it up, make it part of her repertoire, and never look back. I now know it was she, along with my three aunts, who gave me my first cooking lessons (although I didn't realize it until I got to France years later and started cooking to impress my dates). We had pilaf three or four times a week when I was growing up; you could make it with white rice, barley, or kasha—another name for buckwheat groats, a staple in Armenia. (*Groats* is the term used to refer to various types of grains after they've been hulled and crushed.) A typical element in the pilafs made by my mom and aunts was noodles fried in butter, to give a crispy contrast and a nutty complement to the grains. Pilafs are great family recipes; they allow you to stretch out a relatively small amount of savory meat to nourish a big crowd, and they also work very well as leftovers.

The key to the cooking process in this recipe is the relatively long, slow application of heat to the duck skin; this renders all the fat so it can be poured off and also crisps the skin nicely. The dark red, sweet, concentrated port wine is a natural to deglaze the pan and make a sauce for the duck.

TIMING NOTE The duck breasts in this recipe are marinated overnight in a spice rub.

SHORTCUT If you want to skip the pilaf, simply serve the duck on a bed of rice or even on its own.

PREPARE THE SPICE RUB Combine the cumin, allspice, fennel, coriander, cloves, cardamom, star anise, and bay leaves in a small skillet and toast over medium heat until fragrant, about 5 minutes. Allow the mixture to cool, then grind it in a clean coffee or spice grinder or with a mortar and pestle. Add the turmeric and curry powder, and mix well.

SEASON THE DUCK BREASTS Score the skin in a crisscross pattern, cutting through the fat but stopping short of the meat. Coat the skin with the spice

continued

mixture and rub it well. Wrap the duck breasts in plastic and refrigerate for 12 to 24 hours.

COOK THE DUCK Preheat the oven to 350°F. Allow the duck to come to room temperature before cooking.

Heat the duck fat in an ovenproof skillet large enough to hold all the duck breasts without crowding. Add the breasts, skin side down, and cook over low heat until the skin is deep amber, about 20 minutes, pouring off any accumulated fat from time to time.

FINISH AND SERVE Once the duck is browned, season the breasts with salt and pepper, pour off any fat from the pan, and place it in the oven to roast, about 7 minutes for medium-rare. Transfer the duck to a cutting board to rest. Return the skillet to the stove over medium heat. Add the port and simmer until reduced by two thirds, about 5 minutes. Whisk in the butter and season with salt and pepper to taste. Keep the sauce warm over very low heat.

To serve, spoon equal portions of warm pilaf onto each of six warm dinner plates. Cut the duck breasts into ½-inch-thick slices and arrange them on top of the pilaf. Spoon a little sauce over the duck and serve.

BUCKWHEAT PILAF

SERVES 6

- **About 30 strands uncooked angel-hair pasta**
- **1 tablespoon extra-virgin olive oil**
- **1 large shallot, minced**
- **1½ cups whole buckwheat groats (preferably untoasted)**
- **3 cups Chicken Stock (page 262, or low-sodium canned)**
- **¼ cup finely chopped flat-leaf parsley**
- **3 tablespoons fresh lemon juice (1 lemon)**
- **Kosher salt and freshly ground black pepper to taste**

Break the pasta into small pieces. Toast the broken pasta in a dry skillet over medium heat until lightly browned, about 7 minutes; set aside. Heat the oil in a large saucepan over medium heat. Add the shallots and cook, stirring occasionally until they are soft, about 10 minutes. Stir in the buckwheat and cook, stirring, until lightly browned. (If using toasted buckwheat groats, simply continue without browning the groats.) Add the stock and pasta, and simmer, uncovered, until most of the liquid is absorbed, 10 to 12 minutes. Remove from heat, fold in the parsley and lemon juice, season with salt and pepper to taste, and serve (or reserve in a warm place until ready to serve).

EGGPLANT

TOWN

Roasted Four-Spiced Eggplant Purée

MAKES ABOUT 4 CUPS

4 medium eggplants

6 cloves garlic, halved

2 tablespoons extra-virgin olive oil, plus additional for garnish

1 tablespoon unsalted butter

1 teaspoon fine sea salt, or to taste

1 tablespoon quatre épices, or to taste

Pinch of cayenne

Toasted pita wedges or sliced baguette, for serving (optional)

As Parmesan cheese and pasta are to Italian families, so eggplant is to an Armenian family like mine—it was all over the house. When I was between jobs a few years back, I did a *stage* in the kitchen of Alain Passard at Arpège restaurant in Paris; it was an exciting, inspirational midcareer refresher. This is an adaptation of a recipe for my beloved eggplant that I learned while working with Chef Passard. It's particularly suitable as a side dish for freshly caught, simply prepared fish. Don't worry about making too much; the leftovers store well, covered and refrigerated, and can be reheated easily. To serve it as a dip, simply allow it to come to room temperature, freshen it up with some extra-virgin olive oil, parsley, and a pinch or two of cayenne or paprika, and serve with toasted pita wedges.

INGREDIENT NOTE *Quatre épices* ("four spices" in French) is a blend available in the spice section of most markets. Generally, it consists of nutmeg, ginger, cinnamon, white pepper, and/or cloves. If you can't find any or if you prefer to blend your own, go for it.

Preheat the oven to 375°F.

Using a small knife, make three cross-shaped cuts, deep enough to hold a garlic clove, into the skin of each eggplant. Place half a garlic clove in each cut. Rub the eggplants all over with olive oil and place them in a baking dish. Roast until the eggplants are deflated and a knife inserted comes out clean, at least 1 hour.

Allow the eggplants to cool for 15 minutes. Remove the garlic cloves and reserve. Scoop the pulp of the eggplants from their skins and place it in a colander, allowing it to drain of excess water for at least 15 minutes. Place the pulp in a blender with the butter and garlic cloves, and purée. Season to taste with salt, quatre épices, and cayenne. Serve at room temperature as a dip for toasted pita, or warm as a side dish garnished with a drizzling of olive oil.

Country Eggplant Bisque

SERVES 4

3 medium eggplants

3 tablespoons extra-virgin olive oil

2 medium leeks, white parts only, chopped

2 tablespoons chopped garlic (2 large cloves)

Pinch of hot red pepper flakes

½ teaspoon cumin seeds

1 teaspoon Madras curry powder

½ cup dry riesling

3 medium tomatoes, peeled, seeded, and roughly chopped

½ cup heavy cream

3½ cups Chicken Stock (page 262, or low-sodium canned)

2 tablespoons fresh thyme leaves

2 tablespoons fresh oregano leaves

Leaves of 1 sprig rosemary

1 fresh bay leaf

¼ cup chopped flat-leaf parsley

Fine sea salt and freshly ground black pepper to taste

High-quality Spanish sherry vinegar to taste

¼ cup crème fraîche

1 tablespoon hazelnut oil

A traditional bisque is a rich, cream-based shellfish soup flavored with white wine and Cognac. This variation obtains its character from the mildly smoky flavor of eggplant, and its flair from a Middle Eastern–accented blend of spices. If you've ever contemplated a raw eggplant—or even taken a little taste—it's bitter, spongy, and not at all palatable. Cooking one, however, releases its precious essence—the earth, water, and sun that made it grow—miraculously transforming this bulbous nightshade into delicious food. As with virtually all of my soups, this bisque can be served hot (but never *too* hot) or cool (just 10 or 15 degrees below room temperature).

Preheat the oven to 400°F.

Wrap the eggplants in aluminum foil and bake until soft, about 1 hour. In the meantime, place the olive oil and leeks in a large pot over medium heat; sweat until the leeks are slightly browned and soft, about 5 minutes. Add the garlic and cook until fragrant, 1 to 2 minutes more. Add the red pepper flakes, cumin, and curry powder. Cook until the spices are fragrant, about 2 minutes. Add the wine and simmer until the pot is almost dry, about 5 minutes. Add the tomatoes and cook, stirring occasionally with a wooden spoon, until the tomatoes begin to stick to the bottom of the pot, about 10 minutes. Add the cream, stir well, and scrape free any bits of vegetables or spices that have stuck to the bottom of the pot. Simmer for 1 to 2 minutes, then add the stock and bring back to a simmer.

Scoop the pulp from the eggplants and spoon into the soup. Add the thyme, oregano, rosemary, bay leaf, and parsley. Simmer the soup for 20 minutes, then purée it in a blender. Season to taste with salt and pepper. Sharpen it up with a little sherry vinegar and smooth it out with the crème fraîche and hazelnut oil. If you like your soup extra-smooth, pass it through a fine strainer (china cap or chinois). Serve hot or cool.

EGGS

TOWN

Basted Eggs with Lobster Hash

SERVES 6

6 large eggs, at room temperature, cracked into individual cups

4 tablespoons extra-virgin olive oil

Fine sea salt and freshly ground black pepper

Lobster Hash (recipe follows)

Horseradish Cream (recipe follows)

My goal here was to create a dish for special occasions when you want to say "I love you" to your guests with food. What could be more indulgent than jazzing up some lobster meat (leftover or store-bought) and serving it alongside eggs that have been prepared and presented in a thoughtful way? In conceiving the perfect food, it would be hard to improve on the beauty, simplicity, and sheer nourishment value of the egg—not to mention the extreme pleasure of consuming a well-prepared one. Almost anybody can fry or boil an egg; the trick is to coax it along with a gentler treatment—in this case, basting it in olive oil—that will give you a brand-new appreciation of an old treat. Of course, you can also serve these eggs more simply, with toast or English muffins for breakfast; I like to serve them as a luxurious treat for brunch or lunch alongside this lobster hash.

Place 2 tablespoons of the oil in a medium skillet over medium heat. When the oil is hot, pour one egg carefully from its cup into the skillet. Allow the white to set for a few seconds, then pour another egg into the pan. (The eggs may be cooked in batches of two or three.) The eggs should cook gently; the oil should be active—that is, it should move across the pan easily, but it should not spit, spatter, or smoke. Baste the yolks with the hot oil until the whites are set and slightly puffed and the yolks are done as desired, 2 to 4 minutes. Using a spatula, lift the eggs out of the oil to drain on a plate lined with paper towels. Season each egg lightly with salt and pepper.

Place one Lobster Hash patty and one basted egg on each plate. Spoon some Horseradish Cream on top and serve.

MAKES 6 PATTIES

6 small Yukon gold potatoes, peeled, washed, and steamed until fork-tender

¼ pound cooked lobster meat, diced (from a 1½- to 2-pound lobster)

3 scallions, white and light green parts, washed and finely chopped

Leaves of 1 bunch of tarragon, chopped

Leaves of 1 bunch of cilantro, chopped

1 teaspoon hot paprika

Pinch of cayenne pepper

Fine sea salt and freshly ground black pepper

Wondra flour, for dusting

1½ tablespoons extra-virgin olive oil, plus additional if needed

1 tablespoon unsalted butter, plus additional if needed

LOBSTER HASH

Place the steamed potatoes in a large mixing bowl and mash them well with a fork. Add the diced lobster meat and stir to combine. Add the scallions, tarragon, cilantro, paprika, and cayenne. Season to taste with salt and black pepper. Line six 4-inch ring molds with plastic wrap. Spoon the mixture into the molds, filling each mold to the top. Press to form compact patties. (Alternatively, form the patties with your hands, using plastic wrap and a dish or shallow bowl.) Carefully turn out each hash patty into a shallow pan of Wondra and dust with the flour.

Preheat the oven to 400°F. Place the olive oil and butter in a large sauté pan over high heat. Allow the butter to brown lightly, then place the lobster hash patties in the pan and brown them, about 3 minutes per side. (If necessary, work in batches, wiping out the pan and refreshing the oil and butter as needed.) Transfer the patties to an ovenproof skillet, then place them in the oven for 5 to 6 minutes to heat through. Transfer them to a plate lined with paper towel, to drain off excess butter and oil, and reserve in a warm place until ready to serve.

MAKES ABOUT 1 CUP

½ cup heavy cream, chilled

1 tablespoon prepared horseradish

2 tablespoons sour cream

1 tablespoon chopped fresh chives (¼ to ⅓ of a small bunch)

HORSERADISH CREAM

Place the heavy cream in a chilled stainless-steel or other nonreactive bowl and whip with a whisk until soft peaks form. Add the horseradish, sour cream, and chives, and stir well to combine. Reserve, covered, in a cool place until ready to serve.

For a smoother, milder cream, pass the horseradish through a strainer into the whipped cream and discard the solid bits; for more bite, increase the amount of horseradish to 1½ tablespoons.

Country
Coddled Eggs with Wild Mushrooms

SERVES 4

- **1 tablespoon extra-virgin olive oil**
- **¼ cup minced shallots (about 3 shallots)**
- **½ teaspoon minced garlic (about ½ clove)**
- **2 sprigs fresh thyme**
- **1 cup finely chopped mixed wild mushrooms (about ½ pound)**
- **1 cup Chicken Stock (page 262, or low-sodium canned)**
- **1¼ cups heavy cream**
- **½ cup whole milk or skim milk**
- **4 large eggs**
- **Fine sea salt and freshly ground black pepper**
- **4 slices baguette, toasted**
- **Blanched Asparagus Tips (recipe follows; optional)**

I love the word *coddled* because it embodies an important element of my cooking philosophy, which is to try to find a gentler, less aggressive, less intrusive treatment than the norm. In the culinary lexicon, *coddling* is a specific way of preparing eggs (and other foods) by cooking them gently in a water bath—somewhere between baking and poaching. There's a special type of lidded cooking vessel called an egg coddler to achieve this. My aunt Anna used to make baked eggs with feta cheese and tomatoes and serve them with toasted homemade bread for breakfast, which is what introduced me to this kinder, gentler way of cooking eggs. Here, I've created a kind of deconstructed custard, featuring baked eggs and wild mushrooms, meant for a hearty country brunch. In classic French cuisine, the preparation of chopped mushrooms, shallots, and onions sautéed in butter is called a *duxelles*. In this recipe, we take the concept of a duxelles one step further, whipping it into a delicious froth and using it to garnish the coddled eggs.

Preheat the oven to 400°F.

Place the oil in a skillet over low heat. Add the shallots, garlic, thyme, and mushrooms and cook, stirring occasionally, until the mushrooms are tender, approximately 7 minutes. Add the stock, raise the heat to medium, and cook until the pan is almost dry, about 10 minutes. Add the heavy cream and milk.

Simmer, stirring occasionally, until the cream has reduced by about one third, 20 minutes or so. Pass the preparation through a fine strainer, reserving about ½ cup of the cream and the mushrooms separately; discard the thyme.

Divide the strained cream mixture among four 4-ounce ramekins. Crack the eggs carefully into small bowls, then pour one into each ramekin. Season the eggs lightly with salt and pepper, then place them in the oven to bake until they set, 5 to 9 minutes.

Meanwhile, place the ½ cup reserved cream in a small saucepan over medium-low heat and simmer for 1 to 2 minutes; place an immersion blender in the cream and agitate until the cream is frothy. (Alternatively, whip the cream with a whisk.)

Spoon the frothy mushroom cream and reserved mushrooms over each coddled egg; top each with a slice of toasted baguette and 2 blanched asparagus tips (if using) and serve in the ramekins.

BLANCHED ASPARAGUS TIPS

MAKES 8

8 tips from medium to large asparagus spears

Bring a small pot of salted water to a boil and prepare an ice-water bath. (If the asparagus tips have large, tough-looking leaves, trim them a bit as needed.) Blanch the asparagus tips by plunging them in the boiling water until bright green and tender, about 1 minute. Drain the tips, refresh them in the ice water, and reserve.

FENNEL

TOWN

Fennel Bisque with Tomato-Olive Relish

SERVES 6

FOR THE SOUP

3 tablespoons extra-virgin olive oil

1 cup chopped onions (1/2 medium onion)

6 cloves garlic, chopped

1/2 cup chopped celery (1 stalk)

8 cups chopped fennel (4 large bulbs, fronds trimmed)

1/2 cup chopped parsnips (1 medium parsnip, about 1/4 pound)

1 cup Pernod

1 1/2 cups dry white wine

2 cups Chicken Stock (page 262, or low-sodium canned)

2 cups plain whole-milk yogurt

Fine sea salt and freshly ground black pepper

About 1/2 cup dry vermouth, for garnish

FOR THE SACHET

2 tablespoons fennel seeds

2 tablespoons white peppercorns

2 allspice berries

4 juniper berries

Zest of 2 oranges

1 fresh bay leaf

Tomato-Olive Relish (recipe follows; optional)

At the Royalton Hotel, we used to order a huge amount of fennel for our popular fennel and cucumber salad, and I was always looking for interesting ways to use the extra bulbs. There are many ways to bring out fennel's various traits, and this is one of my favorites, a nice twist on the traditional concept of a bisque. The fennel is sweated and then slowly simmered so its anise perfume begins to emerge and meld beautifully with the other aromatic vegetables. This bisque gets its richness from a touch of yogurt. Both the Pernod and the parsnips provide excellent complementary flavors. You can serve this warm or cool, on its own or with the Tomato-Olive Relish, which can be made up to three days in advance. The bisque gets better on the second and third day, so don't hesitate to refrigerate it first. You can also turn it into a sauce for poached, steamed, or grilled fish by boiling it down until it's reduced by a third to a half.

Place the oil, onions, garlic, celery, chopped fennel, and parsnips in a large pot over medium-low heat and sweat for 30 minutes, until translucent and very soft. Be extra careful not to brown or color the vegetables; reduce the heat if necessary. Add the Pernod and cook until it is completely reduced, about 10 minutes. Add the white wine and cook until it is reduced by two thirds, about 20 minutes.

Make a sachet by tying the fennel seeds, white pepper, allspice berries, juniper berries, orange zest, and bay leaf in a bundle of cheesecloth. Add the sachet, stock, 2 cups of water, and the yogurt to the soup. Bring to a simmer, and season with salt and pepper to taste. Simmer the soup for 20 minutes more; remove the sachet and squeeze its juice into the bisque. Purée the bisque in a blender. Season to taste with additional salt and pepper. If you like your soup extra-smooth, pass it through a fine strainer (chinois or china cap).

Place equal portions of hot soup in each of six bowls; garnish each serving with a drizzle of dry vermouth. Add a large dollop of Tomato-Olive Relish, if using, and serve hot. (Alternatively, thin the relish with extra marinade and vermouth to drizzle onto the soup before serving.)

TOMATO-OLIVE RELISH

MAKES ABOUT ¾ CUP

- 8 Cerignola olives, pitted and coarsely chopped
- ¼ cup Tomato Confit (page 265), coarsely chopped, or 2 tablespoons tomato paste
- 3 tablespoons extra-virgin olive oil
- 1 piece star anise, ground
- 1 teaspoon ground fennel seeds
- Pinch of cayenne pepper
- 2 teaspoons dry vermouth
- ¼ cup fromage blanc or crème fraîche
- 2 tablespoons coarsely chopped fresh dill
- Grated zest of 1 lemon

INGREDIENT NOTE Cerignola are relatively big, hard green olives that have good, strong flavor and texture; they hold their own in an assertive marinade like this relish.

Place the olives, tomato confit, oil, ground star anise, ground fennel, cayenne, and vermouth in a glass or other nonreactive container. Cover and refrigerate for up to 3 days.

Prior to serving, remove the olives and tomatoes from the relish marinade, and place them in a bowl; add the fromage blanc, dill, lemon zest, and 1 tablespoon of the marinade, and mix well.

FENNEL

Country
Fennel Gratin with Gruyère

SERVES 4 TO 6

- **3 cups ½-inch cubes brioche or country bread (4 to 6 slices, depending on the size of the loaf; remove the crust)**
- **½ cup extra-virgin olive oil**
- **½ cup unsalted butter**
- **1½ teaspoons minced garlic (1 medium clove)**
- **½ teaspoon cayenne pepper**
- **1 dried bay leaf**
- **Small pinch of freshly grated nutmeg**
- **4 medium bulbs fennel, trimmed and sliced thin across the grain**
- **2 medium Yukon gold potatoes, peeled and sliced ¼ inch thick**
- **6 cups heavy cream**
- **1 teaspoon kosher salt**
- **½ teaspoon freshly ground black pepper**
- **¼ pound Gruyère cheese, shredded (about 1 cup)**

A gratin, to me, is a great way to magically transform a relatively mundane vegetable—even one that's been overcooked—into a delicate and luxurious treat. This gratin is a straightforward side dish, featuring a two-stage cooking process, inspired by something I had in Italy back in the 1980s. Dishes involving two distinct methods are potentially a lot more interesting than any once-baked or quick-fried item. Here, the fennel and potatoes are first simmered in cream, which helps gently infuse them with spice flavors, in preparation for the second, baking-and-melting stage. Serve this gratin as an accompaniment to a roasted leg of lamb, pork shoulder, or pork ribs.

INGREDIENT NOTE As a lighter alternative, simmer the fennel and potatoes in chicken stock instead of cream.

Preheat the oven to 375°F.

Soak the bread cubes in the olive oil.

Melt the butter in a medium pot over medium-low heat (do not allow it to color or sizzle). Add the garlic, cayenne, bay leaf, and nutmeg. Cook for about 1 minute, then add the fennel and potatoes. Add just enough cream to cover the fennel and potatoes. Season with the salt and pepper, then bring to a simmer over medium heat and cook until the potatoes are nearly tender, about 5 minutes. Drain the potatoes and fennel, discarding the cream and bay leaf.

Spoon half the vegetables into a medium gratin or baking dish. Sprinkle with a bit more than half the cheese. Cover with the remaining fennel and potatoes, followed by the remaining cheese. Top with the oil-soaked bread cubes.

Place the dish in the oven, uncovered, and bake until the cheese is melted and the gratin is nicely browned on top, 30 to 40 minutes. Serve directly from the oven.

GRAPEFRUIT

SERVES 6

FOR THE SORBET
(MAKES ABOUT 1 QUART)

½ cup sugar

1½-inch piece ginger, peeled and thinly sliced

4 cups fresh pink grapefruit juice, strained (about 4 grapefruits)

FOR THE GRATIN

6 pink grapefruits

¼ cup sugar

TOWN

Grapefruit Gratin with Grapefruit-Ginger Sorbet

This dessert is my Town takeoff on grilled grapefruit with brown sugar, a traditional English dish. While much of my inspiration for savory dishes—soups, appetizers, pastas, main courses—comes from classic French and Italian cuisine, a lot of my desserts are adaptations of old English favorites. There's something about those British comfort desserts that gets me revved up. Most people think of grapefruits as sour, but the best ones—like any good fruit, really—have a strong dose of both sour and sweet in exquisite balance. This recipe also offers a nice hot-cold contrast—another very desirable dessert feature—between the sorbet and gratin.

PREPARE THE SORBET Place the sugar and ½ cup water in a medium saucepan over high heat and bring to a boil. Add the ginger and boil for 1 minute. Remove the pan from the heat and set it aside to cool. Once it is cool, strain the ginger syrup. Combine the grapefruit juice and the ginger syrup in an ice cream maker and process according to manufacturer's directions. Freeze for at least 1 hour before serving.

PREPARE THE GRATIN Preheat the broiler and arrange a rack near the flame. With a very sharp knife, cut about ½ inch off the top and bottom of each grapefruit. Carefully cut off the peel, removing the pith as well, following the curve of the grapefruit. Carefully cut the segments apart by slicing down along either side of the membrane. Once all the grapefruit segments are filleted in this manner, arrange equal portions in 6 flameproof ramekins or place them in rows in a single large flameproof gratin dish. Sprinkle the grapefruit with a good coating of sugar and place under the broiler until browned, 4 to 10 minutes depending on the broiler heat and the rack height.

Serve the gratin immediately, topped with scoops of grapefruit sorbet.

GRAPEFRUIT

Country Grapefruit Ambrosia

SERVES 6

FOR THE GINGER SYRUP

- ½ cup sugar
- 1 2-inch piece of ginger, peeled and thinly sliced

FOR THE GRAPEFRUIT CURD

- 1 cup sugar
- 6 large egg yolks
- 1 cup fresh ruby red grapefruit juice, strained (about 2 grapefruits)
- 8 tablespoons (1 stick) unsalted butter, roughly chopped

FOR THE AMBROSIA

- 2 cups heavy cream
- Superfine sugar to taste
- 4 ruby red grapefruits, segmented (see instructions under Prepare the Gratin, opposite)
- 2 cups sliced pitted mixed fruit, such as plums, nectarines, or cherries
- ½ cup Ginger Syrup
- 1 cup sweetened shredded coconut, plus additional for garnish

I grew up in my mom's kitchen with fresh, homemade puddings—particularly tapioca, rice, and chocolate—and I've been a big fan of pudding-type desserts ever since I can remember. I've also sampled many an excellent parfait in Britain and other parts of Europe, all of which inspired me to create modern versions of the desserts I loved as a kid. This one is a kind of deconstructed, rustic grapefruit tart: the grapefruit is definitely the headliner, but there are several strong supporting characters, including the mixed fruits, coconut, and ginger. I first served this dish at the Royalton Hotel in 1990, and the crowd there really enjoyed it.

PREPARE THE GINGER SYRUP Place the sugar, ginger, and ½ cup of water in a saucepan over medium heat and bring to a boil. Remove the pan from the heat and let steep for 15 minutes. Allow the syrup to cool completely, then strain, cover, and refrigerate until ready to use.

PREPARE THE GRAPEFRUIT CURD Set up a double boiler over medium-low heat so the water in the bottom section is gently simmering and not touching the bottom of the top section. (If you don't have a double boiler, simply use a metal bowl and a saucepot.) Combine the sugar, egg yolks, and grapefruit juice in the top of the double boiler and whisk well. Place over the simmering water and, whisking constantly, cook until the mixture froths, then thickens enough to coat the back of a spoon, about 10 minutes. Whisk in the butter one piece at a time. Remove the curd from the heat. Working quickly, strain the curd through a fine sieve into a bowl. Place a piece of waxed paper or plastic wrap directly on the surface of the curd to prevent a skin from forming, cool to room temperature, and refrigerate.

ASSEMBLE THE AMBROSIA Chill 6 parfait glasses. Whip the heavy cream until soft peaks form, adding a little sugar to taste. In a large mixing bowl, combine the grapefruit segments, sliced fruit, ½ cup of the ginger syrup, and coconut, and toss to coat the fruit. Place a spoonful of this mixture in the bottom of each glass, and top with a spoonful of grapefruit curd, then whipped cream. Repeat the layers until you reach the top of the glass. Garnish with shredded coconut and serve.

HALIBUT

TOWN

Halibut Poached in Olive Oil with Braised Fennel and Tomato-Orange Marmalade

SERVES 6

FOR THE HALIBUT

- 6 6-ounce boneless, skinless halibut fillets (each about 1½ inches thick)
- 1 teaspoon kosher salt, plus more to taste
- ½ teaspoon freshly ground black pepper, plus more to taste
- 1½ tablespoons anise seeds
- 4 cups extra-virgin olive oil
- 2 sprigs thyme
- 1 fresh bay leaf
- 1 piece star anise
- 1 head of garlic, halved crosswise
- 4 shallots, sliced thin
- 1 tablespoon coriander seeds
- 1 tablespoon fennel seeds
- Braised Fennel (recipe follows; optional)

FOR THE TOMATO-ORANGE MARMALADE

- 3 medium navel oranges
- 3 tablespoons extra-virgin olive oil
- 4 large ripe beefsteak tomatoes, peeled, seeded, and diced
- Kosher salt and freshly ground black pepper
- 30 pitted niçoise olives, plus additional for garnish

Halibut is a fish I learned to love relatively recently, but one that has shot right to the top of my list. Its fillets are big, meaty slabs that can be treated in much the same way as a good cut of steak. The flesh is white, mild-flavored but dense, and substantial enough to hold up to searing, grilling in its skin, steaming, or sautéing in butter. But rather than resorting to those standard treatments, why not try one of the best and most underutilized cooking techniques among home chefs? Poaching in olive oil is a gentler process. I think of it as an "instant confit"—nothing is lost, and the fish retains its moist essence. Furthermore, the flavor of a high-quality olive oil lends a delicious perfume without penetrating the fish and rendering it heavy and oily.

In Middle Eastern cuisines, fruits and vegetables are often combined to create relish-type condiments for meats; the tomato-orange marmalade here echoes that approach. The braised fennel is an optional bed for the fish, with its reduced braising liquid providing an extra sauce.

PREPARE THE HALIBUT Season the halibut fillets on both sides with the salt and pepper, then sprinkle with the anise seeds. Place the seasoned fillets on a plate, cover with plastic wrap, and cure in the refrigerator for about 40 minutes. Meanwhile, place the oil, thyme, bay leaf, star anise, garlic, shallots, coriander seeds, and fennel seeds in a deep skillet or Dutch oven large enough to hold the fish in a single layer. Season the oil lightly with salt and pepper, and bring it to a gentle simmer over medium heat. Reduce the heat to low and cook for 30 minutes to combine the flavors.

PREPARE THE TOMATO-ORANGE MARMALADE Use a vegetable peeler to remove the zest of the oranges, then cut the oranges in half and squeeze out about ¾ cup of their juice; reserve their zest. Place 1 tablespoon of the oil in a large skillet over high heat. When the oil is hot, add the tomatoes, season with salt and pepper, and cook, stirring frequently, until the tomatoes release their juices, about 5 minutes. Remove the skillet from the heat; transfer the tomatoes to a strainer set over a bowl and allow them to drain for several minutes. Return the strained juice to the skillet over medium heat and reserve the tomatoes. Cook the strained tomato juice until the pan is almost dry, then add the orange juice. Simmer the mixture until it reduces by one third (to about ½ cup),

SERVES 6

2 large or 3 small bulbs fennel, washed and trimmed

2 tablespoons unsalted butter

1 teaspoon sea salt

½ teaspoon freshly ground white pepper

⅓ cup dry white wine

1½ cups Chicken Stock (page 262, or low-sodium canned)

about 7 minutes. Add the orange zest and the reserved tomatoes, and simmer for about 5 minutes to combine the flavors, then stir in the remaining 2 tablespoons of oil and the olives. Season the marmalade with salt and pepper, and set aside in a warm place until ready to serve. (The marmalade can be made in advance, refrigerated, and reheated prior to serving.)

COOK THE HALIBUT About 15 minutes before you plan to serve the dish, heat the seasoned 4 cups of poaching oil to a steady temperature of 160° to 175°F.; at this temperature, it will not simmer but occasional small bubbles will appear. Use a spatula to gently slide the halibut fillets into the oil. Poach until the fish is almost cooked through, about 5 minutes. Carefully remove the fillets, transfer them to a plate lined with paper towels to drain, and set them aside to rest in a warm place for 5 minutes.

Using a very sharp knife, slice each halibut fillet lengthwise into pieces about 1 inch thick. Spoon equal portions of the tomato-orange marmalade onto each of six warm dinner plates. (Arrange equal portions of braised fennel, if using, on each plate.) Place a sliced halibut fillet on each plate and drizzle a small amount of the reduced braising liquid, if using, and some of the remaining flavored olive oil on top. Season with a sprinkling of additional salt, garnish with additional olives, and serve.

BRAISED FENNEL

Cut the fennel bulbs in quarters (or halves, if they are small), then slice them lengthwise, about ½ inch thick. Melt the butter over medium heat in a skillet large enough to hold the fennel slices in a single layer. (If necessary, divide the butter and fennel between two skillets.) Add the fennel slices, season with the salt and pepper, and brown evenly on both sides, 12 to 15 minutes. Add the wine and simmer until the pan is almost dry. Add the stock and raise the heat to bring it to a simmer. Reduce the heat slightly, cover the pan, and braise the fennel slices for about 20 minutes. Turn the fennel slices over and continue to braise until they are tender, about 15 minutes more. Remove the fennel from the braising liquid and reserve. Raise the heat to medium-high and reduce the braising liquid until it thickens to your preference, 5 to 10 minutes. Serve the braised fennel with the reduced braising liquid as a sauce.

HALIBUT

Country

Halibut Roasted with Garlic Cloves and Artichokes

SERVES 6

FOR THE SACHET

- 1 teaspoon black peppercorns
- 1 teaspoon white peppercorns
- 1 dried bay leaf
- 2 sprigs thyme
- 1 piece star anise
- 1 teaspoon fennel seeds

FOR THE ARTICHOKES AND THE HALIBUT

- 4 medium to large artichokes
- 1/3 cup fresh lemon juice (1 1/2 lemons), plus additional for the artichoke hearts
- About 2 cups extra-virgin olive oil
- 6 medium pearl onions, peeled and sliced thin
- 8 cloves garlic, left whole
- 2 medium carrots, halved lengthwise and sliced very thin
- 1 medium bulb fennel, trimmed and sliced very thin lengthwise (about 1 1/2 cups)
- Kosher salt and freshly ground black pepper
- 6 5 1/2-ounce portions skinless halibut fillets (each about 1 1/2 inches thick)
- 1 tablespoon crumbled dried lemon verbena
- 1 tablespoon unsalted butter
- 2 sprigs thyme
- 1/4 cup torn basil leaves in 1/2-inch pieces
- 1 teaspoon ground toasted coriander seeds

Halibut and artichoke hearts have complementary subtle flavors; this recipe is a longtime favorite, simple and easy to make, designed to take good advantage of this excellent pairing. With its delicately textured, mild-flavored flesh, halibut takes very well to roasting, as do several other white-fleshed varieties including monkfish and various members of the cod family. This is actually a three-step process: first a sauté, then roasting in the oven, and finally basting in the pan. Basting is really the best way to finish a piece of fish; it's important to baste continuously, keeping those juices flowing, and to cook to only 80 or 90 percent of your desired doneness. Always remember: carryover cooking is a slippery slope to overdoneness, particularly with fish.

INGREDIENT NOTES Dried lemon verbena is available in health-food stores in the tea section.

The recipe calls for skinless halibut fillets, but you can also cook it with skin-on fillets, in which case you can cook them a bit more on the skin side, allowing it to begin browning.

PREPARE THE SACHET Place the black peppercorns, white peppercorns, bay leaf, thyme, star anise, and fennel seeds inside a piece of cheesecloth and tie it up with twine. Reserve.

PREPARE THE VEGETABLES Using a small, sharp paring knife, cut all the leaves and the stems off the artichokes. Trim all the tough green parts from around the hearts to expose the light green flesh underneath, but do not cut into the hearts themselves. Cut the chokes away from the tops of the hearts, then slice the hearts about 1/4 inch thick. Reserve the sliced artichoke hearts in a bowl of water with 1 to 2 tablespoons of lemon juice.

Warm 1/4 cup of the olive oil in a large deep skillet over medium-low heat. Add the onions and sweat until they soften, about 12 minutes. Add 6 of the garlic cloves and continue to sweat, stirring frequently, until the garlic is fragrant, about 5 minutes more. Drain and add the reserved artichoke hearts and the carrots and fennel. Sweat the vegetables, stirring frequently, until they are well coated with oil, about 5 minutes more. Add 1¼ cups of the oil. Increase the heat to medium-high and bring the ingredients to a simmer. Lower the heat and stir in the ⅓ cup of lemon juice and enough water to barely cover the vegetables (about 1 cup). Season lightly with salt and pepper, and add the sachet. Gently simmer the stew until the artichokes are tender, about 35 minutes. (The stew can be made up to a day in advance, stored in the refrigerator, covered, and warmed over low heat just before serving.)

COOK THE HALIBUT Preheat the oven to 350°F.

Season the halibut fillets moderately with salt and pepper and sprinkle with the lemon verbena. Place 2 tablespoons olive oil in a large, ovenproof skillet (or 2 skillets) over medium-high heat. (The skillet should be large enough to hold the halibut fillets in one layer with at least 1 inch of space all around each; crowding the fillets will cause them to steam, begin to break up, and become difficult to remove from the pan.) Add the halibut fillets, skinned side up (interior side down), and cook for 1 minute. (Because the halibut flesh is delicate, the fillets should be cooked without turning or moving them in the pan.) Reduce the heat to medium, add about 1 tablespoon of oil, and cook, basting the fish with the hot oil, until the flesh no longer appears completely raw, about 2 minutes. Transfer the pan to the oven and roast the fish until each piece is nearly opaque, from the bottom to the top, about 7 minutes. (Check for doneness after 5 minutes; thinner pieces may take less time.) Return the pan to the stove over medium heat. Add the butter, the remaining 2 cloves of garlic, and the thyme. Cook, basting the fillets repeatedly with butter, until the halibut gives easily when gently pressed, about 2 minutes more. (The butter will turn light brown.) Transfer the fillets to a warm platter and pat with a paper towel to remove excess oil.

Remove the sachet from the vegetable stew. Add the basil and ground coriander, and season to taste with salt and pepper. Place equal portions of the vegetable stew in each of six shallow bowls with one halibut fillet on top. Spoon a little of the braising liquid from the vegetable stew onto each fillet and serve immediately.

HAM

TOWN

Ham and Stilton Brioche Sandwiches with Endive Salad

SERVES 4

- **½ pound Stilton, sliced ¼ inch thick**
- **1 loaf brioche, cut into 8 slices (each about ½ inch thick)**
- **¼ pound sliced smoked or cured ham, such as Black Forest, Westphalian, Bayonne, or Serrano**
- **¼ pound (1 stick) unsalted butter**
- **1 large egg yolk**
- **2 tablespoons sherry vinegar**
- **1 tablespoon fresh lime juice**
- **2 tablespoons mustard**
- **2 tablespoons honey**
- **Fine sea salt and freshly ground black pepper to taste**
- **3 tablespoons extra-virgin olive oil**
- **4 heads of endive, julienned lengthwise**
- **10 ounces arugula (about 2 bunches), cleaned and trimmed**

At Restaurant 44, positioned in the lobby of the high-profile Royalton Hotel, which catered to the power elite of the media and fashion industries, business lunches were a huge ticket for us. As far as I'm concerned, the perfect meal for such an occasion is a sandwich and a salad. This recipe merges the two into a one-plate luncheon dish. It's descended from the classic croque-monsieur (fancy grilled ham-and-cheese sandwich), which has been served in the bistros and cafés of Paris for nearly a hundred years. It also takes a cue from the composed salads of nouvelle cuisine, as well as capturing the flavors of a traditional raclette (melted cheese served with vinegary pickles and pickled onions).

PREPARE THE SANDWICHES Lay the Stilton slices on half the brioche slices, making sure to cover the bread. Top the cheese with ham, evenly dividing it among the sandwiches. Place another slice of cheese on top of the ham and then close the sandwich. Spread about a tablespoon of butter on top of each sandwich.

PREPARE THE DRESSING Place the egg yolk, vinegar, lime juice, mustard, and honey in a bowl. Season with salt and pepper to taste, and whisk to combine. Whisk continuously while gradually adding the oil.

PREPARE THE SALAD Combine the endive with the arugula in a mixing bowl. Add 4 tablespoons of dressing, season with salt and pepper to taste, and toss to mix well. (The remaining dressing can be refrigerated for use within the next day or so.)

FINISH AND ASSEMBLE THE DISH Preheat the oven to 350°F.

Place 2 tablespoons of butter in each of two large skillets over medium heat. Add 2 sandwiches to each pan, buttered side down, and cook until they are crisp and golden, 2 to 3 minutes. Turn the sandwiches over and cook for 2 minutes more. Transfer the sandwiches to the oven and bake until the cheese is thoroughly melted, about 5 minutes.

Cut the sandwiches in quarters. Arrange four sandwich quarters on each of four plates. Mound salad in the middle of each plate and serve.

Country
Serrano Ham with Cavaillon Melon

SERVES 6

1 Cavaillon melon (or 1 small, ripe cantaloupe)

$1\frac{1}{2}$ teaspoons honey

1 tablespoon extra-virgin olive oil

2 tablespoons yuzu juice or lime juice

Fine sea salt and freshly cracked black pepper

12 thin slices serrano ham (about $\frac{1}{2}$ pound)

About 1 packed cup micro mustard greens, arugula, or baby arugula

$\frac{1}{4}$ cup crushed toasted pistachios (preferably Sicilian)

This recipe takes a time-honored pairing—prosciutto and melon—and cranks up the volume across the board. Cavaillon is a small, very sweet, and utterly captivating French melon with an intoxicating perfume. You can substitute Charentais, a more common French melon from the cantaloupe family, or an Israeli melon; just be sure it's perfectly ripe and very sweet. Serrano ham is Spain's answer to Italian prosciutto; genuine serrano is drier, saltier, nuttier, and gamier-tasting than the more delicate Parma or San Daniele hams from Italy.

INGREDIENT NOTE Yuzu is a Japanese citrus fruit about the size of a tangerine; its rind is used as a garnish, and its juice is sour and delicious. If you can't find any, lime juice is a good substitute. This recipe calls for 2 tablespoons of yuzu juice, but feel free to adjust the quantity to suit your taste.

Slice the melon in half. Scoop out and reserve the mass of seeds and fibrous pulp. Slice the flesh into 12 wedges; trim off and discard the rind. Press the seeds and pulp into a strainer positioned over a bowl to collect the juices. Create a melon vinaigrette by combining about ½ cup of this melon juice with the honey and olive oil. Add the yuzu juice, and season with salt and pepper.

Arrange two slices of melon on each of six plates; sprinkle lightly with additional salt and the melon vinaigrette. Lay slices of ham over the melon slices. Garnish with the greens, drizzle the greens with a little of the vinaigrette, and serve topped with pistachios.

LAMB

SERVES 4

FOR THE CRUST

- 6 tablespoons chopped pitted green olives
- 3/4 cup (1 1/2 sticks) unsalted butter, at room temperature
- 2 small cloves garlic, diced
- 1/4 cup chopped thyme leaves
- 3/4 cup chopped flat-leaf parsley leaves
- 3/4 teaspoon freshly ground toasted cumin
- 3/4 teaspoon freshly ground toasted coriander seeds
- 1 teaspoon Madras curry powder
- 1/4 teaspoon freshly ground white pepper
- 3/4 teaspoon ground mustard seeds
- 1 1/2 cups coarse bread crumbs

FOR THE LAMB

- 2 racks (7 to 8 bones each) New Zealand lamb, Frenched (see Ingredient Note, page 136) and trimmed of all fat
- 1 teaspoon kosher salt
- 1/2 teaspoon freshly ground black pepper
- 4 tablespoons unsalted butter, very cold

TOWN

Rack of Lamb with Mustard and Green Olive Crust

There were so many lamb recipes in my family growing up, but the expensive rack was a little out of reach, the dream of a far-off financially secure future, which is one of the reasons why I appreciate it so much today. Mustard crust is an old French recipe; here I've livened it up with a few extra spices and some olives.

A rack of lamb is quick, easy, and elegant, but it's also a cut that is subject to a fair amount of abuse, particularly by way of overcooking. For me, the keys are to (1) bring it to room temperature before putting it in the oven; (2) not overcook it (if it's underdone, you can always put it back in the oven); and (3) let it rest before serving. To determine whether it's cooked to your preference, you can use a meat thermometer (about 125°F. is medium-rare), but I strongly recommend you trust your powers of observation at least as much as the scientific instrument.

INGREDIENT NOTE It's always best to grind your spices (in a clean electric coffee grinder or by hand with a mortar and pestle) and toast them at home for each dish. For the convenience of using store-bought preground spices, you will sacrifice some flavor. Likewise, it's best to make your own bread crumbs, using day-old, hardened (or lightly toasted) country-style white bread, crushed or coarsely ground in a food processor.

Place the olives, softened butter, garlic, thyme, parsley, cumin, coriander, curry powder, white pepper, and mustard in the bowl of a food processor. Pulse until the ingredients are well combined and the butter turns green. Add the bread crumbs and pulse until the mixture is thick and pasty. Spoon the crust out onto a sheet of parchment paper; using a spatula, spread it evenly and relatively thin. Cover with another piece of parchment paper and roll it flat with a rolling pin to an even thickness of about 1/4 inch, about 9 inches square. Chill completely in the refrigerator for at least 30 minutes.

Preheat the oven to 375°F.

Allow the lamb to come to room temperature. Season the lamb with the salt and pepper. Lay the racks bone side down (meaty side up) in a roasting pan. Cut the rolled-out crust mixture into two pieces. Fit the crust over the exposed meaty parts of the racks and press into the meat. Roast the lamb for 30 to

40 minutes for medium-rare; a meat thermometer inserted into the thick part of a rack should read 125°F.

Allow the racks to rest for 10 minutes in a warm place. Meanwhile, preheat the broiler. Dot the crust of each rack of lamb with thin slices of the cold butter. Place the racks under the broiler, about 6 inches from the heating element, until the butter is melted and the crust is brown, 3 to 5 minutes. Slice the racks apart into lamb-chop portions and serve immediately.

LAMB

Country

Grilled Double Lamb Chops with Tomato-Bread Pudding

SERVES 6

- **1 teaspoon minced fresh rosemary**
- **1 clove garlic, minced**
- **1 teaspoon minced shallots (½ small shallot)**
- **1 tablespoon extra-virgin olive oil, plus additional for brushing the grill rack**
- **1 teaspoon Pommery or other whole-grain mustard**
- **6 double lamb rib chops (each about 8 ounces), Frenched (see Ingredient Note, page 136)**
- **Kosher salt and freshly ground black pepper**
- **6 small sprigs flat-leaf parsley**
- **Tomato-Bread Pudding (recipe follows)**

It's nearly impossible to cook thin lamb chops so they're nicely caramelized, lightly charred, and tasty on the outside without overdoing them on the inside. This recipe solves that dilemma by calling for double chops, which have two rib bones each and are at least 2 inches thick. The extra thickness translates to longer cooking time on the grill, which means better flavor development. With just one double chop per entrée serving, each diner gets a big, juicy dose of lambiness.

Make sure you buy really good, ripe tomatoes for the pudding. It's a lovely rustic accompaniment for the lamb: imagine the best tomato and bread sandwich or a perfect bruschetta, baked in the oven to lock in all the flavors, and that's what you have.

TIMING NOTE The lamb chops are marinated in their rub overnight in the refrigerator. The tomato-bread pudding should also be prepared in advance; you can time it to finish baking and rest just as you're grilling the lamb chops (preferable) or you can complete the entire process in advance and then reheat the pudding.

continued

INGREDIENT NOTE Lamb chops come from either the shoulder, rib, or loin section of the animal. The loin chops are from farther back on the animal and have a T-bone; they contain more fat and are therefore the tastiest in simple preparations. The rib chops comprise a rack before it's sliced into chops; they are leaner and very tender. For this recipe, you can use almost any type, but I recommend rib chops. Have your butcher French the chops, which means to trim them in the same manner as a crown rack of lamb, removing all excess fat and gristle from the bones (and exposing them as perfect little "handles" to pick up the chop if you like). Lamb chops can range in thickness from 3/4 of an inch to 1 1/4 inches; the thicker the better, especially for grilling medium-rare. I prefer imported New Zealand lamb; it's naturally raised, grass-fed, and very consistent.

MARINATE THE LAMB CHOPS OVERNIGHT Place the rosemary, garlic, shallots, olive oil, and mustard in a small mixing bowl; stir until thoroughly combined. Rub the mixture all over the lamb chops, place them in a dish, cover with plastic wrap, and refrigerate overnight. (The chops can also be marinated in large resealable plastic bags.)

GRILL THE LAMB CHOPS Prepare a hardwood charcoal fire in an outdoor grill. Allow the coals to burn down until they're grayish white on the outside and glowing red on the inside. Position the rack 4 to 5 inches above the coals. The fire should be hot—you should be able to hold your hand 5 inches above the grill for no more than 5 seconds (any longer and the fire isn't hot enough). Season the lamb chops generously with salt and pepper. Lightly oil the rack. Place the lamb chops on the rack and grill until medium-rare (a meat thermometer inserted into the thickest part will indicate a temperature of 125°F.), about 5 minutes per side. Transfer the lamb chops to a platter, lightly cover with aluminum foil, and allow to rest for 5 minutes. Garnish the chops with parsley sprigs and serve with the tomato-bread pudding.

SERVES 6

12 ripe medium tomatoes (about 3½ pounds)

3 cloves garlic, minced

Kosher salt and freshly ground black pepper

¼ cup plus 2 tablespoons extra-virgin olive oil, plus additional for greasing the dish

1 large baguette, sliced on the bias about ¾ inch thick

5 tablespoons minced flat-leaf parsley

5 tablespoons finely chopped basil

TOMATO-BREAD PUDDING

Bring a pot of water to a boil. Core the tomatoes, then blanch them in the boiling water for about 30 seconds to loosen the skins. Transfer the tomatoes to a strainer. When cool enough to handle, peel off the skins. Cut the tomatoes in half horizontally and position the strainer over a medium bowl; scoop the seeds and pulp from the tomatoes into the strainer. Press the pulp to extract as much of the juice as possible.

Arrange the tomato halves, cut side up, on a large plate. Sprinkle with the garlic and season moderately with salt and pepper. Drizzle with 2 tablespoons of the olive oil and allow to stand for 30 minutes. Pour any juices that accumulate on the plate into the strained tomato juice.

Preheat a cast-iron grill pan or preheat the broiler. Brush the baguette slices on both sides with the remaining ¼ cup of olive oil and grill or broil until toasted, 1 to 2 minutes per side. Season the toasts with salt and pepper and transfer to a large plate. Grill or broil the tomatoes on one side until lightly charred, about 3 minutes, then return to the plate.

Preheat the oven to 350°F. Lightly oil a shallow 3 × 9-inch baking dish. Arrange half the tomatoes on the bottom, pressing them down with a spatula. Sprinkle the tomatoes with 2 tablespoons each of the parsley and basil; season generously with salt and pepper. Top the tomatoes with half the toasted baguette slices. Repeat the procedure with the remaining tomatoes, 2 tablespoons each of the parsley and basil, and the remaining toast. Pour about 1 cup of the juice evenly over the bread pudding. Place a piece of aluminum foil over the pudding, then weight it with another pan.

Place the dish in the oven and bake until the liquid is absorbed and the tomatoes are very soft, about 30 minutes. Remove the weight and foil and bake until the top of the pudding is crisp, about 10 minutes more. Allow to stand for 15 minutes, sprinkle with the remaining 1 tablespoon each of parsley and basil, and serve.

LAMB

TOWN

Basted Lamb Loin with Herbs and Citrus-Eggplant Purée

SERVES 6

FOR THE LAMB

2 boneless loins of lamb (about 1 pound each)

½ cup flat-leaf parsley leaves

2 tablespoons fresh thyme leaves

2 tablespoons fresh rosemary leaves

3 large shallots, finely chopped

4 medium cloves garlic, finely chopped

1 cup extra-virgin olive oil

Kosher salt and freshly ground white pepper

2 tablespoons salted butter, plus additional if needed

Juice of 2 lemons

FOR THE SALAD AND TO SERVE

½ pound small yellow wax or green beans, cut into 1-inch pieces

1 lime, peeled, sliced very thinly, then each slice quartered

2 cups peppercress leaves or watercress leaves

Citrus-Eggplant Purée (recipe follows; optional)

Careful pan-browning and basting is the best way to control the cooking process and avoid overdoneness. You're literally and figuratively on top of it the whole time, and it doesn't take all that long. This recipe uses that technique to yield a light, lemony lamb dish, ideal for late spring or early summer. Although the dish stands very well on its own, I like to serve it with an eggplant purée because lamb and eggplant work so well together. They find many happy partnerships, especially in Middle Eastern cuisine, which is one of my fundamental influences.

INGREDIENT NOTES A loin of lamb is a filet from the T-bone section, the lamb equivalent of beef tenderloin; two loins comprise a saddle of lamb. Since it's a lean cut, it benefits a lot from the marinating. A loin weighs about 1 pound, give or take a few ounces.

Peppercress, also known as peppergrass, is an edible weed native to North America that grows wild in fields and meadows—as opposed to on the banks of streams and rivers, which is where you find watercress. As the name implies, it has a nice peppery flavor to it. If you can't find it, watercress is a perfectly acceptable substitute.

TIMING NOTE The lamb is marinated in the refrigerator overnight beforehand. If you're using the purée, it can be made well in advance.

MARINATE THE LAMB OVERNIGHT Place the parsley, thyme, rosemary, shallots, garlic, and ¾ cup of the oil in a blender and purée until a paste is formed. Spread the paste all over the lamb loins, wrap them in plastic, and refrigerate for at least 12 and up to 24 hours.

COOK THE LAMB Remove the lamb loins from the refrigerator and allow them to come to room temperature before cooking. Brush off and reserve any excess marinade. Generously season each loin with salt and pepper. Place the butter in a large sauté pan over medium-low heat; when the butter foams, place the lamb loins in the pan (work in batches if necessary). Cook the loins until lightly browned, about 8 minutes, basting continuously with the butter and pan juices. Turn the loins over and cook, continuing to baste, until medium-rare, about 6 minutes more (a thermometer inserted into the thickest part will indicate a temperature of 125°F.). If the pan becomes too dry during the cooking process, add more butter as needed. Transfer the loins to a platter and reserve in a warm place.

Pour off all the fat from the pan; add the lemon juice and remaining ¼ cup oil, along with 2 tablespoons of the reserved lamb marinade. Bring to a simmer over medium heat; stir in the juices from the resting lamb loins, simmer for 1 to 2 minutes, season with salt and pepper, and keep warm at the back of the stove as a sauce for the finished dish.

PREPARE THE SALAD Blanch the beans in boiling, salted water for about 20 seconds. Drain the beans, pat them dry with paper towels, and place them in a mixing bowl with the sliced lime and peppercress.

FINISH AND SERVE Drizzle some of the warm lamb sauce onto the salad and toss gently to combine. Arrange equal portions of the salad on each of six dinner plates. Slice the lamb loin ⅛- to ¼-inch thick. Spoon a portion of Citrus-Eggplant Purée (if using) on each plate, top with slices of lamb arranged in a fan pattern, drizzle sauce around the plate, and serve immediately.

CITRUS-EGGPLANT PURÉE

MAKES ABOUT 2 CUPS

- 2 medium domestic or Italian eggplants (about 1 pound each)
- 3 tablespoons extra-virgin olive oil
- Kosher salt and freshly ground black pepper
- 1 quart orange juice (preferably fresh)
- ¼ pound (1 stick) salted butter

Preheat the oven to 375°F.

Cut the eggplants in half lengthwise and score the flesh, making crosshatch incisions stopping short of the skin. Season the eggplants with the oil, salt, and pepper. Place the eggplants in the oven to bake until soft, about 45 minutes. While the eggplants are baking, place the orange juice in a medium nonreactive saucepan over medium-high heat, bring to a boil, adjust the heat to maintain a steady boil, and cook until reduced to ¾ cup, about 45 minutes. Allow the eggplant halves to cool for about 10 minutes, then scrape the pulp and juices out into the cup of a blender; discard the skins. Add the reduced orange juice and butter, and blend on high until a very smooth, creamy purée is formed. Set the purée aside at room temperature until ready to serve. Just before serving, season to taste with salt and pepper, and warm in a saucepan over low heat.

Country Braised Lamb Shanks

SERVES 6

- **3 tablespoons ground cumin**
- **3 tablespoons ground coriander**
- **2 tablespoons Madras curry powder**
- **2 tablespoons minced fresh rosemary**
- **2 tablespoons minced fresh thyme**
- **2 tablespoons minced garlic (2 large cloves)**
- **1 tablespoon coarsely ground black pepper, plus more to taste**
- **½ cup plus 2 tablespoons extra-virgin olive oil**
- **1 tablespoon kosher salt, plus more to taste**
- **6 lamb shanks (1 to 1¼ pounds each), trimmed of excess fat**
- **2 stalks celery, coarsely chopped**
- **1 large yellow onion, coarsely chopped**
- **1 large carrot, coarsely chopped**
- **1 cup dry white wine**
- **2 quarts Chicken Stock (page 262, or low-sodium canned)**

Braised lamb shanks represent the ultimate in simple, country comfort, and they're a great addition to your home-kitchen repertoire. I honed my recipe for the opening of the Blue Door restaurant at the Delano Hotel, Miami Beach, in 1995. But the idea was planted years ago when I had *gigot à sept heures* ("seven-hour lamb") in France; it was so tender that they served it without a knife.

The crucial flavor-building step here is to create a spice rub and allow the lamb to marinate well in advance. The rest of the procedure involves straightforward braising: it takes a long time, but once you've put the pan in the oven, you leave it alone and can go about your other business. (In fact, it's best not to disturb the shanks much at all.) Once you've reduced the braising liquid to a sauce—another simple procedure that leaves you free to make other preparations—the meal is ready to serve. Like most braised or stewed meat dishes, this one actually improves if left in the fridge for a day or two and served reheated. Be sure to wash it down with a bottle of hearty Rhône red or some equivalent wine.

MARINATE THE LAMB SHANKS Place the cumin, coriander, curry powder, rosemary, thyme, garlic, and pepper in a small mixing bowl, and stir to combine well. Stir in 6 tablespoons of the oil to make a paste. Season the paste with 1 tablespoon salt. Rub the lamb shanks with the spice rub, place them in a dish, and cover with plastic wrap (or in a large resealable plastic bag), and refrigerate overnight.

BROWN AND BRAISE THE LAMB SHANKS Preheat the oven to 350°F.

Wipe the spice paste from the shanks with a paper towel and discard. Heat 2 tablespoons of the oil in a large ovenproof skillet over medium heat. (Choose a pan that is large enough to hold the shanks in a single snug layer, or use a separate larger roasting pan for braising.) Working in batches if necessary, brown the shanks on all sides, about 20 minutes. Wipe out the skillet. (It is important to discard any burned spices.) Add the remaining 2 tablespoons of oil with the celery, onion, and carrot, and cook over medium heat until the veg-

etables begin to soften and brown, about 12 minutes. Return the shanks to the pan, add the wine, and simmer until the pan is almost dry, about 8 minutes. Add the stock and bring to a simmer. Cover the pan and place it in the oven to braise for 1 hour. (If using a separate roasting pan, transfer all contents before placing in oven.) Turn the shanks and cook until the lamb is very tender, about 1 more hour. Remove the pan from the oven and allow the shanks to cool in their cooking liquid.

Transfer the shanks to a plate or bowl and pass the braising liquid through a strainer into a saucepan. Discard the solids. Bring the braising liquid to a simmer over medium-high heat. Skim the fat as it rises. (Alternatively, chill the sauce so the fat hardens on top and can be removed.) Reduce the braising liquid to about 2 cups of sauce, approximately 15 minutes. Season the sauce with salt and pepper to taste. Return the shanks to the cooking pan. Pour the sauce over the shanks and reheat in the oven, basting with sauce frequently. Serve the shanks on a platter or in large bowls topped with sauce.

LAMB

TOWN

Lamb Bolognese with Egg Noodles and Fresh Mint

SERVES 6 TO 8

- **3 tablespoons extra-virgin olive oil**
- **½ pound coarsely ground lamb shoulder**
- **½ pound coarsely ground turkey leg meat**
- **½ pound coarsely ground veal shoulder**
- **4 tablespoons (½ stick) unsalted butter**
- **1½ cups finely chopped sweet onion, such as Vidalia (1 small to medium onion)**
- **¼ cup chopped garlic (4 large cloves)**
- **½ teaspoon hot red pepper flakes (or to taste)**
- **¾ cup diced carrot (1 large carrot)**
- **¾ cup diced celery (1 large stalk)**
- **¾ cup diced celery root (½ small celery root)**
- **½ teaspoon ground toasted cumin**
- **1 teaspoon ground toasted coriander**
- **½ teaspoon ground star anise**

I love everything about Italy, especially its rich tapestry of regional cuisines. Every time I've visited the country, it's been incredibly inspirational. By the same token, part of me always remains true to my Middle Eastern roots. So here is a hybrid sauce, applying a regional Italian specialty (Bolognese sauce) to a Middle Eastern favorite (lamb) to create a hearty yet sophisticated dish. It's probably the closest thing I do now to all those great lamb recipes my mother and aunts used to serve when I was growing up. The egg noodles and mint lend it an elegant "town" veneer.

This recipe yields about 5 cups of sauce, which is a generous amount for 2½ pounds of noodles. Remember, it's always good to err on the side of caution when saucing pasta; the ideal amount of sauce is usually somewhat less than what we Americans consider normal. Also, bear in mind that fresh noodles will absorb more sauce than the dried variety. I have absolutely no preference or recommendation between the two: fresh noodles are nice, but there are so many good brands of dried noodles that you really don't sacrifice anything for their convenience.

INGREDIENT NOTES For the ground lamb, I recommend using a lamb shoulder, trimmed of any sinew and excess fat. For the turkey, use leg meat, skinless and trimmed; and for the veal, use shoulder as well. All three meats should be coarsely ground. It's best to either do this at home yourself or have your butcher do it to order. You can buy prepackaged ground meats from the supermarket display, but they will be fattier and mushier, and will diminish the recipe somewhat.

- 1 cinnamon stick
- 2 fresh bay leaves
- 3 tablespoons tomato paste
- 1 cup dry white wine
- Grated zest of 2 lemons
- 2 cups fresh tomatoes, peeled and coarsely chopped (2 medium tomatoes)
- 2 cups Chicken Stock (page 262, or low-sodium canned)
- Kosher salt and freshly ground black pepper to taste
- 1 cup heavy cream
- 1 cup fresh flat-leaf parsley leaves, chopped
- 1 cup fresh mint leaves, chopped
- ¼ cup fresh rosemary leaves, chopped
- 2½ pounds egg noodles (fresh or dried)

Place the oil in a large heavy saucepot or Dutch oven over medium-high heat. Add the lamb, turkey, and veal. Brown the meat, stirring and breaking it up with a wooden spoon, until no longer pink, about 7 minutes. Spoon the meat into a colander placed over a bowl, to drain any excess fat.

Discard the fat from the pot and return it to medium heat. Add the butter and onions, and cook over medium heat, stirring frequently, until the onions are soft and brown, about 10 minutes. Add the garlic and hot pepper flakes, and cook, stirring often, until the garlic is fragrant, about 3 minutes. Add the carrots, celery, celery root, cumin, coriander, star anise, cinnamon, and bay leaves. Increase the heat to medium-high, and cook, stirring, until the vegetables begin to brown, about 5 minutes. Stir in the tomato paste and cook for another 5 minutes. Add the wine and lemon zest. Bring to a simmer and cook, stirring, until the wine has reduced by about one third, 5 to 7 minutes.

Return the meat to the pot and add the tomatoes and stock. Bring to a simmer, cover, reduce the heat to low, and simmer until the tomatoes have released all their juices, about 45 minutes. Stir the pot frequently to ensure that none of the sauce sticks to the bottom.

Uncover the pot and season to taste with salt and pepper. Stir in the cream, parsley, mint, and rosemary. Simmer, uncovered, until the liquid has reduced by about two thirds and the sauce looks moist but not liquid, about 45 minutes more. Remove and discard the bay leaves and cinnamon stick.

Cook the egg noodles in a pot of boiling, salted water to the desired doneness (al dente is best). Drain the noodles, return to the pot, add the sauce, toss well to combine, and serve immediately in warm bowls.

Country Lamb Sandwiches

SERVES 4

- **8 slices crusty bread, ½ inch thick each**
- **1 large clove garlic, halved**
- **Fine sea salt and freshly ground black pepper**
- **¼ cup Mayonnaise (page 264, or Hellman's)**
- **1 large or 2 small celery root(s), peeled and julienned (about 1 pound)**
- **1 tablespoon chopped fresh tarragon**
- **1 tablespoon minced fresh chives**
- **1 tablespoon minced shallots (1 medium shallot)**
- **1 teaspoon freshly squeezed lemon juice (½ small lemon)**
- **8 leaves romaine or other crisp lettuce**
- **1½ to 2 pounds leftover cooked lamb, at room temperature, trimmed of fat and sliced thin**

Calvin Trillin often applies his wry humor to food and writes as brilliantly as anyone else on the subject. One of my favorite quotes from him goes something like this: "My mother was remarkable in that during her whole life she served nothing but leftovers. In fact, we're still searching for the original meal." If you're Calvin's mom—or anybody else—it's nice to have some foolproof recipes for leftovers. There's no reason they can't taste at least as good as, if not better than, the original; I think this lamb sandwich is a good example.

For a great sandwich, you need plenty of crunch and a good allotment of flavor and texture contrasts. Here, the tender, tasty lamb meat contrasts with the toasted bread and the crunchy, moist celery root salad. It's important to place a lettuce leaf on either side of the lamb and celery root salad to keep the bread from getting soggy. Serve these sandwiches with some crispy gherkins and a glass of good ale.

INGREDIENT NOTE You can use various types of leftover lamb—leg, rack, shank—for this recipe. If you use the crusted rack, leave the crust on when you slice it. Leftovers from any of the lamb recipes in the book—the rack, the basted loin, or the braised shanks—can be used; simply double one of those and use the excess to make these sandwiches the next day.

Rub the bread slices lightly with the garlic and season moderately with salt and pepper, then toast them to your liking. (The best way to do this is on an outdoor charcoal grill; otherwise, do it in the oven at 350°F. or on a griddle pan.)

Place the mayonnaise, celery root, tarragon, chives, and shallots in a bowl. Add the lemon juice, toss well to combine, then season to taste with salt and pepper. Make sandwiches layered as follows: 1 slice of bread, 1 leaf of lettuce, a portion of lamb, a portion of celery root salad, another leaf of lettuce, and a second slice of bread. Any excess salad can be served on the side or refrigerated for up to two days.

TOWN

Lemon and Yogurt Trifle

SERVES 6

FOR THE LEMON CREAM

3 large eggs

1 large egg yolk

½ cup sugar

½ cup fresh lemon juice

3 tablespoons unsalted butter, diced, at room temperature

FOR THE YOGURT CREAM

1 cup heavy cream

½ teaspoon vanilla extract

1½ teaspoons sugar

½ cup plain whole-milk yogurt (preferably Greek, such as Fage)

FOR THE GARNISH

2 pints raspberries

6 Shortbread Cookies (recipe follows, or store-bought)

More often than not, I'll answer my "What's for dessert?" question with the answer "Lemon." I'm also a big yogurt fan, so as far as I'm concerned, this dessert is blessed with a double Yummy Factor. Traditional English trifles have sponge cake soaked in sherry or perhaps some liqueur, layered with various combinations of whipped cream, custards, chopped nuts, shaved chocolate, and fresh or candied fruits. This recipe represents a lighter approach, but still offers a lot of visual appeal and elegance. Although it consists of several component recipes, all are quite simple and can be executed in advance. The finished trifles can be prepared and assembled before dinner, then stored in the fridge until serving time.

INGREDIENT NOTE It's just fine to buy the shortbread cookies, but I'm providing a recipe below if you want to make them. The quantities called for yield about 4 dozen little shortbread cookies; the excess cookies can accompany various desserts, including many types of ice cream and sorbet. You can also make festive little dessert sandwiches with two cookies and your favorite jam or fruit preserve between them.

PREPARE THE LEMON CREAM Place the whole eggs, egg yolk, sugar, and ¼ cup of the lemon juice in a large stainless-steel mixing bowl or the top of a double boiler, and whisk to combine. Set over a pot of boiling water and whisk vigorously until the mixture is frothy, about 5 minutes. Add the remaining lemon juice. Continue whisking until the mixture is thick and creamy, about 4 minutes more.

Remove the bowl from the heat and whisk in the butter bit by bit. Continue to whisk the cream until it cools to room temperature. Transfer it to a glass or other nonreactive container, cover with plastic wrap, and refrigerate until cool.

FOR THE YOGURT CREAM Combine the cream, vanilla, and sugar in a bowl. Using a whisk, whip until soft peaks form. Add the yogurt and continue whipping until well blended. Cover the bowl with plastic wrap and refrigerate.

ASSEMBLE THE TRIFLE Place several raspberries in the bottom of each of six wine or martini glasses. Spoon about 2 tablespoons of the yogurt cream on top of the berries (to a depth of about 1 inch). Place a shortbread cookie in each glass, pressing gently to flatten the cream. Arrange 5 more berries around the perimeter of the cookie, making sure they touch the side of the glass. Spoon about 3 tablespoons of lemon cream into each glass. Top each trifle with 2 to 3 tablespoons of the yogurt mixture. Garnish each glass with more berries.

SHORTBREAD COOKIES

MAKES ABOUT 4 DOZEN 1½-INCH COOKIES

- **12 tablespoons (1½ sticks) unsalted butter, at room temperature**
- **½ cup sugar**
- **1½ cups all-purpose flour**
- **⅓ cup cornstarch**

Place the butter and sugar in a large mixing bowl and beat with a spoon until smooth and creamy. Sift the flour and cornstarch together, add them to the butter mixture, and stir together until they form a smooth dough. Wrap the dough in plastic and refrigerate for 1 hour.

Preheat the oven to 300°F. Roll the dough out to a thickness of ⅛ inch. Use a cookie cutter to cut out cookies 1½ to 2 inches in diameter. Arrange the cookies on baking sheets and bake until they begin to turn golden, 15 to 25 minutes. Allow the cookies to cool for about 5 minutes on the sheets, then transfer to a rack to cool completely. They can be stored in an airtight container away from heat and light for a couple of weeks.

Country Caramelized Lemon Tart

MAKES ONE 10-INCH TART

FOR THE DOUGH

3/4 cup (1 1/2 sticks) unsalted butter, at room temperature

1/3 cup confectioners' sugar

1 large egg yolk

1 1/2 cups all-purpose flour

1 tablespoon heavy cream

FOR THE FILLING

3 lemons, washed

5 large egg yolks

3/4 cup plus 3 tablespoons sugar

1/2 cup plus 2 tablespoons heavy cream

Fresh berries and Whipped Cream (page 19), for serving

My family probably did more to promote lemons than any other fruit in our neighborhood. (We were always carting in vegetables and fruits by the box-load, and I'm sure our neighbors thought we were loony.) We made fresh lemonade, baked lemons, steamed lemons, preserved them in salt, made lemon marmalade, used them for traditional remedies . . . and then, of course, there were the desserts. Aside from fresh berries or ripe fruit in season, it's really tough to find a better after-dinner treat than a delicious lemon tart. Too many lemon desserts leave their beautiful lemony essence locked up inside a lackluster cake or heavy custard. But this tart is simple and light, with a finishing touch of lightly caramelized sugar to highlight its smooth filling and give it an extra burst of sweetness and crunch.

PREPARE THE DOUGH, APPROXIMATELY 4 HOURS IN ADVANCE Place the butter and confectioners' sugar in the bowl of an electric mixer. Using the paddle attachment on low speed, mix until just combined, taking care not to overmix. (The mixture should not turn creamy.) Add the egg yolks and gradually mix until just combined. Add the flour all at once and combine until the flour is incorporated three fourths of the way. Turn off the mixer and add the cream. Restart the mixer on low and continue to mix the dough until it just comes together. Remove the dough from the mixer. Flatten it into a disk, wrap it in plastic wrap, and chill in the refrigerator for 2 to 3 hours.

BAKE THE DOUGH Preheat oven to 375°F. Bring the dough to room temperature.

Roll the dough out to a thickness of approximately 1/8 inch. Gently fit it into a 10-inch fluted tart pan. Be careful: the dough is quite fragile. Save any scraps and use them to patch the crust if it tears. Place the tart pan in the freezer for about 15 minutes to chill the dough, then line it with parchment paper or aluminum foil. Weight the tart dough with dried beans or rice and bake in the oven for approximately 10 minutes. Remove the lining and beans or rice and bake until the crust is light golden, about 10 minutes more.

PREPARE THE FILLING Meanwhile, finely grate the zest of one of the lemons. Squeeze the juice of all three lemons through a strainer into a small bowl. Place the egg yolks and ¾ cup plus 1½ tablespoons of the sugar in another bowl and whisk together until thoroughly combined. Add the lemon juice and zest, and continue whisking. Next, whisk in the cream. Transfer the mixture to a pitcher or other container suitable for pouring.

FINISH AND SERVE THE TART As soon as the crust is baked, reduce the oven temperature to 250°F. Pull the tart halfway out of the oven and pour the filling into it almost to the top. Gently slide the oven rack back into the oven and bake for about 30 minutes, or until the filling is barely set. Shake the tart gently: the filling should still jiggle. (It will continue to set outside the oven.) Remove the tart from the oven and allow it to cool for approximately 30 minutes.

Move the oven rack to its uppermost notch and turn on the broiler. Sprinkle the remaining 1½ tablespoons of sugar evenly over the top of the tart. Place the tart under the broiler to lightly caramelize the sugar; this should take about 7 minutes. Watch carefully and turn the tart as necessary, as it can go from nicely browned to burned very fast. Cut the tart into wedges and serve with fresh berries and whipped cream.

LOBSTER

TOWN

Lobster Ginger Royale

SERVES 8

FOR THE GINGER BROTH

2 tablespoons unsalted butter

1 medium white onion, thinly sliced

2 cups peeled, sliced fresh ginger (2 6- to 8-inch pieces, about ½ pound total)

1 large or 2 medium sweet potatoes, peeled and thinly sliced

2 quarts Chicken Stock (page 262, or low-sodium canned)

FOR THE ROYALE

2 tablespoons unsalted butter

3 shallots, sliced

¼ cup minced fresh peeled ginger (1 4-inch piece)

1 sprig thyme

1 cup coconut milk

1 cup heavy cream

2 large eggs

1 teaspoon kosher salt, plus more to taste

½ teaspoon freshly ground white pepper, plus more to taste

TO FINISH AND SERVE

1 cup whole milk

¾ cup sweet white dessert wine, such as Coteaux du Layon

¼ to ½ pound cooked lobster meat

Like many foods possessing a high degree of the Yummy Factor, lobsters left me with a distinct memory when I discovered them at a young age. For my twelfth birthday, my parents took me to Anthony's Pier 4 restaurant, right on the harbor in Boston. I had a steamed lobster with a big plate of rice; I wonder if my parents suspected my future was sealed right then and there. This royale is very much a grown-up recipe, but it has its roots in that night, when I fell in love with lobster.

In classic French cuisine, a *royale* is a custard made in a mold and used to garnish a consommé or other clear soup. The royale is baked in a bain-marie (water bath), then unmolded and cut into little cubes or other more fanciful shapes. Borrowing staples of upscale Asian cuisine—lobster and ginger—I've created a ginger custard (royale) here, but left it whole, surrounded by a bowl of fragrant broth. This is a festive dish I developed in the late 1980s, and it has been one of our bestsellers at Town; I think it's ideal for the first course of a fancy dinner party at home.

PREPARE THE GINGER BROTH, UP TO 1 DAY IN ADVANCE Melt the butter in a large saucepan over medium heat. Add the onion, ginger, and sweet potato, and sweat until the vegetables are tender, about 20 minutes. Add the stock, bring to a simmer, and cook until the sweet potatoes are very soft, about 20 minutes more. Allow the broth to cool slightly, then transfer it to a blender and purée. Press the broth through a fine strainer (chinois or china cap) into a clean saucepot and reserve until ready to reheat. (Once cooled to room temperature, the broth can be refrigerated until ready to use.)

PREPARE THE ROYALE Preheat the oven to 300°F.

Bring a teakettle of water to a boil. Melt 1 tablespoon of the butter in a medium saucepan over medium-low heat. Add the shallots, ginger, and thyme, and sweat until the shallots are tender, about 10 minutes; do not allow them to color. Add the coconut milk and heavy cream. Allow the mixture to simmer gently until it reduces by about one third, about 15 minutes. Allow the mixture to cool for 1 to 2 minutes, then place it in a blender and purée, adding the eggs one at a time while the blender is running. Season the mixture with the salt and pepper, and pass it through a fine strainer. Place eight 2-ounce ramekins in a roasting pan. Evenly divide the mixture among the ramekins. (You may have a little left over.) Place the roasting pan in the oven on the middle rack. Add enough of the boiling water from the teakettle to come three quarters of the way up the sides of the ramekins. Cover the roasting pan with aluminum foil and bake the custards in the water bath until just set, about 25 minutes. Remove the roasting pan from the oven, take the custards out of the water bath, and allow them to cool for 1 to 2 minutes. Run a paring knife around the edge of each ramekin and gently turn each royale out into a soup bowl.

FINISH AND SERVE Bring the ginger broth to a boil over medium-high heat, add the milk and wine, then blend the broth again so it becomes foamy on top. (This is best accomplished with an immersion blender; if you don't have one, feel free to skip this step.) Season to taste with salt and pepper. Meanwhile, melt the remaining tablespoon of butter in a skillet over medium heat. Warm the lobster meat in the butter. Place equal portions of the lobster meat in each bowl around a royale. Spoon warm, foamy broth into each bowl and serve.

LOBSTER

Country Lobster Roll

SERVES 4 TO 6

2 1½-pound lobsters (to yield 1½ to 2 cups cooked lobster meat)

1 teaspoon chopped fresh chives

½ teaspoon celery salt

1 teaspoon chopped fresh tarragon

2½ tablespoons Hellman's or homemade Mayonnaise (page 264), or more to taste

Squeeze of lemon (at least a dash but up to ½ lemon, according to taste)

Fine sea salt and freshly ground black pepper

Several tablespoons butter, softened

4 to 6 hot dog rolls

8 to 12 small leaves romaine lettuce, washed and cut to fit rolls

Lobster roll is one of those deceptively simple delights that when done right is a joy. But when botched, it can be a disaster. Ironically, growing up in New England, I encountered many lousy lobster rolls, which compels me to do this American classic justice here. Just pay attention to a few basics: make sure the lobster meat is well drained; don't overdress it with mayonnaise; and make the salad an hour or less before putting together the rolls. Wash them down with good beer or, for more special occasions, prosecco or Champagne.

INGREDIENT NOTES First of all, that is not a misprint: yes, I am calling for Hellman's mayo, because I think it's really one of the best commercial food products out there.

The amount of lobster meat called for can fill 4 rolls very generously; it can also easily be stretched to fill 6, in which case you'll need some extra lettuce leaves.

Fill a large pot with salted water and bring it to a boil over high heat. Plunge the lobsters into the pot and cook for about 10 minutes. Remove the lobsters from the pot, drain, and allow them to cool.

Preheat a grill or oven to 400°F.

Crack the lobster open, allow the juices to run out, then extract the meat from the tail, claws, and body, and chop it into large bite-size chunks. Place the lobster meat, chives, celery salt, tarragon, mayonnaise, and lemon juice in a large bowl, and mix well. Season the salad to taste with salt and pepper. Spread a little butter on the inside of each hot dog roll. Place the rolls on a grill or in the oven for a brief period to lightly toast. Line each roll with 2 trimmed lettuce leaves, mound lobster salad on top, and serve.

MACKEREL

TOWN

Mackerel Escabeche with Zucchini Noodles

SERVES 8

FOR THE SACHET

1 teaspoon black peppercorns

1 teaspoon coriander seeds

1 dried bay leaf

2 sprigs thyme

FOR THE MARINADE

3 tablespoons extra-virgin olive oil

1 medium red bell pepper, cored, seeded, and cut into ¼-inch-thick strips

1 medium carrot, peeled and cut into ¼-inch-thick strips

1 small bulb fennel, cored and thinly sliced

2 small shallots, thinly sliced

Kosher salt and freshly ground black pepper

2 cups fresh orange juice

2 cups high-quality dry white wine

¼ cup white wine vinegar

FOR THE FISH AND ZUCCHINI

3 pounds mackerel fillet, cut into 16 3-ounce pieces

6 small to medium "fancy" (smooth and unblemished) zucchini

2 tablespoons unsalted butter

My family didn't eat mackerel, but we did eat plenty of sardines (often marinated with onions), anchovies, and salt cod—all of which were inexpensive and delicious ways to incorporate very nutritious fish into our diets. Mackerel is another "poor man's" seafood that's also very tasty whether marinated or cooked conventionally (with heat). So this is a nice shift of gears on all those dishes I had as a kid.

Traditional escabeches consist of fish fillets that have been browned and then marinated in a vinegary solution with onions and a few other ingredients. A ceviche, on the other hand, is "cooked" in an acidic marinade—without sautéing, grilling, or frying it. This recipe actually falls somewhere between the two. Mackerel is a flavorful, oily fish with a pleasingly dense texture. (Fish oil is a good thing!) This recipe is a great way to coax out its best features.

INGREDIENT NOTE When you buy the mackerel fillets, ask your fishmonger to remove any tiny pin bones remaining in the fish; you might also want to double-check yourself, and simply pull out any leftover ones with tweezers.

PREPARE THE SACHET Gather the peppercorns, coriander seeds, bay leaf, and thyme sprigs in a 6-inch square of cheesecloth and tie it up with a piece of twine.

MARINATE THE MACKEREL, 1 DAY IN ADVANCE Place the oil in a large skillet over medium heat. When the oil is hot, add the peppers, carrots, fennel, and shallots, and sweat, stirring frequently, until the vegetables begin to soften, about 7 minutes. Season the vegetables liberally with salt and pepper, and add the orange juice and white wine. Add the sachet, then simmer the marinade until the vegetables are very tender, about 7 minutes more.

Place the mackerel in a single layer, skin side up, in a deep glass or other nonreactive dish. Pour the hot marinade over the fish. Allow the marinade to cool to room temperature, then cover the container with plastic wrap and refrigerate for 12 to 24 hours.

FINISH AND SERVE Shortly before serving, cut the ends off the zucchini. Stand a zucchini up (the newly flat surface makes this easier) and carefully shave off the green skin, continuing to shave until you reach the seeds. Give the zucchini a quarter turn and repeat until only the seedy core remains; discard the core. Repeat until all the zucchini have been reduced to thin sheets. Using a sharp knife, cut the zucchini sheets into long, spaghetti-thin strands. (Alternatively, if you have a mandoline, fit it with the medium teeth and slide each zucchini lengthwise across the blades to create the strands.)

Melt the butter in a sauté pan over medium heat. Add the zucchini and sauté until tender, 1 to 2 minutes. Season the zucchini with salt and pepper to taste. Mound equal portions of zucchini on each of 8 small plates. (For a more elaborate presentation, twirl the zucchini strands around a fork, creating cylinders, then arrange the cylinders on plates.)

Place the mackerel fillets and the marinade in a large, deep nonreactive skillet over medium-low heat. Heat the mackerel, basting with the marinade, until it is warmed through, 3 to 5 minutes. Arrange 2 mackerel fillets on each plate and serve.

MACKEREL

Country

Warm Mackerel with Basil Chiffonade and Zucchini Vinaigrette

SERVES 4

FOR THE SALAD (OPTIONAL)

1 medium carrot

1 small zucchini

1 small knob celery root, or 1 small yellow squash

FOR THE DRESSING

1 very large or 2 medium zucchini squash (1 pound)

3 tablespoons rice wine vinegar

¼ cup extra-virgin olive oil

Fine sea salt and freshly ground black pepper

FOR THE MACKEREL

About 30 fresh basil leaves (3 branches)

2 pounds mackerel fillets (8 fillets), skin on

1 teaspoon kosher salt

½ teaspoon freshly ground black pepper

6 tablespoons extra-virgin olive oil

Fried Celery Leaves (recipe follows; optional)

A mackerel is like a turbocharged sardine; it's one of the best, most satisfying, and most underused fish available. It takes very well to a number of treatments, including grilling and sautéing. But like any other fish, it's still important to avoid overcooking. The idea for a zucchini vinaigrette alongside fish was inspired by a dish I had at the Michelin three-star Oustau de Baumanière in Les Baux de Provence, dining on the terrace on a gorgeous summer evening. They served theirs with *rouget* (red mullet); this is my attempt to re-create that magical moment.

INGREDIENT NOTE Mackerel must be handled carefully as it spoils easily. A clean cutting board and knife are essential. The mackerel works well on its own, so if you'd like to take a shortcut just skip the salad.

PREPARE THE SALAD (IF USING) Cut the carrot into small dice. Cut the green skin and outer layer of the zucchini from the seedy core. Discard the core, or use it for another purpose. Dice the green part of the zucchini the same size as the carrot. Cut off the tough outer layer of the celery root, then dice the inner white flesh the same size as the other vegetables. (If substituting yellow squash, treat it the same as the zucchini.) Refrigerate the vegetables in a sealed container.

PREPARE THE DRESSING Cut the green exterior off the large zucchini and chop it coarsely. (Again, discard the seedy center or reserve it for another use.) Place the chopped zucchini, vinegar, and oil in a blender and purée. Thin out the dressing, if necessary, with up to 2 tablespoons of water, then season to taste with salt and pepper.

COOK THE MACKEREL Slice the basil leaves into thin lengths (julienne).

Cut each mackerel fillet on the bias into two equal pieces. Season both sides of each fillet with the salt and pepper. Lay the fillets flesh side down on the cutting board and scatter basil chiffonade on the skin side. Place 2 tablespoons of the oil in a large skillet and warm over high heat. Working in batches, carefully add the seasoned mackerel fillets to the pan, skin side down. (Only cook as many fillets as will comfortably fit in the pan without crowding.) Cook the fish over high heat until the skin crisps, about 2 minutes. Reduce the heat to medium and turn each fillet over. Cook until the fish is opaque and flaky, about 3 minutes more. Transfer the cooked fillets to a plate or platter and reserve in a warm place while cooking the other fillets; wipe out the pan between batches.

TO FINISH Dress the diced vegetables (if using) with about 4 tablespoons of the zucchini vinaigrette and season to taste with salt and pepper. Arrange equal portions of the salad onto each of 4 dinner plates. Stack 3 pieces of mackerel on each plate, skin side up, in a spiral pattern. Drizzle a little of the remaining dressing around the rim of the plate, garnish with fried celery leaves (if using), and serve.

FRIED CELERY LEAVES

MAKES ABOUT 1 CUP

About 1½ cups fresh celery leaves (1 medium bunch), washed and thoroughly dried

About 3 cups neutral vegetable oil, such as canola or safflower

Fill a large pot with at least 2 inches of vegetable oil. Heat the oil over a medium-high flame until it reaches a temperature of 350°F. (check with a thermometer or drop a celery leaf in the oil; if it begins to fry immediately, the oil is ready). Working in batches, carefully add the leaves to the pan and fry them until crisp and light brown, about 2 minutes. Transfer the fried leaves to a large plate lined with paper towels to drain.

MUSSELS

TOWN

Mussels in a Pot with Kaffir Lime and Coconut Broth

SERVES 6

FOR THE KAFFIR LIME BROTH

1 tablespoon vegetable oil

5 shallots, sliced thin

Pinch of ground turmeric

3 dried kaffir lime leaves

1 tablespoon black peppercorns

Kosher salt

1 tablespoon coriander seeds

Juice of 2 limes

1 cup sweet white wine

1 cup dry white wine

1 quart Fish Stock (page 263)

¾ cup coconut milk

½ cup heavy cream

Freshly ground black pepper

FOR THE MUSSELS

Garlic Butter (recipe follows), or ¼ pound (1 stick) unsalted butter

6 pounds P.E.I. mussels, well rinsed

2 cloves garlic, sliced paper-thin

Leaves of ½ bunch of cilantro, chopped

Leaves of 1 bunch of flat-leaf parsley, chopped

2 medium tomatoes, peeled, seeded, and diced

Sea salt and freshly ground black pepper

Toasted baguette slices, for serving

My first taste of mussels was at Caserta's Pizzeria in Providence, Rhode Island. Then, believe it or not, I had another mussel pizza—in northern France. There, and also in Belgium, eating mussels is almost a religious experience; they must have four hundred ways of cooking them. As my career developed, mussels remained fascinating to me, and I experimented with a lot of recipes. This is my Indonesian-accented version of the standard bistro dish *moules à la marinière*. I created it at Patroon in the late 1990s; I remember there was an A-list of media and fashion types—including Graydon Carter, Oscar de la Renta, and Michael Douglas—who ate them at lunch with a gleeful lack of inhibition.

INGREDIENT NOTES Kaffir lime leaves are available through Kalustyan's (and other Middle Eastern and/or Indian spice sources) online or by phone (see "Sources and Resources," page 266).

P.E.I. mussels, named after their original source, Prince Edward Island, Canada, are farm-raised and beardless, making them plump, consistent in shape and size, and easier to wash than their less reliable and tougher wild cousins.

PREPARE THE KAFFIR LIME BROTH Heat the oil in a medium saucepan over medium heat. Add the shallots and cook, stirring frequently, until they begin to soften, about 3 minutes. Add the turmeric, kaffir lime leaves, peppercorns, 1 teaspoon salt, and the coriander seeds, and cook until the shallots are translucent, about 3 minutes more. Add the juice of 1 lime, and the sweet and dry white wines. Raise the heat to medium-high and simmer the ingredients until the pan is almost dry, about 20 minutes. Add the fish stock, reduce the heat to medium, and simmer until reduced by about half, about 20 minutes. Pour in the coconut milk and cream, and again reduce by half, another 20 minutes or so. Season the broth to taste with salt and pepper, then add the remaining lime juice. Pass it through a fine strainer and reserve.

COOK THE MUSSELS Melt half the garlic butter in a large heavy pot over medium heat. Add the mussels and the garlic. Cook, stirring, for about 1 minute, then pour in the strained broth. Cover and cook the mussels, lifting the lid from

time to time to stir, until they open, about 7 minutes. Discard any unopened mussels. Add the remaining garlic butter, the cilantro, parsley, and tomato and mix well. Season with salt and pepper to taste. Spoon the mussels and broth into bowls and serve warm with toasted baguette slices.

GARLIC BUTTER

MAKES ABOUT 1/4 POUND (1 STICK)

10 cloves garlic

1 cup whole milk

1/4 pound (1 stick) unsalted butter, at room temperature

1/2 cup chopped flat-leaf parsley

Fine sea salt and freshly ground black pepper to taste

Place the garlic cloves and milk in a small saucepot over medium-low heat. Cover the pan and gently simmer until the garlic is soft, about 45 minutes. Allow the garlic to cool in the milk, then transfer both ingredients to a food processor and purée the garlic. Add the butter and pulse until the mixture is smooth. Pulse in the parsley. Season the garlic butter with salt and pepper to taste, wrap it in plastic, and refrigerate.

Country
Mussel Potage "Billy B."

SERVES 6

2 tablespoons plus 1 teaspoon extra-virgin olive oil

6 medium shallots, diced

5 cloves garlic, sliced thin

1 sprig thyme

1 sprig rosemary

2 pounds P.E.I. mussels, rinsed and drained (about 5 dozen; see Ingredient Note, page 158)

1 cup dry white wine

1 dried bay leaf

6 tablespoons Pernod

1 tablespoon peppercorns in a sachet, or 1 teaspoon freshly ground black pepper

2 cups Chicken Stock (page 262, or low-sodium canned)

2 cups clam juice

2 cups heavy cream, plus additional for the mashed potato

1 medium Yukon gold potato (about 4 ounces)

1 teaspoon kosher salt

Fine sea salt, freshly ground black pepper, and cayenne to taste

2 tablespoons diced Tomato Confit (page 265), or 1 medium tomato, peeled, seeded, and diced

6 sprigs chervil, roughly chopped

I love this recipe: it's an updated classic and another expression of my mussel madness. Culinary lore has it that "Billy B." (often transcribed as "billibi" or "billi by") was a favored customer, very possibly the American tycoon William B. Leeds, after whom Chef Louis Barthe of Maxim's in Paris named this type of mussel soup. A *potage* falls somewhere between a thin, clear consommé and a thick, hearty soup. The standard "Billy B." features mussels with shallots, onions, and white wine, thickened with cream and egg yolks; it can be served hot or cold. My version, which features a taste of Pernod, is designed to be served hot. It's thickened by adding some cream and mashed potatoes, and "countrified" with tomato and rosemary.

PREPARE THE SOUP Warm the oil in a large pot over medium heat. Add the shallots, followed by the garlic, thyme, and rosemary, and cook until the shallots are translucent, about 5 minutes. Add the mussels, wine, bay leaf, and 3 tablespoons of the Pernod. Add the sachet of black pepper, stir the pot, cover and steam the mussels until they open, about 5 minutes.

Using a pair of tongs or a slotted spoon, transfer the mussels to a bowl. Remove the herbs from the pot and discard the sachet of pepper. Add the stock and clam juice to the mussel juices remaining in the pot. Bring to a gentle simmer, then add the cream. Allow the soup to simmer, stirring occasionally, until it has reduced by about one quarter, about 20 minutes.

Meanwhile, remove the mussels from their shells, discarding any unopened ones, and reserve.

PREPARE THE MASHED POTATO Place the potato in a pot. Add water to cover, season with 1 teaspoon kosher salt, and bring to a simmer over medium heat. Simmer the potato until it is tender, about 30 minutes. Drain the potato, peel it, return it to the pan, and mash it. Stir in the remaining 3 tablespoons of Pernod, 1 teaspoon of oil, and about 1 tablespoon of cream, and mix until smooth. Season the potato with sea salt and pepper to taste, cover the pan, and reserve in a warm oven on its lowest setting.

TO FINISH Use an immersion blender to smooth out the consistency of the soup (alternatively, pulse in a food processor or blender). Reheat if necessary over medium heat. Season the soup to taste with sea salt, black pepper, and cayenne. Warm the mussels in the oven for a few minutes, then divide them equally among 6 soup bowls. Ladle the soup over the mussels, garnish with a dollop of warm mashed potato, a teaspoon of tomato confit, and chervil, and serve.

OLIVE OIL

TOWN

Olive Oil Gelato

MAKES ABOUT 1 QUART

6 large egg yolks

1 cup sugar

½ cup extra-virgin olive oil

1 cup heavy cream

3 cups whole milk

1 vanilla bean, split

Olive oil ice cream—how's that for a novel dessert concept? It's kind of whimsical and—I hope you agree—very appealing. Sometimes the best recipes come from unexpected, even slightly weird-sounding twists like this one. I was playing around with ideas for olive oil in 2003 and found some Italian references to gelato; pastry chef Luci Levere and I developed this recipe. Serve it with biscotti and/or a garnish of toasted pine nuts.

Place the egg yolks and sugar in the bowl of an electric mixer with the whisk attachment, and beat until frothy, at least 5 minutes. With the mixer still running, drizzle in the oil, then add the cream and milk. Transfer the mixture to a nonreactive saucepan over medium heat, add the vanilla bean, and cook, stirring constantly, until it thickens slightly and coats the back of a spoon, about 10 minutes. Remove the pan from the heat, pass the mixture through a strainer into a bowl set over ice; let cool, then chill thoroughly. Process the gelato in an ice cream machine according to the manufacturer's instructions, then freeze until ready to serve.

OLIVE OIL

Country

Black and White Olive Oil Yogurt Bruschetta

MAKES ABOUT 2 CUPS OF SPREAD FOR APPROXIMATELY 30 CROSTINI

3 cups plain whole-milk yogurt (preferably Greek, such as Fage)

¼ cup Lemon-Infused Grapeseed Oil (recipe follows)

In the ethnic cuisines of my youth, olive oil and yogurt are both tremendously important staple ingredients. Here's a way to combine the two to make a versatile hors d'oeuvre spread. It can also serve the same purpose as compound butter: simply place a generous spoonful on top of your steamed, broiled, or grilled fish, or a piece of grilled chicken or veal, and let it melt to a saucelike consistency.

Crostini, or "little toasts" in Italian, are canapés of a savory spread on small slices of toasted bread. *Bruschetta* is a somewhat larger (often full-

½ cup pitted, chopped kalamata olives, or other flavorful black olives

¾ cup extra-virgin olive oil

¼ pound soft, fresh goat cheese

1 tablespoon fresh thyme leaves

Fine sea salt and freshly ground black pepper to taste

1 large crusty loaf peasant bread

1 clove garlic, halved

sized) slice of toasted bread, traditionally rubbed with garlic and olive oil, and spread with chopped tomatoes. Crostini place more emphasis on the spread, while a bruschetta is more about the bread. This recipe is a combination of the two, with a savory Greek-accented spread. Note that the first few steps of this recipe are executed a day in advance to allow for marinating overnight.

INGREDIENT NOTE Genuine Greek kalamata olives give this spread its optimum kick; they are assertive and fruity, dark blackish purple, and come packed in a wine-vinegar marinade and/or olive oil.

Spoon the yogurt into a fine strainer lined with cheesecloth set over a bowl. Put the strainer and bowl in the refrigerator and allow the yogurt to drain overnight. Prepare the lemon oil. Combine the olives and 5 tablespoons of the olive oil in a bowl. Cover and set aside to marinate overnight.

Combine the strained yogurt and goat cheese in a metal or heat-resistant glass bowl, or the top of a double boiler. Set over a pan of simmering water and beat the mixture together until it is smooth. Remove the cheese mixture from the heat and whisk until it is cool. While continuing to whisk, gradually drizzle in 3 tablespoons of the olive oil, followed by the strained lemon oil. Whisk in the thyme and season to taste with salt and pepper. Spoon the spread into a shallow serving bowl. Cover with plastic and refrigerate for at least 2 hours.

Preheat the oven to 350°F. Slice the bread into approximately 30 squares or rounds about 2 inches across and ½ inch thick. Place the bread on a baking sheet, drizzle on both sides with the remaining ¼ cup of olive oil, and toast it in the oven until light brown, about 5 minutes per side. Rub 1 side of each toasted bread slice with the garlic, then season it with salt and pepper. Drizzle the black olive–olive oil mixture over the cheese-yogurt mixture, then spoon equal portions (about 1 tablespoon per serving) onto the toasts and serve.

LEMON-INFUSED GRAPESEED OIL

MAKES ¼ CUP

Peel of 1 lemon, julienned

¼ cup grapeseed oil

Place the lemon peel and grapeseed oil in a container, cover, and allow to marinate overnight in a cool place. Strain the lemon oil and refrigerate until needed.

OLIVES

TOWN

Green Olive and Artichoke Stew with Purple Basil

SERVES 6

FOR THE SPICE SACHET

1 tablespoon coriander seeds

1 tablespoon fennel seeds

1½ teaspoons white peppercorns

2 dried bay leaves

3 lemons, halved

FOR THE ARTICHOKES

18 baby artichokes

¾ cup extra-virgin olive oil

1 medium bulb fennel, trimmed and sliced

1 medium yellow onion, sliced

2 cloves garlic, lightly crushed

1½ cups (½ bottle) dry white wine

1½ cups pitted green olives (preferably Cerignola or other large, meaty variety)

2 cups Chicken Stock (page 262, or low-sodium canned), plus additional if necessary

1 teaspoon kosher salt

1 teaspoon freshly ground black pepper

1 small bunch of flat-leaf parsley, tied together with twine

¼ pound (1 stick) unsalted butter, cut into small pieces

2 medium tomatoes, peeled, seeded, and diced

6 leaves purple basil, torn into ½-inch pieces

¼ cup freshly grated Pecorino Romano (optional)

Some of my most vivid and lasting food impressions come from the times I spent exploring southern France when I was supposed to be hitting the books for my graduate degree in economics. This recipe is based on a Provençal dish called *barigoule,* which features artichokes braised in white wine and olive oil with mushrooms and ham or bacon. This is a great side dish for a simple entrée of roast chicken, pork, or even a whole roasted fish.

TIMING NOTE The stew is steeped in its pot for at least an hour before finishing and serving. It can be made a day in advance, allowed to cool to room temperature, then covered and refrigerated until you're ready to reheat and serve.

PREPARE THE SPICE SACHET Place the coriander seeds, fennel seeds, white peppercorns, bay leaves, and 2½ lemons in a piece of cheesecloth. (Reserve half of 1 lemon to rub the artichokes.) Gather the cheesecloth up and tie it into a bundle with twine.

PREPARE THE ARTICHOKES Wash the baby artichokes, cut the sharp tips off their leaves, trim off and discard the tough outer leaves to reveal the tender, pale-green inner leaves, then rub them with the reserved half lemon.

Place ¼ cup of the oil in a medium to large saucepot over medium heat. Add the fennel, onion, garlic, and spice sachet, and sweat until the vegetables are soft, about 15 minutes. (Do not allow the vegetables to color; reduce the heat if necessary.) Add the artichokes, wine, olives, the remaining ½ cup of oil, and the stock. The liquid should just cover the vegetables; if not, add water so it does. Season with the salt and pepper and add the parsley. Adjust the heat so the liquid gently simmers and cook, uncovered, until the artichokes are tender, about 35 minutes. Remove the pot from the heat and allow the ingredients to steep, undisturbed, for 1 hour so flavors meld as the pot cools.

Shortly before serving remove the sachet and parsley and bring the stew to a simmer over medium heat. Reduce the heat to low and swirl in the butter, one piece at a time, swirling the pot. The butter should add a nice sheen to the stew. Remove the pot from the heat and stir in the tomatoes. Using a ladle, transfer the artichokes, olives, and some of the braising liquid to a warm serving dish, sprinkle with purple basil and grated cheese, and serve.

Country Olive-Clam Dip

MAKES 4 CUPS

- 1 pound cream cheese (preferably Philadelphia), at room temperature
- 1/4 cup sour cream
- 1 cup mixed pitted, diced black and green olives
- 1 cup minced clams (canned, frozen, or freshly steamed; see Ingredient Note), juice reserved
- 1 tablespoon Worcestershire sauce
- 1/4 teaspoon Tabasco sauce
- 2 shallots, finely minced
- Pinch of hot red pepper flakes
- 1 tablespoon sevruga caviar (optional)
- 1 tablespoon lemon juice (1/2 lemon)
- Fine sea salt and freshly ground black pepper to taste
- Potato chips

I grew up in a working-class neighborhood in Worcester, Massachusetts, where an olive-clam dip would find an honored place on the sideboard at just about any occasion. This is a true blue-collar dish that also happens to be one of my all-time sentimental favorites. The classic accompaniment would be Cape Cod brand potato chips—the type seasoned with malt vinegar. But if you want to make life a little more interesting, make the chips at home (see Buttered Chips, page 52). The dip also goes very well with a plate of crudités—called "raw vegetables" where I come from.

INGREDIENT NOTE The minced clams can come from a 16-ounce can or, if you prefer to steam them yourself, from about 4 dozen littlenecks (shells 2 inches across) or 2 to 3 dozen quahogs (3 inches across).

Place the cream cheese and sour cream in the bowl of a mixer with the paddle attachment, and mix on low speed until velvety smooth. (Alternatively, mix by hand with a whisk.) Fold in the olives, clams, Worcestershire sauce, Tabasco, shallots, hot pepper flakes, and caviar (if using). Use the reserved clam juice to thin the dip as necessary to your desired consistency. Season the dip with lemon juice, salt, and pepper to taste. Serve the dip in a bowl with potato chips on the side.

ORANGES

TOWN

Saffron-Poached Clementines

SERVES 4

8 clementines or other small sweet oranges, peeled and kept whole with stem intact

4 cups sugar

1 vanilla bean, split and scraped, seeds discarded

1 piece star anise

1 cinnamon stick

Pinch of saffron threads

Clementines were a childhood favorite of mine, brightening up many a dreary winter day. I know our neighbors were aghast at the number of lemons and oranges we used to bring into our house—as many as we could persuade my parsimonious uncle Simon, who ran a produce business, to part with. My mother and aunts would cook them every way they knew, often poaching the damaged or bruised ones and serving them with yogurt. (Now there's an ethnic breakfast for you!) Adding cinnamon, saffron, and sugar enhances their best attributes and lends an attractive, slightly exotic air. I like to serve them with a cheesecake or some other fairly dense, rich confection, but they're also great on their own for a light, elegant dessert.

INGREDIENT NOTE Clementines are grown mostly in Spain and North Africa; they're a seedless member of the Mandarin orange family, another of which is the tangerine.

Place the clementines, stem end up, in a large pan at least 2 inches deep. Combine the sugar, vanilla bean, star anise, cinnamon, and saffron in a medium skillet. Add 2 cups of water to the sugar mixture and bring to a boil over medium-high heat. Reduce the heat to low and cook gently for 5 minutes to make a syrup. Pour the syrup over the clementines and allow them to marinate, turning them from time to time, until the syrup has cooled. Serve 2 per plate with some syrup.

Country Orange-Rosewater Wine

MAKES 8 TO 10 GLASSES

4 juice oranges, plus 1 or 2 additional for garnish

2 750-milliliter bottles rosé wine

2 whole cloves

½ teaspoon rosewater

¼ cup sugar

I was inspired to create this refreshing and mildly intoxicating concoction by all the fanciful house wine blends offered in the old inns and sidewalk cafés I visited during my formative summers traveling around France. Plus, I remember my family never wasted anything: all the damaged fruit would go into infusions with rosé wine, or grain alcohol, which makes for great party drinks. Think of this as a Francophile version of sangria with a Middle Eastern twist (the rosewater). It's equally appropriate before, during, or after a meal. I often serve it as an after-dinner drink with an assortment of madeleines, macaroons, or other little cookies, or as an apéritif before a casual but elegant summer meal.

INGREDIENT NOTE Rosewater is available from Kalustyan's online (see "Sources and Resources," page 266), and at many gourmet food shops. An inexpensive table rosé such as Tavel is appropriate for this recipe.

Cut each orange into about 8 slices. Place the wine, oranges slices, cloves, and rosewater in a large bowl, and stir well to combine. Cover the bowl and refrigerate overnight.

Place the sugar in a small saucepan, add ¼ cup water, and bring to a boil over medium-high heat, stirring well so the sugar melts completely into the water. Remove the syrup from the heat and allow it to cool, then add it to the wine mixture. Transfer the orange-rosewater wine to a decanter, iced-tea pitcher, or other decorative container, discarding the cloves but leaving in the orange slices. Slice additional oranges and place one slice in each of 8 to 10 heavy wineglasses along with several cubes of ice. Pour the orange-rosewater wine into the glasses and serve.

TOWN

Oyster Tempura with Vermouth Aïoli

SERVES 6

FOR THE VERMOUTH AÏOLI

1 teaspoon chopped fresh chives

1 teaspoon chopped fresh tarragon

1 teaspoon chopped fresh dill

1 teaspoon chopped flat-leaf parsley

½ cup crème fraîche

1 tablespoon dry vermouth

1 small clove garlic, minced

½ cup Mayonnaise (page 264, or store-bought, preferably Hellman's)

1 tablespoon reserved oyster juice, or to taste

Fine sea salt and freshly ground white pepper

Early in my career, beginning in 1982, I worked at Le Cirque, much of the time under Chef Alain Sailhac. He helped me develop a profound appreciation for oysters and showed me how to cook them many different ways, always emphasizing the importance of preserving their fresh flavor. (I was also blown away—and still am—by the incredible knowledge French chefs possess regarding all the different oyster types.) In 1984, Alain was deep-frying oysters in batter—very forward-thinking for a classically trained French chef at that time. This tempura is motivated by all the bad fried seafood I had as a kid in New England, and spurred to greater heights by Alain's example. The key to a good tempura is to fry the food hot and fast, in fresh oil. The batter should be white and thin; the oil should be light and neutral-tasting. I find peanut oil works very well.

INGREDIENT NOTE Among the best oysters for eating raw on the half shell are the small to medium East Coast types, such as Blue Point and Malpeque. For frying, the traditional choices are usually larger, plumper oysters. For tempura, you want to revert to those smaller, more delicate types. That's all you need to know about oysters to make this dish a success.

PREPARE THE VERMOUTH AÏOLI Combine the chives, tarragon, dill, and parsley in a bowl with the crème fraîche, vermouth, and garlic. Cover and place in the refrigerator until well chilled. (The aïoli will be finished just before serving.)

FOR THE TEMPURA BATTER

½ cup cornstarch, plus additional for dusting the oysters

½ cup cake flour

Pinch of cayenne pepper

Pinch of kosher salt

½ teaspoon baking powder

1 cup seltzer water

24 small oysters, such as Kumamoto, Blue Point, or Fisher Island, in their shells

Approximately 2 cups peanut oil, for frying

Fine sea salt

PREPARE THE TEMPURA BATTER Sift the cornstarch with the flour, cayenne pepper, salt, and baking powder into a mixing bowl. Gradually whisk in the seltzer until the mixture attains the consistency of thin pancake batter; it should coat a spoon without being too clumpy or runny. If the batter is too thick, add a little more seltzer; if too thin, add some flour. Allow the batter to rest at room temperature for about 10 minutes.

PREPARE AND COOK THE OYSTERS Open the oysters, carefully disconnecting each one from its base shell without cutting into the flesh. Reserve any of the liquid and all the base shells. Strain the liquid and rinse the shells under running water, then wipe them clean with a paper towel.

Fill a heavy pot to a depth of at least 3 inches with peanut oil and place the pot over medium heat. Heat the oil until a drop of water in the pot immediately sizzles. (Alternatively, use a frying thermometer or an electric deep fryer and bring the oil to a temperature of 350°F.) Blot the oysters dry, then sprinkle them with cornstarch. Working in small batches, coat the oysters in batter, then fry until crisp, about 2 minutes. Remove the oysters to a plate lined with paper towels to drain off excess oil. Season lightly with fine salt while still hot.

FINISH AND SERVE Fold the vermouth–crème fraîche mixture into the mayonnaise to finish the aïoli. It should have the consistency of a somewhat runny mayonnaise; add some of the reserved oyster juice to thin it if necessary. Season the aïoli with salt and pepper to taste. Place each oyster on a cleaned, dried half shell. Spoon some vermouth aïoli onto half of each oyster, allowing some of the aïoli to collect in a pool in the shell. Serve immediately.

OYSTERS

Country

Oyster Tartare Cocktail with Fresh Cilantro and Almonds

SERVES 2

- **6 medium oysters, carefully shucked (so as not to mutilate the bivalve—or your hand), with 6 oyster half-shells**
- **2 small shallots, finely diced**
- **Cracked black pepper to taste**
- **Balsamic vinegar to taste**
- **1 tablespoon roughly chopped, lightly toasted almonds**
- **1 ripe plum, peeled, pitted, and finely diced**
- **1 tablespoon chopped fresh cilantro**

The oyster is one of nature's perfect inventions, so I like to leave it alone as much as possible, with minimal preparations that highlight its sweet, fresh, juicy, subtly briny qualities. With good raw oysters, you even have to be careful with how much lemon or vinegar you add: literally just a drop is usually enough; any more is almost always too much. For this recipe, assemble all the ingredients in advance and pull them together at the last moment. And try this fun presentation: place the oysters in large, chilled porcelain Chinese soup spoons, add the garnishes, and serve with a chilled glass of Sancerre or a crisp rosé.

INGREDIENT NOTES Although good fresh oysters are available year round (contrary to certain old wives' tales), they are best in fall and winter as opposed to during the summer spawning season, when they turn somewhat fatty and overly plump. It's a good idea to buy oysters preshucked at your fish market; keep them very cold and resting in plenty of their liquid until moments before serving. The liquid should be clear and fresh-smelling—not cloudy or fishy.

Arrange the oyster half-shells on a plate on a bed of crushed ice, seaweed, or rock salt. Chop the oysters roughly (three to five times each at most). Divide equal portions of the roughly chopped oysters among the six oyster shells. Top each portion of oysters with minced shallot, cracked pepper, a few drops of balsamic vinegar, and chopped almonds. Garnish each portion with diced plum and chopped cilantro, and serve immediately.

PARMESAN

TOWN

Parmesan and Pancetta Gnocchi with White Truffle Oil

SERVES 8

FOR THE GNOCCHI (MAKES ABOUT 15 DOZEN OR 180 GNOCCHI)

- 3 pounds russet or Idaho (baking) potatoes
- 2 dried bay leaves
- 1 teaspoon fine sea salt
- Pinch of freshly grated nutmeg
- ½ teaspoon freshly ground black pepper
- 3 large egg yolks, lightly beaten
- About 2 cups "00" pasta flour (see Ingredient Note for Pasta Dough, page 265), or all-purpose flour

FOR THE PANCETTA–WHITE TRUFFLE SAUCE

- ¼ pound pancetta, diced
- 2 tablespoons minced shallots (2 medium shallots)
- 1 cup dry white wine
- 1 quart heavy cream
- ¼ teaspoon freshly grated nutmeg (½ whole nutmeg)
- ½ cup fresh sage leaves, torn into small pieces
- 2 sprigs thyme
- 1 garlic clove
- 1 tablespoon white truffle oil, or to taste
- Fine sea salt and freshly ground black pepper

- ½ pound high-quality aged Parmigiano-Reggiano
- White truffle slices (optional)

This recipe makes me think of a cold winter evening and a good glass of Barolo or Barbaresco. It was inspired by some potato gnocchi made by Thomas Keller when he was at Rakel in New York City in the late 1980s. I was amazed at how happy a person could become from eating these little lumps of flour and potato. I think most people, if they asked an expert to name the best cheese in the world, would expect to hear about some fairly obscure, exotic delicacy. But in fact, a great percentage of cheese gurus will answer, "Parmesan."

The quantities here yield about 15 dozen gnocchi, or 8 generous portions of nearly two dozen gnocchi per hungry diner. If you're serving this as an opening course, I recommend halving the recipe; or you can freeze the extra. If you make the full quantity of sauce, just refrigerate the excess and serve it on pasta a day or two later.

INGREDIENT NOTES White truffles, a specialty of Piedmont, are to me the eighth wonder of the world. You can summon an intoxicating hint of their musky, earthy flavor by using a small amount of white truffle oil any time of year; but for an extra treat, shave paper-thin slices of fresh white truffle on top of your dishes as a garnish. The season for fresh white truffles is late fall and early winter, so take the opportunity and gobble them up while you can. Gnocchi (pronounced "NYOH-kee") can be made from flour, but I much prefer the potato version.

MAKE THE GNOCCHI Place the potatoes in a pot of cold water. Add the bay leaves and bring to a boil over medium-high heat. Reduce the heat and simmer the potatoes until tender, about 30 minutes (a thin knife should penetrate the skin easily). Drain the potatoes and discard the bay leaves. While they are still warm, peel away the skin and any discolorations. Cover a large, flat work surface with parchment paper. (Marble is best; smooth butcher block or a synthetic is acceptable.) Pass the hot potatoes through a ricer onto the parchment paper. Spread the potatoes out in a thin, even layer and allow them to cool. Sprinkle the potatoes with the salt, nutmeg, and pepper. Spread the lightly beaten egg yolks over the potatoes. Use your hands to combine the ingredients into a large ball. Sprinkle half the flour on the parchment and press the ball down to form a rectangle. Sprinkle a small amount of flour on top of the rectangle and fold it into itself. Move the dough from the parchment to the work surface and knead for 4 to 5 minutes, incorporating just enough flour to prevent the dough from turning sticky. Wrap the dough in plastic and put it in the refrigerator to rest for about 10 minutes.

To form the gnocchi, slice the rectangle of dough into six equal pieces. Flour your hands and roll a slice of dough from the center outward to form a cylinder about ½ inch in diameter. Cut the rolled dough into pieces about 1 inch long. Roll each piece of dough into a ball, then press the balls with the back of a fork so they are somewhat flattened. Transfer the gnocchi to a lightly floured tray or baking sheet. Repeat this process with the remaining dough. (The gnocchi may be frozen until ready to use: line a baking sheet with plastic wrap, place the gnocchi on the sheet, cover with another layer of plastic, then freeze them. Once they're frozen solid, they can be transferred to a resealable, freezer-safe plastic bag for easier storage.)

PREPARE THE SAUCE Place the pancetta in a medium saucepan over medium heat and sweat, rendering the fat but not allowing the pancetta to brown, 3 to 5 minutes. When the pancetta is rendered there should be just enough fat to coat the bottom of the pan; pour off any excess. Add the shallots and sweat until soft, about 3 minutes, lowering the heat if necessary to ensure they do not color. Add the wine and reduce until the pan is dry, about 12 minutes. Add the cream, nutmeg, sage, thyme, and garlic. Gently simmer the sauce until the cream thickens enough to coat the back of a spoon (it will have reduced by about one third), about 15 minutes. Remove and discard the garlic and thyme sprigs. Season the sauce with the truffle oil, and salt and pepper to taste. Cover and reserve in a warm place.

FINISH AND SERVE Bring a large pot of boiling, salted water to a boil. Drop in the gnocchi and wait until all of them float for several seconds together. Carefully transfer them to a large bowl or platter with a slotted spoon, allowing any excess water to drain off. Pour enough sauce on top of the gnocchi to cover them, but not so much that the dish becomes soupy. Turn the gnocchi over gently to coat well, divide into equal portions in serving bowls or plates, grate 1 tablespoon of Parmesan on top of each portion, garnish with paper-thin slices of white truffle (if using), and serve.

PARMESAN

Country

Parmesan and Swiss Chard Soufflé

SERVES 6

1½ pounds Swiss chard or spinach, veins trimmed and leaves coarsely chopped

¼ pound (1 stick) unsalted butter, plus additional for greasing soufflé dishes

½ cup all-purpose flour, plus additional for dusting the soufflé dishes

2 cups heavy cream

1 teaspoon ground allspice

Kosher salt and freshly ground black pepper

5 large eggs, separated

½ cup freshly grated Parmigiano-Reggiano cheese

½ cup freshly grated Emmenthaler cheese

When I was working at Le Cirque in the early 1980s, the pastry chef burned his hand one day. Chef Alain Sailhac turned to me and said, "You're making the soufflés now." Suddenly I was responsible for a hundred or more of them at every meal, and I had no choice but to learn fast. I think the biggest fear of any amateur soufflé–maker is that their precious concoction won't rise and attain that state of perfect puffiness they've seen in restaurants. Here are a few hints to ensure success: First, make sure your roux cooks but doesn't brown; stir the flour well and keep the heat low. Second, start with your egg whites at room temperature and don't overwhip them (soft peaks are enough); and take your time folding the whipped whites gently and gradually into the mixture so it contains some air. And finally, check your soufflés while they're baking. If they stick, simply use the tip of a knife to lift them up a little and separate them from the sides of their dishes. This soufflé, which highlights the simple goodness of its main ingredients, is light and airy yet satisfying and filling—the perfect lunchtime entrée.

INGREDIENT NOTES Any top-quality French or Swiss hard mountain cheese such as Gruyère or Emmenthaler will do alongside the Parmesan in this recipe. There are so many really good frozen vegetable products in markets today, so feel free to use frozen spinach or chard for this soufflé. I can't decide whether this dish is better with spinach or chard; it's really a matter of personal preference.

Preheat the oven to 375°F.

Bring a large pot of salted water to a boil over high heat. Place the Swiss chard in the pot and blanch it until it is wilted and tender, about 2 minutes. Drain the Swiss chard in a colander, refresh under cold, running water, squeeze out excess water, and set aside.

Place the butter in a medium saucepan over medium-low heat. When the butter is melted, whisk in the flour. Cook the flour mixture (roux), stirring constantly with a wooden spoon, until it is bubbly, pulls from the edges of the pan, and no longer smells raw, about 7 minutes. Do not allow the roux to brown; lower the heat if necessary. Whisk in the cream and simmer over medium heat, stirring constantly with a wooden spoon, until the mixture is smooth and thick, about 5 minutes. Remove the pan from the heat and immediately pass the mixture through a fine strainer into a bowl to make a smooth soufflé base. Stir in the allspice, then season the mixture lightly with salt and pepper. Whisk in the egg yolks, one at a time. Allow the soufflé base to cool to room temperature, then stir in the Parmesan and Emmenthaler. Fold in the Swiss chard, cover with plastic wrap, and reserve.

Place the egg whites in a bowl (copper is best, stainless steel is fine, and even glass will work), add a pinch of salt, and whip until the whites form soft peaks. Use a spatula to gently fold the whipped egg whites into the soufflé base in three equal portions.

Butter and lightly flour six 6-ounce soufflé dishes. Fill each dish about halfway, place the dishes in the oven, and bake until the soufflés are puffed and slightly golden, about 20 minutes; serve immediately.

PEAS

TOWN

Chilled Pea Soup

SERVES 6

- **2 pounds fresh or frozen shelled English peas**
- **Kosher salt and freshly ground black pepper**
- **3 slices applewood-smoked bacon**
- **2 tablespoons extra-virgin olive oil, plus additional for garnish**
- **1 medium Vidalia onion, thinly sliced**
- **1 tablespoon fresh thyme leaves**
- **Ham-Cream Garnish (recipe follows; optional)**

My childhood recollections of pea soup, like those of so many people in my generation, are pretty dreary. Here's a recipe to erase all those dim memories and conjure up visions of the sweet arrival of spring. I had an unforgettable pea soup at the Quai des Ormes restaurant in Paris, made by my friend Georges Masraff. It was so good I couldn't wait to get home and try to come up with my own version. The first thing you'll notice about this soup is its electric kelly green color (chilling the pea purée in an ice-water bath accomplishes this), which shouts "fresh peas!" I like to serve it in demitasse or espresso cups or even wineglasses as an opening course. It's easy and convenient to make; it also stores well refrigerated or frozen. Use a simple garnish of fresh thyme leaves and a drizzle of extra-virgin olive oil; or, if you're feeling somewhat ambitious, try the optional fancy garnish below.

INGREDIENT NOTE With the availability of so many excellent brands of fresh-frozen, organic peas in the market, you can use this recipe to dial up spring any time of year.

Bring 4 cups of salted water to a boil in a large pot over high heat. Add the peas and cook until they are tender, about 8 minutes for fresh or 3 to 5 minutes for frozen. Drain and reserve about ⅓ cup of the peas for garnish. Purée the remaining peas with the cooking water in a blender. Strain the soup through a fine sieve into a bowl resting in ice water. Season the soup with salt and pepper to taste, then refrigerate until ready to serve.

Cut the bacon crosswise into thin strips. Place the bacon in a small saucepan over medium heat and cook until its fat is rendered, about 7 minutes. Continue cooking, stirring occasionally, until the bacon is crisp, then transfer it onto a plate lined with paper towels to drain. Reserve the bacon for use in the onion garnish and the bacon fat for use in the Ham-Cream Garnish (if using).

Heat the 2 tablespoons of oil in a large skillet over medium-low heat. Add the onions and season with salt and pepper. Cook the onions, stirring occasionally, until they are soft and translucent, about 20 minutes. Mix in the reserved bacon and set aside to cool.

To serve, place a portion of the bacon-onion mixture in the center of each of four or six chilled soup bowls. Ladle a portion of soup into each bowl, then garnish each serving with thyme leaves, a drizzle of olive oil, and the Ham-Cream Garnish (if using).

HAM-CREAM GARNISH

This can be prepared up to several hours in advance.

MAKES ABOUT 2 CUPS

- 2 large slices serrano ham, sliced paper-thin
- 1 cup heavy cream, or a combination of heavy cream and crème fraîche
- Bacon fat (from recipe above)
- 1 pinch of Aleppo pepper flakes, or other hot red pepper flakes

INGREDIENT NOTE Aleppo pepper flakes are available from Kalustyan's by phone order or online (see "Sources and Resources," page 266) as well as at Middle Eastern and gourmet specialty stores. Regular hot red pepper flakes are an acceptable substitute; taste them carefully first, though, to judge the amount of heat you're comfortable using as a garnish for your soup.

Preheat the oven to 200°F. Cut the ham into thin strips and arrange it in a single layer on a baking sheet. Dry the ham in the oven until firm and chewy, about 45 minutes. Reserve the ham at room temperature.

Stir the cream into the pan containing the bacon fat and simmer gently for 5 minutes. Remove the bacon-flavored cream from the heat and place it in a stainless-steel or other nonreactive bowl; allow it to cool to room temperature, cover, then chill it in the refrigerator until shortly before serving.

To serve, whip the bacon-flavored cream with a whisk until it forms stiff peaks. Garnish each portion of soup with dried ham, a dollop of the whipped cream, and a pinch of the red pepper flakes.

Country

Sweet Pea and Crab Toasts with Fresh Herbs

MAKES ABOUT 1½ CUPS SPREAD, FOR 18 TO 24 TOASTS

FOR THE TOASTS

- 18 thin slices baguette
- 1½ tablespoons hazelnut or extra-virgin olive oil
- Kosher salt and freshly ground black pepper

FOR THE CRAB SALAD

- ½ cup (about ¼ pound) fresh shelled or frozen English peas
- ½ pound jumbo lump crabmeat, picked through to remove any shell fragments
- ½ teaspoon celery salt
- ½ teaspoon hazelnut oil
- ¼ cup Champagne Mayonnaise (recipe follows) or store-bought mayonnaise
- Fine sea salt and freshly ground black pepper
- 2 tablespoons chopped fresh dill leaves
- 2 tablespoons chopped fresh tarragon leaves
- 2 tablespoons chopped fresh celery leaves

I was messing around in the kitchen at the Royalton Hotel one day, munching on some leftovers while trying to come up with new hors d'oeuvres recipes. I stumbled on this fantastic combination of fresh green peas—the essence of spring—and briny crabmeat—a hint of the sea. Together, they sang a beautiful, harmonious duet, one ever-so-sweet sweet, and the other just salty enough. If you use one heaping tablespoon of pea-crab salad per toast, you'll need about 18 toasts; if you prefer to use less salad per toast, simply slice and toast more bread. The pea-crab salad also works well as a sandwich filling or the topping for a bed of greens lightly dressed with vinaigrette. Be sure to cook the peas until just tender (al dente)—no more.

INGREDIENT NOTE The Champagne Mayonnaise is strictly a fancy option; feel free to substitute regular mayo, either homemade (page 264) or store-bought (preferably Hellman's).

PREPARE THE TOASTS Preheat the oven to 350°F.

Arrange the slices of bread on a baking sheet; drizzle them with hazelnut oil, then sprinkle them lightly with salt and pepper. Bake in the oven until they are crisp and golden brown, 5 to 8 minutes. Remove from the oven, allow to cool to room temperature, and set aside.

PREPARE THE CRAB SALAD AND ASSEMBLE THE TOASTS Bring a medium pot of water to a boil over high heat. Add the peas and cook until they are just tender, about 5 minutes for large, fresh peas, or 1 minute for frozen. Drain the peas, refresh them under cold running water, and drain again well. Combine the crabmeat, peas, celery salt, and hazelnut oil in a bowl. Add about ¼ cup mayonnaise and mix gently to coat the crabmeat with the mayonnaise. Season to taste with salt and pepper. Arrange the toasts on a serving dish or tray. Spoon about 1 heaping tablespoon of pea-crab salad onto each toast, garnish with dill, tarragon, and celery leaves, and serve.

MAKES ABOUT $1\frac{1}{2}$ CUPS

2 shallots, roughly chopped

½ small clove garlic, roughly chopped

1 large egg yolk

1 tablespoon Champagne vinegar, or top-quality chardonnay or other white wine vinegar

1 teaspoon honey

Juice of 1 lime

1 cup grapeseed oil, or other light vegetable oil

Fine sea salt and freshly ground black pepper

CHAMPAGNE MAYONNAISE

Place the shallots, garlic, egg yolk, vinegar, honey, and lime juice in the jar of a blender. Turn the blender on high speed for 1 to 2 minutes, until the ingredients are well combined. With the blender still running, add the oil in a slow, steady stream, and continue to run the blender until the mixture attains the consistency of a light mayonnaise. (The mayonnaise can also be made by hand-whisking it in a bowl.) Season to taste with salt and pepper, transfer to a glass or other nonreactive container, cover, and refrigerate until ready to use (up to 24 hours).

PORK

TOWN

Braised Stuffed Pork Bellies

SERVES 6

FOR THE STUFFING

2 tablespoons unsalted butter

1 cup finely diced yellow onion (1 medium onion)

1 teaspoon kosher salt

½ teaspoon freshly ground black pepper

Pinch of quatre épices

1½ cups diced bread

1 large egg

1 cup whole milk

1 tablespoon chopped fresh marjoram, plus additional chopped leaves for garnish

FOR THE PORK

4½ pounds pork belly, cut into 6 equal pieces

1 teaspoon kosher salt

½ teaspoon freshly ground black pepper

2 tablespoons extra-virgin olive oil

1 cup roughly chopped yellow onion (1 medium onion)

½ cup roughly chopped carrot (1 medium carrot)

½ cup roughly chopped celery (1 medium stalk)

¼ cup roughly chopped turnips (½ small turnip)

½ cup peeled, seeded, chopped tomatoes (1 small tomato)

1 teaspoon tomato paste

2 cups dry white wine

6 cups Chicken Stock (page 262, or low-sodium canned)

Pork belly represents old-fashioned, primal French cooking at its best. It's a "cheap" cut of meat that's recently been elevated to near-cult status by a few clever restaurant chefs. My mentors—particularly Alain Sailhac and Daniel Boulud—used pork belly as a base or flavoring agent for many dishes. I always cooked with bacon, lardons, and pancetta, but it was not until the beginning of the "Offal Revolution"—around the mid-1980s—that I started experimenting with pork bellies as a stand-alone dish. This recipe is one of my favorite results. It's a great way to put the somewhat lost art of braising—very long, slow cooking in some liquid—to use. Once you've done the prep, you can just forget about it and let it quietly braise away for hours. One warning: it will fill your house with incredibly delicious aromas, so don't invite anybody over you don't like a lot, because it'll be almost impossible to convince them to leave. These braised pork bellies are about as close to flavor perfection as you can get. Serve with Mashed Potatoes (page 51) or Rosemary Crushed Yukon Gold Potatoes (page 190) on the side.

INGREDIENT NOTES Pork belly can be special-ordered from your local butcher shop; it is essentially uncured, whole, raw bacon. Use peasant-style bread or brioche, crust removed.

PREPARE THE STUFFING Melt the butter in a small sauté pan over medium heat. Add the onions and sweat, stirring frequently, until translucent and tender, about 8 minutes. Reduce the heat as necessary so the onions don't brown. Season the onions with the salt and pepper; add a pinch of quatre épices and the bread, and cook until the bread softens, about 3 minutes. Transfer the contents of the pan to a mixing bowl. Cool almost to room temperature, then stir in the egg, milk, and marjoram until well combined. Cover the bowl with plastic wrap and place it in the refrigerator until well chilled.

STUFF THE PORK BELLIES Lay each pork belly flat, skin side up, on a cutting board. Using a sharp knife, carefully cut a pocket into the belly along one edge, about midway through the meat and at least ½ inch from the skin on top; be sure to keep the knife parallel to the cutting surface so it creates a pocket inside without poking through the top or the underside of the belly. The pocket should be about 3 inches wide and run almost the entire length of the belly. Spoon just enough stuffing into each pocket so it is full but not bursting (the filling will expand during cooking). Close the incisions with toothpicks or by sewing them shut with a needle and twine.

Season the pork bellies with the salt and pepper. Heat the oil in a large Dutch oven or high-sided skillet over medium heat. Add the stuffed pork belly pieces and cook until brown on all sides, about 15 minutes total. (Brown the skin sides first.) Remove the pork from the pan. Discard all but 2 tablespoons of fat; add the onions, carrots, celery, and turnips, and cook, stirring occasionally, until they are soft and lightly colored, about 15 minutes. Add the tomatoes and tomato paste, and cook, stirring constantly, for another 3 minutes. Add the wine and cook until it is completely reduced, about 10 minutes. Return the pork to the pan. Add the stock and enough water to cover the pork. Bring the contents of the pan to a simmer over medium heat. Lower the heat, cover, and simmer for 3 hours. Uncover the pan and continue braising until the meat is very tender, about 1 more hour.

FINISH THE SAUCE Allow the pork to cool in the braising liquid, then remove it from the pan. Strain the braising liquid into a clean pot and return it to the stove. Bring the liquid to a simmer and skim off the fat (alternatively, chill the liquid and lift off the hardened fat). Simmer the braising liquid until it thickens slightly, about 30 minutes.

FINISH AND SERVE Preheat the oven to 400°F. Score the skin of each piece of braised pork belly, making cross-hatch incisions and stopping just short of the fat. Place the pork in a single layer in a roasting pan, skin side up. Add the sauce and simmer in the oven, basting every 20 minutes or so until the pork is heated through and the skin crisp and brown, about 25 minutes. Transfer the pork to a cutting board and remove the toothpicks. Cut each piece into ¾-inch to 1-inch slices and arrange on warm dinner plates. Spoon sauce over the pork and garnish with chopped marjoram.

Country Pork Chops with Apple Cider and Rosemary

SERVES 6

6 center-cut pork chops, about 1 inch thick each

5 tablespoons extra-virgin olive oil

2 medium shallots, minced

1 tablespoon minced fresh rosemary leaves

1 teaspoon kosher salt

½ teaspoon freshly ground black pepper

2 tablespoons unsalted butter

⅔ cup apple cider

¼ cup crème fraîche, or plain whole-milk yogurt

2 tablespoons Calvados (optional)

Pinch of ground turmeric

2 tablespoons chopped flat-leaf parsley

I have intense childhood memories of smelling pork fat stewing in the kitchen as I bounded in the back of the house—the screen door slamming shut—on a Saturday afternoon. My mother often smothered her pork in onions to keep it moist. This is another Mama's Boy recipe, but I'm taking a detour to northern Europe, where apples are a traditional accompaniment to keep this lean meat from drying out. In this simple concoction, we've got apples in two liquid forms—the cider and the Calvados—both of which contribute to a delectable pan sauce. In keeping with the hearty, Northern European theme, I like to serve this dish with fried apples and/or some red cabbage braised in red wine, alongside a nice bottle of Riesling.

INGREDIENT NOTES Organic pork chops are best; my preferred brand is from Niman Ranch (see "Sources and Resources," page 266).

Calvados is a type of dry apple brandy from Normandy, on the northern coast of France, where apples reign supreme.

MARINATE THE PORK CHOPS, AT LEAST 8 HOURS IN ADVANCE OR UP TO OVERNIGHT Lightly score both sides of each pork chop, using a small sharp knife to make cross-hatch patterns in the meat. Place 1 tablespoon of the oil in a small mixing bowl with the shallots and rosemary, and stir thoroughly to combine. Rub the shallot-rosemary mixture into the pork chops; cover them tightly in plastic wrap (or seal them in large resealable plastic bags) and refrigerate for at least 8 hours to marinate.

COOK THE PORK CHOPS Allow the pork chops to come to room temperature before cooking. Season them with the salt and pepper on both sides. Place 2 tablespoons of the oil in a large sauté pan over medium-high heat. (Work in batches or use two pans.) When the pan is hot, add three of the pork chops. Reduce the heat to medium and cook the pork chops until nicely browned, about 5 minutes. Turn the chops over and add 1 tablespoon of the butter. Continue cooking the chops, basting them with the butter, until they attain medium doneness (just slightly pink in the center with an internal temperature of 155°F. on a meat thermometer), about 5 minutes more. Transfer the pork chops to a platter and reserve in a warm place. (If cooking in batches, wipe out the pan between batches and repeat the procedure.)

PREPARE THE SAUCE, FINISH, AND SERVE Pour off any fat remaining in the pan, add the cider to the pan, and deglaze, stirring with a wooden spoon to loosen any browned bits stuck to the bottom. Reduce the cider until it is syrupy, about 5 minutes. Stir in the crème fraîche, Calvados (if using), and turmeric, and cook until the sauce is slightly reduced, about 3 minutes. Return the pork chops to the pan and cook until they are warmed through and nicely coated with pan sauce, about 2 minutes. Place 1 pork chop on each of six warm dinner plates, drizzle with sauce, sprinkle with chopped parsley, and serve immediately.

TOWN

Grilled Roquefort-Flavored Pork Chops

SERVES 4

FOR THE ROQUEFORT BUTTER

¼ pound (1 stick) unsalted butter, at room temperature

¼ pound Roquefort cheese, crumbled, at room temperature

Juice of ¼ lemon (about 2½ teaspoons)

Pinch of hot red pepper flakes

1 small clove garlic, minced

5 drops of Tabasco sauce, or to taste

¼ cup roughly chopped flat-leaf parsley leaves

FOR THE CHOPS

4 8-ounce pork chops

Vegetable oil, for oiling the grill rack

½ teaspoon kosher salt

½ teaspoon freshly ground black pepper

This recipe features an easy, effective way to flavor just about any kind of grilled meat. It's a variation on a classic method of preparing steak, which is to grill or pan-fry it, then simply top it with a dollop of parsley-, garlic-, or herb-butter—the seasoned butter melts and imparts its perfume as you get ready to serve it. Here, the creamy, pungent flavors of the Roquefort work well with the mild pork. In addition, since pork is inherently lean, it can use some additional fat (by way of the melted butter). Serve with roasted potatoes, or a tomato and onion salad.

INGREDIENT NOTES The pork chops should be nicely marbled, and you should trim most but not all of their fat. As with similar meat recipes, this is best prepared on an outdoor grill with genuine hardwood charcoal.

The Roquefort butter can be taken directly from the fridge and placed on the hot meat as it rests after grilling. The resting period—one of the most important and overlooked aspects of grilling or roasting meats—should be 5 to 7 minutes for these chops. Their internal temperature should be 145°F., which will increase to about 150°F. from the carryover cooking, and they should be medium to medium-rare or slightly pink in the center.

MEAT DONENESS

This is an area of great pitfalls and stress-related anxiety for many home cooks. But if you pay attention, you can easily learn how to cook all kinds of meats like a pro, and avoid over-doneness.

Very few—if any—professional chefs use meat thermometers to check doneness. We do it by feel, by sight, sound, smell, touch—and of course taste. I realize that may seem like a bit of mumbo jumbo, a kind of

PREPARE THE ROQUEFORT BUTTER Place the butter, Roquefort, lemon juice, red pepper, garlic, and Tabasco in the bowl of a food processor, and process until thoroughly combined. Fold in the parsley. Place the mixture on a sheet of plastic wrap and form it into a cylinder 2 inches in diameter. Refrigerate until ready to use.

COOK THE PORK CHOPS Preheat the oven to 375°F. Prepare a charcoal grill and position the rack about 5 inches above medium-high heat. (If you can hold your hand 5 inches above the grill for longer than 5 seconds, the grill isn't hot enough.) Lightly oil the rack or griddle pan. Season the pork chops with the salt and pepper. Grill the chops for 2 minutes, rotate 45 degrees (to give them nice grill marks), then cook for 2 minutes more. Turn the chops over and repeat the process. Transfer the chops to the oven and continue cooking until a meat thermometer registers 145°F., about 7 minutes. (If you're judging by touch, they should be about as firm as the flesh at the base of your thumb, just under the joint.) Remove the chops from the oven and allow them to rest in a warm spot for about 5 minutes. As the meat rests, cut four slices of Roquefort butter, transfer the chops to a platter, place a round of butter on each chop, and serve.

sixth sense, beyond the reach of anyone but the experienced pro. In fact, it's not all that hard. Anyone can develop a reliable ability to test and determine doneness by feel. Poke the meat. If necessary, cut a slit, and peek inside. Let the food speak to you. Smell it, look at it, taste it.

I'm not saying you shouldn't use a meat thermometer; it's a helpful tool. But don't make it your only one, a crutch. Pay attention to the entire process of cooking and be fully aware of the transformations that occur. You should be able to determine doneness by feel about the third time you cook a dish.

Don't ever forget the vital importance of the resting period for meats after you remove them from the heat. This is actually part of the cooking process, and all good chefs factor it into the equation. As meat or fowl rests, its juices collect and emerge. The meat also continues to cook, and its internal temperature will actually rise a few degrees. This is called carryover cooking, and is the reason why it's important to slightly undercook a piece of meat, allowing it to reach ideal doneness as it rests.

Country
Ancho Chile Pork Chili

SERVES 6

4 tablespoons extra-virgin olive oil

3 pounds ground pork (from the shoulder)

½ tablespoon kosher salt, plus more to taste

½ tablespoon freshly ground black pepper, plus more to taste

1 large white onion, chopped

3 large cloves garlic, minced

1 tablespoon ancho chili powder (see Ingredient Note)

1 tablespoon Worcestershire sauce

2 cups White Beef Stock (page 261, or low-sodium canned)

1 tablespoon green Tabasco, or equivalent green hot pepper sauce

6 chopped canned tomatoes or fresh peeled, seeded medium tomatoes (about 3 pounds)

1 tablespoon tomato paste

½ pound blue cheese, at room temperature, crumbled into small pieces, for garnish

1 small bunch of scallions, chopped, for garnish

I had pork chili once at a barbecue at my good friend Bobby Flay's house. It was so good I was jealous, and I told Bobby I was going to steal his idea and come up with my own recipe. Here it is, Bobby. I hope it's at least as good as the one you made. Chili, in general, is one of the unsung heroes of the kitchen. This variation is meant to bring out the best in pork: it's lean and mild yet tasty, and has a finer, denser, potentially smoother texture than beef. It's like a south-of-the border Bolognese without the cream; the smoky ancho chiles and pork are a dynamite pairing. I like to eat a bowl of this reheated for breakfast, inside or alongside an omelet, or just on its own. If I'm not sure when I'll find time for my next meal, it's an energy-boosting start to the day.

INGREDIENT NOTE Ancho chiles are the dried form of poblano chiles, which are among the sweeter, fruitier peppers and are generally mild to moderately spicy. They are one of the most commonly used chiles in Mexican cuisine and a key ingredient in certain mole sauces. Poblanos start out green when fresh, ripen to a reddish brown, and acquire a moderately smoky paprikalike flavor when dried. They're 3 to 4 inches long and relatively broad, about 2½ inches, hence the designation *ancho,* which means "wide" in Spanish. This recipe calls for anchos in their dried, ground form. If you like, you can substitute a whole dried one; simply soak it in hot water for 10 minutes, then scrape out the seeds, cut off the stem, dice it, and add it to the chili mixture prior to the simmering process.

Place 2 tablespoons of the oil in a Dutch oven or large heavy pot over medium-high heat. When the oil is hot, add the meat and cook, stirring frequently, until brown all over, about 10 minutes. Season the meat with the salt and pepper and transfer to a colander set over a bowl to drain.

Wipe out the pot, place it over medium heat, and add 2 more tablespoons of the oil. Add the onions and cook, stirring frequently, until they soften, about 8 minutes. Add the garlic and cook until fragrant, about 2 minutes, then add the chili powder. Toast the chili powder, stirring, until it darkens slightly, about 2 minutes. Add the Worcestershire sauce, stock, Tabasco, tomatoes, and tomato

paste. Adjust the heat to bring the contents of the pot to a gentle simmer. Return the meat to the pot and simmer the chili, stirring occasionally, until the liquid is reduced and the flavors combined, about 40 minutes. Season the chili to taste with salt, pepper, and additional Tabasco if desired. Spoon the chili into bowls, top with crumbled blue cheese and chopped scallions, and serve.

POTATOES

TOWN

Rosemary Crushed Yukon Gold Potatoes

SERVES 6

- $3\frac{1}{2}$ pounds Yukon gold potatoes (6 large), skins on
- 1 head of garlic
- 8 sprigs rosemary plus $\frac{1}{4}$ cup rosemary leaves
- 2 teaspoons caraway seeds
- Kosher salt
- 1 cup extra-virgin olive oil
- Freshly ground black pepper
- 4 to 6 tablespoons unsalted butter, at room temperature

These potatoes recall a dinner I had under the stars at La Bastide de Moustiers, Alain Ducasse's deluxe country inn in Provence, with my good friends the Blackburns. I had a dish of crushed potatoes that was heady, creamy, and utterly remarkable. I've tried to duplicate it many times, and this is my closest effort. A great many potato recipes come out best when the skins are left on; this is definitely one of them.

Place the potatoes in a large pot and cover with cold water. Add the garlic, rosemary sprigs, and caraway seeds, and season liberally with salt. Bring the potatoes to a simmer over medium-high heat, reduce the heat to medium, and simmer until a thin knife easily penetrates to the center of a potato and effortlessly slides out, about 25 minutes.

In the meantime, combine the oil and rosemary leaves in a small pot over medium heat. Heat the oil until it is warm to the touch (it should not simmer). Turn off the heat, and allow the herbs to steep for 15 to 20 minutes. Strain the oil, season with salt and pepper, and reserve.

Drain the potatoes, reserving the head of garlic but discarding the rosemary and caraway seeds. Allow the potatoes to cool until they are not too hot to handle; peel them while they are still warm. Return the peeled potatoes to the pan. Slice off the top of the head of garlic and squeeze it into the potatoes. Mash the potatoes with a potato masher, whisk, or fork. Gradually add the rosemary oil, then the butter (add more butter for richer potatoes). Season the potatoes with salt and pepper to taste and serve.

Country
Avocado and Potato Salad

SERVES 6

1 pound Red Bliss potatoes, scrubbed and dried

¼ cup finely chopped red onion

1 large avocado, peeled and cut into 1-inch cubes

¼ cup chopped fresh cilantro

1 tablespoon puréed chipotle peppers (purchase canned chipotles and purée with some of their liquid)

¼ cup red wine vinegar

½ cup Mayonnaise (page 264, or Hellman's)

Fine sea salt and freshly ground black pepper

Like many of my favorite recipes, this one is simple, direct, and relies on a delicious if somewhat unconventional pairing of two fundamental ingredients. I don't remember exactly where or when I developed this dish, but it probably came about by accident because both potatoes and avocados are very high on my list of favorites. I do know my childhood memories of potato salad—and also my portliness as a youngster—hinge on the fact that I ate large bowls of the stuff. What I remember most is the creaminess. Because this version contains avocado, it's creamy without relying on excess eggs or mayonnaise. It's the ultimate summer side dish for cook-outs, potlucks, and outdoor parties.

INGREDIENT NOTES Feel free to use Hellman's mayonnaise or make your own fresh at home. Be sure the red onions are firm and fresh; if you want to take away some of their bite, slice them before dicing and soak the slices in ice water for about 10 minutes.

Place the potatoes in a medium pot of salted water over medium heat. Bring the water to a simmer and cook until they are tender, about 20 minutes. Drain the potatoes thoroughly and cut them into 1-inch cubes. Place the potatoes, onion, avocado, cilantro, and chipotles in a large bowl. Drizzle the red wine vinegar into the bowl and set aside for 10 minutes. Add the mayonnaise and mix well to combine all ingredients; season to taste with salt and pepper, and serve. The salad can also be refrigerated, covered in its bowl, but be sure to allow it to come to room temperature before serving.

QUAIL

SERVES 6 AS AN APPETIZER

FOR THE QUAIL

- 1 tablespoon Orange Powder (recipe follows), or minced zest of 1 orange
- 2 teaspoons ground coriander
- 2 teaspoons fresh thyme leaves
- ½ teaspoon freshly ground black pepper
- 6 semi-boneless quails
- 4 tablespoons Clarified Butter (page 264), or extra-virgin olive oil
- 1 teaspoon kosher salt
- 2 tablespoons unsalted butter
- 6 bunches of watercress, leaves only, trimmed, washed, and dried

FOR THE VINAIGRETTE

- ¼ cup fresh orange juice (1 small juice orange)
- 2 tablespoons fresh grapefruit juice (½ small grapefruit)
- 1 tablespoon fresh lemon juice (½ lemon)
- 2 shallots, minced
- 1 tablespoon hazelnut oil
- 1 tablespoon extra-virgin olive oil
- Fine sea salt and freshly ground black pepper to taste

TOWN

Quail with Orange-Lime Reduction Sauce

While I was waiting to open Town in 2000, I worked with Chef Alain Passard at Arpège in Paris. He showed me how to cook quail his way and inspired this recipe. Alain may be the greatest chef I've had the pleasure to know. He's a cerebral man with a true love of life and a bit of Hollywood in him; in the kitchen, he knows when to keep it simple and how to coax the best out of an ingredient.

Don't fall prey to the misconception that quail is either gamey or problematic to cook and eat. Quite the contrary: it's highly accessible, lean, and mildly flavored. I like putting poultry on top of a salad—in this case, a bed of baby greens lightly dressed with a lively citrus vinaigrette. This dish is a great appetizer for a three- or four-course meal, but it also works as a main course for a light lunch or supper. Simply allot 2 quails per person, increase the amount of spice rub slightly (1½ tablespoons orange powder, 2½ teaspoons ground coriander, 1 tablespoon thyme, ¾ teaspoon pepper) and double the quantities for the vinaigrette.

INGREDIENT NOTES Semi-boneless quail is flattened, with the legs and wings intact, making it convenient for grilling or sautéing (as opposed to quail left whole, for roasting). It's available either in stock or by special order at most butcher shops and fine supermarkets; you can also order it online or by phone from D'Artagnan (see "Sources and Resources," page 266).

The orange powder is fun and challenging to make; you can do it once a month and use it to flavor all kinds of marinades. If you'd prefer not to bother, you can order it from Whole Spice online or by phone (see "Sources and Resources," page 266), or simply substitute minced orange zest.

SEASON THE QUAILS Place the orange powder, coriander, thyme, and pepper in a bowl and mix well. Rub the quails all over with the mixture, then refrigerate for at least 2 hours but preferably overnight.

MAKE THE VINAIGRETTE Place the orange juice, grapefruit juice, and lemon juice in a small nonreactive pot over medium heat. Bring to a simmer, then reduce to a glaze, about 5 minutes. Add the shallots, remove the pot from the heat, and allow the ingredients to cool to room temperature. Add the hazelnut oil and the olive oil, and season to taste with salt and pepper.

COOK AND SERVE THE QUAILS Working in batches or with two large skillets, heat the clarified butter over medium-high heat. Season the quails with the salt, and place them in the pan skin side down to cook until they begin to brown, about 3 minutes. Add the butter to the pan, then turn the birds over and cook, basting with browning butter, until they are browned on the other side and warm at the center, about 3 minutes more. Transfer the quails to a plate lined with paper towels to drain and set them aside to rest for several minutes.

Dress the watercress leaves with about half the vinaigrette, season them with salt and pepper to taste, and arrange equal portions on each of six plates. Cut the quails in half lengthwise and arrange them on top of each portion of watercress salad. Drizzle each plate with a little additional vinaigrette and serve.

ORANGE POWDER

MAKES ABOUT 1/2 CUP

8 orange peels (pith removed)

1 quart sugar water (2 parts water, 1 part sugar), for blanching

In a medium saucepan, blanch the orange peels for 3 minutes in the sugar water until soft and tender. Set aside on a rack on the top of the stove to dry overnight. Grind into fine powder in a clean coffee or spice grinder or by hand with a mortar and pestle.

Country "Barbecued" Quail

SERVES 4

2 teaspoons sweet paprika

2 teaspoons cayenne pepper

2 teaspoons ground coriander

8 whole semi-boneless quails

1 cup extra-virgin olive oil

Leaves from 2 sprigs rosemary

Leaves from 3 sprigs thyme

3 cloves garlic, halved

1 cup flat-leaf parsley leaves

1 teaspoon kosher salt

FOR THE BARBECUE SAUCE

1½ cups ketchup

¼ cup brown sugar

2 tablespoons Dijon mustard

¼ teaspoon (16 drops) Worcestershire sauce

10 drops Tabasco

1 teaspoon celery salt

1 teaspoon freshly ground black pepper

2 teaspoons sweet paprika

1 teaspoon ground coriander

¼ cup finely minced onion

2 cloves garlic, minced

1 bay leaf

3 sprigs thyme

Grated zest of 1 orange

We're obliged to put *barbecued* in quotation marks here because the birds are not actually barbecued. Instead, they're first browned, then sautéed in a hot pan, and basted with a relatively traditional barbecue sauce. I first learned how to cook quail under Pierre Orsi at his eponymous restaurant in Lyons, where he would gently roast it on a grill. This recipe achieves the same result in a pan, where the heat is much easier to monitor and control.

Quail is at least as easy—if not easier—to cook as chicken, and one bird is an ideal appetizer portion. As a variation, try grilling the quail on a lightly oiled rack for 2 to 4 minutes per side. Then either brush on the sauce to finish or transfer the quails to a pan and baste as described below. With this method, you obtain a slightly different flavor but an equally satisfying result. This recipe yields 4 servings (2 quails per person) as a main course and 8 as an appetizer (1 quail per person).

MARINATE THE QUAILS OVERNIGHT Combine the paprika, cayenne, and coriander seeds in a bowl. Coat the quails with the spice mixture, rubbing it all over each bird. Place the quails in a large bowl or resealable plastic bag. Add ½ cup of the oil, the rosemary, thyme, garlic, and parsley, and mix well. Marinate in the refrigerator overnight.

PREPARE THE BARBECUE SAUCE Place the ketchup, brown sugar, mustard, Worcestershire sauce, Tabasco, celery salt, black pepper, paprika, coriander, onion, garlic, bay leaf, thyme, and orange zest in a small saucepan over medium-low heat. Simmer the sauce gently until the flavors blend, about 20 minutes. Strain the sauce, discarding the solids, and set aside.

COOK THE QUAILS AND ASSEMBLE THE DISH Remove the quails from the marinade and pat them dry with a paper towel, cleaning off any herbs that stick to the flesh. Season them with the salt. Place 2 tablespoons of the olive oil in each of 2 large skillets over medium-high heat. (Alternatively, work in batches.) When the oil is nearly smoking, add the quails, one by one, breast sides down. Cook the quails without moving them until the breasts are browned, 1 to 2 minutes. Reduce the heat to medium, add about 1 more tablespoon oil to each pan, and cook the quails, still breast side down, basting them constantly with oil, until the breasts are fully crisped, about 1 minute more. Turn the quails over, and continue cooking until the other sides are brown and the breasts are slightly firm to the touch, 2 to 3 minutes. Pour off any excess oil and add about 3 tablespoons of barbecue sauce to each pan (reserve 1 to 2 tablespoons of sauce to use as a glaze). Turn the quails in the sauce and cook until caramelized, about 1 minute per side. Brush each quail with the reserved sauce. Transfer them to a platter and allow them to rest for 3 minutes in a warm place. Serve the quails hot, whole or halved.

RABBIT

TOWN

Pappardelle with Rabbit Ragù

SERVES 6 TO 8 AS A MAIN COURSE

- 2 tablespoons extra-virgin olive oil
- 1 rabbit, cut into 8 pieces
- ½ tablespoon kosher salt, plus more to taste
- ½ tablespoon freshly ground black pepper, plus more to taste
- 6 cloves garlic, minced
- 1 medium carrot, diced
- 3 stalks celery, diced
- 2 medium leeks, white parts only, thoroughly cleaned, diced
- 2 fresh bay leaves
- 3 sprigs rosemary
- 3 sprigs thyme
- 1½ cups dry white wine
- 1½ cups white vermouth or semisweet white wine
- 1 quart Chicken Stock (page 262, or low-sodium canned)
- 1 cup heavy cream
- 2 tablespoons mascarpone cheese or sour cream, or more to taste
- ¾ teaspoon ground cardamom
- 2 pounds pappardelle, or other equivalent pasta

In Bologna, they usually refer to a meat-based pasta sauce as a *ragù*; elsewhere, of course, the sauce becomes a Bolognese. Once the meat has been browned and rendered of excess fat, it is simmered in some combination of aromatic vegetables, white wine, and cream or milk, restoring its moistness. For a proper Bolognese ragù, the simmering is long and slow, so the meat becomes very tender and all the flavors are thoroughly commingled. Rabbit is a dryish white meat when cooked, so it takes well to stewlike treatments such as this; it soaks up the cream, and benefits from a last-minute flavor boost by way of mascarpone and cardamom.

INGREDIENT NOTE Pappardelle are a broad, flat, somewhat irregular pasta, shaped like big rustic noodles. They're particularly well suited for a ragù. You can also use fettucine, maltagliati, egg noodles, or any other similar shape.

Heat the oil in a large deep skillet over medium heat. Season the rabbit with the salt and pepper. Working in batches if necessary, brown the rabbit on both sides, 15 to 20 minutes. Transfer the rabbit to a plate and reserve.

Add the garlic to the pan and cook, stirring frequently, until it is fragrant, about 3 minutes. Add the carrot, celery, leeks, bay leaves, rosemary, and thyme. Cook, stirring occasionally, until the vegetables are tender, about 15 minutes. Add the wine and vermouth, and reduce until the pan is almost dry, about 20 minutes. Return the rabbit to the pan. Add the stock and enough water to just cover the rabbit. Reduce the heat to medium-low and gently simmer the rabbit until the meat is very tender and beginning to pull away from the bones, about 1½ hours. Remove the pan from the heat and allow the ingredients to cool to room temperature.

Remove the rabbit and vegetables from the braising liquid. Cut the meat from the bones, dice it, then reserve along with the vegetables. Simmer the braising liquid over medium heat, skimming off any fat that comes to the surface, until it is reduced to about 1 cup; it will become darker and slightly thicker. Add the cream and simmer until the sauce coats the back of a spoon, about 10 minutes. Return the rabbit meat and vegetables to the pan and keep warm over very low heat.

Cook the pappardelle in a large pot of boiling salted water until al dente, about 7 minutes for dried pasta, 1 to 2 minutes for fresh. Meanwhile, swirl the mascarpone into the sauce. Add the cardamom and season the sauce to taste with salt and pepper. Drain the pasta, reserving a little of the cooking water. Combine the pasta and sauce in the pan, moistening with cooking water if the sauce seems dry. Increase the heat to medium and cook the pasta in the sauce for 1 to 2 minutes. Spoon the pasta onto warm plates and serve.

RABBIT

Country Rabbit "Coq au Vin" Style

SERVES 4

- **1 4-pound rabbit, bone in, cut into 8 pieces**
- **2 sprigs thyme**
- **2 cups good red wine (Burgundy is preferable)**
- **1/4 pound slab bacon, diced**
- **1 tablespoon extra-virgin olive oil, plus additional if needed**
- **2 tablespoons all-purpose flour**
- **1 teaspoon kosher salt, plus more to taste**
- **1/2 teaspoon freshly ground black pepper, plus more to taste**
- **1/2 cup brandy**
- **3 cloves garlic, whole and unpeeled**
- **2 cups pearl onions, peeled**
- **7 tablespoons unsalted butter**
- **1 1/2 cups sliced mushrooms (preferably morels)**
- **1/4 cup roughly chopped flat-leaf parsley**
- **2 tablespoons chopped fresh chervil**
- **12 slices country bread, 1/2 inch thick, toasted and rubbed with fresh garlic**

Coq au vin is one of the primal dishes of French country cuisine, a time-honored method of preparing a tough old cock (rooster) by marinating it in red wine then braising it in a stew of onions, bacon, and mushrooms. (Nowadays, coq au vin is usually made with a large chicken.) It's a very versatile recipe, appropriate for any moderately tough or gamey meat, including duck, guinea fowl, and rabbit. This is a modern, upscale version—something very old made new—with pearl onions and morel mushrooms. I used to make coq au vin every year for Christmas dinner at home; one year I decided to try it with rabbit, and it came out great. Serve it with your choice of starch—rice, egg noodles, potatoes, or crusty toasted peasant bread—on the side. Either way, it's ideal for a family-style gathering.

INGREDIENT NOTES For the red wine, I recommend a decent bottle of Burgundy or other pinot noir– or gamay-based wine. Morels are an excellent choice for the mushrooms, but you can substitute cremini, buttons, or portobellos, subject to availability and/or economic considerations. You don't want to use porcini or chanterelles, however; their textures and flavors are too subtle and delicate to work well with the hearty red-wine base.

MARINATE THE RABBIT OVERNIGHT. Place the rabbit pieces, thyme sprigs, and wine in a large bowl or resealable plastic bag. Allow to marinate in the refrigerator overnight.

Place the bacon and oil in a large deep skillet or Dutch oven. Render the bacon over medium heat until it is crisp, about 12 minutes. Remove the bacon from the pan and reserve. Pour off all but about 3 tablespoons of fat (enough to liberally coat the bottom of the pan).

Remove the rabbit pieces from the marinade; reserve the marinade. Pat the rabbit dry with paper towels. Sprinkle the rabbit with flour and season with the salt and pepper. Add about half the rabbit to the pan. Brown the rabbit over medium heat, about 7 minutes per side. Remove the browned rabbit from the pan. Add the remaining pieces and brown them, adding a little olive oil if the pan gets too dry. When all the rabbit is browned, add it back to the pan with the reserved bacon. Add the brandy and boil over high heat until the pan is almost dry. (The brandy may ignite. If you feel dramatic, don't hesitate to flambée it; just be careful.) Add the garlic, reserved marinade, and enough water to barely cover the rabbit, about 1 cup. Adjust the heat so the ingredients maintain a slow simmer. Cook, uncovered, on the stovetop for about 1½ hours, skimming occasionally to remove any impurities that rise to the top. The rabbit is done when the meat easily pulls off the bone. Remove the pan from the heat and reserve (the dish can be prepared up to this point 1 or 2 days in advance).

Blanch the pearl onions in a pot of boiling salted water until tender, about 2 minutes. Drain the onions. Melt 2 tablespoons of the butter in a large skillet over medium heat, add the onions, and sauté, jiggling the pan occasionally, until they are lightly brown all over, 5 to 7 minutes. Season the onions with salt and pepper to taste and set aside in a warm place. Wipe out the pan and add 2 more tablespoons of the butter. Add the mushrooms and cook over medium heat until lightly browned all over, about 5 minutes. Season the mushrooms with salt and pepper to taste, and set aside in a warm place.

Reheat the rabbit and sauce (marinade) over low heat. Swirl in the remaining 3 tablespoons of butter, 1 tablespoon at a time. Season the dish with salt and pepper to taste. Ladle the rabbit and pan sauce into the center of a large warm platter. Top with the mushrooms and pearl onions, garnish with generous portions of chopped parsley and chervil, and serve with toasted garlic-rubbed bread to soak up the sauce.

RASPBERRIES

TOWN

Raspberry and Honey Crisps with Greek Yogurt

SERVES 6

FOR THE CRISPS

24 egg roll wrappers (6 inches square)

4 tablespoons (1/2 stick) unsalted butter, melted

1/3 cup sugar

FOR THE BERRIES

4 pints raspberries

1/4 cup mild honey (preferably lavender)

FOR THE YOGURT CREAM

1/4 cup crème fraîche

1 cup plain whole-milk yogurt (preferably Greek, such as Fage)

2 teaspoons mild honey (preferably lavender)

Confectioners' sugar, for garnish

Basil oil (recipe follows; optional)

I learned to make beautifully simple raspberry crisps when I worked with Daniel Boulud at Le Cirque in 1986. I really like composed desserts such as this, consisting of several basic elements put together just before serving (as opposed to those requiring multiple prep and cooking steps). I consider this dish a good example of nouvelle cuisine, American style: it's quick, streamlined, and it borrows from two of our strongest influences—the classic French (in the crisps, which resemble *mille-feuille,* or layered puff pastry) and the rich Greek tradition (yogurt and honey). Not to mention that the egg roll wrappers come from the Chinese section of the supermarket.

INGREDIENT NOTE There are three principle categories of yogurt: fat-free, low-fat, and full-fat (whole-milk) or Greek-style. (Fage is a commonly available brand of the latter.) I much prefer to use a smaller portion of full-fat yogurt rather than more of the diminished type. One good spoonful of Greek-style yogurt is really the right amount to satisfy.

PREPARE THE CRISPS Preheat the oven to 350°F.

On a lightly floured surface, roll out (or trim, as necessary) each egg roll wrapper until it is about 4 inches square. Brush both sides of each wrapper with melted butter. Lay the squares on two large baking sheets (alternatively, work in batches). Sprinkle each square generously with sugar and bake until golden, about 10 minutes. Set aside at room temperature.

MACERATE THE RASPBERRIES Place the raspberries in a large bowl. Add the ¼ cup of honey and mix gently. Allow the raspberries to macerate for about 15 minutes, stirring occasionally to release their juices.

PREPARE THE YOGURT CREAM Place the crème fraîche in a mixing bowl and whisk until it forms soft peaks. Combine the yogurt with the 2 teaspoons of honey, and fold the mixture into the crème fraîche.

TO ASSEMBLE AND SERVE Place one crisp, sugared side up, in the center of each of six dessert plates. Spread a generous tablespoon of yogurt cream on each crisp, followed by a generous tablespoon of macerated raspberries. Repeat this process two more times to form alternating layers of raspberries and honey yogurt. Place a final crisp on top of each layer of raspberries. Dust each dessert with confectioners' sugar, garnish each plate with a light drizzle of basil oil (if using), and serve.

BASIL OIL

MAKES ABOUT ⅓ CUP

1½ tablespoons chopped basil
1½ tablespoons chopped mint
¾ cup extra-virgin olive oil

Place the basil, mint, and oil in a blender and purée for 2 minutes. Place the mixture in a saucepan over medium heat and bring to a boil. Remove from the heat immediately, allow to cool to room temperature, strain through a coffee filter, and store in a covered jar or bottle in the refrigerator until ready to use.

RASPBERRIES

Country

Flourless Raspberry Soufflé

My love for raspberries was cemented when I worked at Le Cirque in the mid-1980s. Not only did we sell a lot of the raspberry crisps (see Town recipe on page 200), but I made this raspbeery soufflé every day for about five years. It's an easy recipe that requires just 15 minutes to cook and is guaranteed to impress your guests. At Le Cirque, we called this a "flourless diet soufflé," somewhat of a marketing ploy, which apparently worked because we sold literally thousands of them. This version calls for creating fancy swirls for the top of the soufflé using a pastry bag; it's a fun, decorative touch but by no means mandatory.

SERVES 6

FOR THE RASPBERRY PURÉE

4 6-ounce containers fresh raspberries

½ cup sugar

1½ tablespoons fresh lemon juice

FOR THE SOUFFLÉS

Butter, for greasing the soufflé dishes

1 cup sugar

18 large egg whites

Confectioners' sugar, for garnish

Set aside 36 of the raspberries for garnish. Place the remaining raspberries, 6 tablespoons of the sugar, and the lemon juice in a saucepan over medium heat and cook until the fruit is very soft, 15 to 20 minutes. Remove the raspberries from the heat and allow them to cool to room temperature. Purée the berries in a blender, stirring, then transfer them to a bowl. Cover the bowl with plastic wrap and refrigerate for at least 1 hour.

Preheat the oven to 400°F.

Prepare six 8-ounce ramekins (or 1½-cup soufflé dishes) by generously buttering them on the inside and then coating the butter lining with 2 tablespoons of the sugar. Place the egg whites in the bowl of an electric mixer with the whisk attachment on low speed. Whip the whites until they form soft peaks, then gradually begin adding the remaining sugar. Continue whipping until the egg whites form stiff, glossy peaks. Remove the egg whites from the mixer and gradually fold in 1¼ to1½ cups of raspberry purée in thirds, taking care to not overfold. (If you like an airy, lighter-flavored soufflé, add the lesser amount of purée; if you prefer more intense fruit flavor, add the greater amount.) Reserve any remaining purée. Using a pastry bag with the large plain tip, pipe the soufflé mixture into the ramekins, swirling it so each soufflé has a peak like a soft ice cream cone. (Alternatively, just spoon the mixture into the soufflé dishes or ramekins, filling them not quite to the top.) Stud the peaks of the soufflés with the reserved raspberries. Place the soufflés in the oven immediately and bake until puffed and golden, about 15 minutes. The center of the soufflé should still be soft. Dust with confectioners' sugar and serve immediately, garnished with any leftover raspberry purée.

SALMON

SERVES 4

FOR THE COURT BOUILLON

- 2 small leeks, whites parts only, split lengthwise, thoroughly washed, and roughly chopped
- 2 tablespoons coriander seeds
- 2 tablespoons hot red pepper flakes
- 1 cup dry white wine
- 1 cup white wine vinegar
- 1 cup kosher salt
- ¼ cup sherry vinegar (optional)
- Dash of Tabasco sauce (optional)

FOR THE SALMON AND GARNISH

- 1½ pounds skinless salmon fillet
- 3 large shallots, minced
- 1 cup loosely packed basil leaves, julienned
- Juice of 3 limes
- ½ cup extra-virgin olive oil
- Fine sea salt and freshly ground black pepper
- 1 medium bulb fennel, trimmed, cored, and thinly sliced (⅛ inch thick) crosswise
- 1 ripe avocado, peeled and diced
- 2 tablespoons capers, drained

TOWN

Poached Salmon Tartare with Avocado, Fennel, and Vinaigrette

I created this perennial favorite at the Royalton in 1990. But I first learned how to poach a salmon the old-fashioned way—whole, in a flavorful court bouillon—from Alain Sailhac when I worked for him as chef de cuisine at Le Cirque in Manhattan. Poaching is a great technique to downplay salmon's heaviness; prepared this way, you can chill it, dress it up, and make it into a wonderful salad or appetizer. The lime juice also lends a refreshing touch. In this case, the salmon is not fully poached, nor is it truly a (raw) tartare, so I attached both labels to it.

A note about the court bouillon: if you want to make it more complex, you can add a carrot, a couple of celery stalks, a handful of white peppercorns, a couple of bay leaves, and a small bunch of thyme. In any case, it's best made a day or two in advance so the flavors can meld and mellow. If you want to take a shortcut, simply use a high-quality store-bought fish stock (or use the one you prepared a week ago and presciently froze for just such an occasion).

INGREDIENT NOTE I recommend Atlantic or farm-raised salmon, the fattier the better.

PREPARE THE BOUILLON Combine the leeks, coriander, hot pepper flakes, white wine, and white wine vinegar in a large pot and bring to a boil over high heat. Reduce the heat to medium and simmer until the liquid has reduced by about half, 15 to 20 minutes. Add 2 quarts of cold water. Bring the bouillon back to a simmer and cook gently until the flavors meld, about 1 hour. Pass the bouillon through a fine strainer. Allow the bouillon to cool, then taste it. It should taste quite salty, sharply acidic, and spicy. If it doesn't, adjust the seasoning with salt, sherry vinegar, and Tabasco. Once the bouillon has cooled to room temperature, refrigerate until ready to use.

PREPARE THE SALMON, UP TO 2 HOURS IN ADVANCE Trim any dark meat from the salmon. Cut the fillet into several pieces, all about the same size, for easy handling during poaching. Place the court bouillon in a large pot and bring it to a boil over high heat. Reduce the heat to medium so the bouillon just simmers, then slide the salmon fillets into the pot. Poach the fillets until medium rare, about 1 minute for smaller pieces and slightly longer for larger pieces. (The exterior should be pale pink; the center should still be bright pink.) Using a spatula, carefully transfer the salmon to a large plate to cool. Once cool, wrap the fillets in plastic wrap and chill in the refrigerator for at least 1 hour.

Shortly before serving, use a paring knife to flake the salmon apart along its natural seams, then place it in a large mixing bowl. Add the shallots and basil to the bowl with the salmon and mix gently. Dress the salmon mixture with lime juice and olive oil to taste, then season with sea salt and pepper to taste.

TO SERVE Divide the salmon into six equal portions. Spoon each portion into a ring mold to form a mound on each of six chilled plates. (Alternatively, place a portion of salmon in a teacup, tamp it down with a teaspoon, then invert the salmon onto each plate; or simply shape the tartare by hand into mounds on each plate.) Garnish each plate with sliced fennel, diced avocado, and capers. Drizzle the fennel and avocado with additional olive oil if desired, season with sea salt and pepper, and serve.

SALMON

Country

Grilled Salmon with Smashed Cucumber–Date Salad

SERVES 6

FOR THE GRILLED SALMON

- **1 2½-pound center-cut skin-on salmon fillet, cut into 6 equal pieces**
- **2 tablespoons extra-virgin olive oil**
- **1 teaspoon kosher salt**
- **½ teaspoon freshly ground black pepper**

FOR THE CUCUMBER-DATE SALAD

- **2 English (hothouse) cucumbers, peeled and cut into 8 pieces**
- **¾ cup finely sliced fennel, feathery fronds reserved for garnish**
- **6 Medjool dates, pitted and cut in slivers**
- **⅓ cup coarsely chopped walnuts**
- **2 tablespoons minced chives**
- **2 tablespoons fresh lemon juice (½ a large lemon)**
- **6 tablespoons fruity olive oil (preferably from Spain)**
- **Medium-coarse sea salt (preferably Maldon from England)**
- **Freshly ground black pepper**
- **Fennel fronds for garnish**

The idea here is to take salmon—an overused and sometimes abused fish—and lighten it up by creating a salad with some Middle Eastern accents (the dates), a refreshing summery element (the cucumber), and some extra added crunch (the walnuts). I think the best way to prepare fish is to lightly grill or sear it, then garnish it cleanly and simply to enhance its natural flavors. This recipe is a good example of what I call Dynamic American Cuisine, a style I was consciously trying to advance when I created this dish for Restaurant 44 at the Royalton Hotel.

INGREDIENT NOTES English (hothouse) cucumbers are long and thin, and have few if any seeds. They are also consistently the most flavorful.

For the olive oil, use a fruity, robust variety (Spanish is good).

PREPARE THE SALMON Prepare a charcoal fire in an outdoor grill (alternatively, cook the salmon indoors on a grill pan); the coals should be medium-hot and the rack should be positioned about 6 inches from the fire. Place the salmon fillets on a cutting board, skin side down. Cut down the center of each fillet lengthwise along the center seam. Cut through the flesh but not the skin. Draw the salmon flesh apart at the incision, flattening the fillets, leaving them skin side down. Fold each fillet into a horseshoe shape, bending it back onto itself, so it resembles a boneless salmon steak. Brush each piece of fish lightly on both sides with extra-virgin olive oil and season with the salt and pepper.

Grill the salmon just until the flesh firms and grill marks appear, about 1 minute. Rotate each fillet one quarter-turn (90 degrees) and grill just long enough to mark the fillets, completing a cross-hatch pattern, less than 1 minute. Turn the fillets over and repeat the grilling and rotating procedure until the other sides show the cross-hatch grill markings. Remove the fish from the grill and reserve. (The salmon can be grilled up to 1 hour in advance of the meal.)

PREPARE THE SALAD Roll the cucumber pieces up in a clean linen napkin, then smash them—press down hard with the heels of your hands while ensur-

ing the towel doesn't unroll—to release the juices. Discard the juice and transfer the crushed cucumber to a cutting board, then coarsely chop it. Combine the cucumbers, sliced fennel, dates, walnuts, and chives in a salad bowl and mix gently.

FINISH COOKING THE SALMON AND DRESS THE SALAD Preheat the oven to 350°F.

Arrange the salmon fillets in a baking dish, brush each one lightly with extra-virgin olive oil, and roast about 3½ minutes for medium-rare.

Meanwhile, dress the cucumber salad with the lemon juice and 4 tablespoons of fruity olive oil, then season with salt and pepper to taste. Toss the salad lightly, then arrange equal portions on each of six plates. Top each portion of salad with a grilled salmon fillet. Drizzle a little fruity olive oil on top of each portion, garnish each plate with fennel fronds, and serve.

SCALLOPS

SERVES 6

3 tablespoons high-quality sherry vinegar

3 tablespoons wildflower honey

1½ teaspoons high-quality peanut oil

⅔ cup grapeseed oil

Fine sea salt and freshly ground white pepper to taste

1 tablespoon finely chopped fresh rosemary leaves

9 fresh diver scallops, each about the diameter of a quarter

Coarse sea salt to taste

TOWN

Carpaccio of Sea Scallops with Sherry Vinegar–Honey Emulsion

For those of you who buy this sort of thing, raw scallops are believed to be an aphrodisiac. In any case, really fresh sea scallops have a smooth, soft texture and a sweetish, very mild hint of ocean brine that tickles all the senses. They require a light, somewhat sweet sauce that won't overpower their delicate flavor—especially when they're served raw, before any application of heat complicates matters by introducing caramelized flavors. The sherry vinegar–honey emulsion here contains two polar opposites, sweet and sour, but leans toward the sweet end of the spectrum. That combination is hard to beat for bringing out the freshness and underlying sweetness of raw seafood treats such as scallops or sushi-quality tuna. The emulsion can be whisked by hand, as described below, or in a blender on low speed. If you want to make it in a blender, you'll need to double the ingredients; it's virtually impossible to make a smaller amount in the machine.

Place the vinegar and honey in a medium bowl and whisk until well combined. Whisking constantly, gradually incorporate the peanut oil. Whisk in the grapeseed oil in a steady stream. Once all the ingredients are well combined, the emulsion should have the consistency of a light mayonnaise. If it is too thick, whisk in a little water; if it is too thin, add a little more oil. Season to taste with fine sea salt and white pepper, then fold in the chopped rosemary.

Using a very sharp paring knife, carefully cut each scallop into 4 thin slices. Arrange six slices of scallop in a thin layer on each of six plates. Season lightly with coarse sea salt, drizzle the emulsion over the scallops, and serve.

Country

Seared Bay Scallops with Brown Butter Emulsion

SERVES 4

FOR THE EMULSION

2 cups balsamic vinegar

¼ pound (1 stick) unsalted butter

1 tablespoon soy sauce

Freshly ground black pepper

FOR THE SCALLOPS

2 pounds bay scallops

½ teaspoon kosher salt

¼ teaspoon freshly ground black pepper

About ¼ cup Clarified Butter (page 264)

2 sprigs thyme

2 cloves garlic

1 tablespoon unsalted butter

Bay scallops are small and delicate. Unfortunately, they often suffer overcooking, oversaucing, or some other cruel fate. Here, they're seared and then quickly basted in butter, bringing out a delicious caramelized flavor, which is also reflected in the balsamic vinegar reduction sauce. This "emulsion" attains a beautifully balanced, almost chocolatelike flavor—somewhat reminiscent of a good Mexican mole sauce—that emphasizes the fresh natural sweetness of the scallops.

PREPARE THE EMULSION Place the vinegar in a medium nonreactive saucepan over high heat and bring to a boil. Reduce the heat to medium-low and simmer, stirring occasionally, until thick and reduced to ½ cup, about 30 minutes. Transfer to a small bowl and allow it to cool to room temperature.

Place the butter in a medium skillet over medium heat, and allow it to melt and turn light brown. Remove the butter from the heat and allow it to cool to room temperature. Gradually whisk the browned butter into the reduced balsamic vinegar. Whisk in the soy sauce and season with pepper to taste. Reserve the emulsion at room temperature.

COOK THE SCALLOPS Pat the scallops dry with paper towels and season them with the salt and pepper. Coat the bottom of 2 large skillets with clarified butter. Place the pans over a medium-high flame and heat until the butter is nearly smoking. Divide the scallops between the pans; do not shake the pans or move the scallops around. Immediately reduce the heat to medium and add a little more clarified butter to each pan. Cook the scallops until they are deeply brown on one side, about 3 minutes. Turn the scallops over, and add a sprig of thyme and a clove of garlic to each pan. Allow the scallops to brown slightly on the other side, continuously basting them with the hot butter, about 2 minutes. Transfer the scallops to a platter with a slotted spoon and reserve in a warm place. Add the 1 tablespoon of butter to the pan and scrape with a wooden spoon to dislodge any browned bits; remove the pan from the heat when the butter is completely melted.

Pour an equal portion of the emulsion onto each plate in a wide stripe down the center. Place an equal portion of scallops, browned side up, in the center of each plate, spoon the pan drippings around, and serve immediately.

SHRIMP

TOWN

Shrimp Scampi with Black Truffles

Scampi in Italy are prawns; in America, the term is used to describe large shrimp that are butterflied and cooked with garlic and oil. For some reason, many American menus list this type of dish as "shrimp scampi," which is kind of like saying "escargots snails." But, just to be sure, I'm going to stick with it.

I offer this recipe with a tip of the hat to Frank Pellegrino of Rao's; it's my interpretation of a scampi dish I once had at his legendary New York restaurant. Like a table reservation at Rao's, black truffles are a rare and special treat.

INGREDIENT NOTE Winter black truffles from France or Italy are the most desirable and expensive; their flavor is subtle and almost indescribably delicious. Summer and Asian truffles are more affordable and you still get great flavor.

SERVES 6 TO 8

- ¼ pound (1 stick) unsalted butter, at room temperature
- 2 heaping tablespoons (about 1 ounce) minced fresh or frozen black truffles
- 3 pounds colossal (U15; see Ingredient Notes, page 213) shrimp, cleaned, tail shells left on, and butterflied
- 2 tablespoons all-purpose flour, for dusting
- ½ cup extra-virgin olive oil
- 1 teaspoon kosher salt, plus more to taste
- ½ teaspoon freshly ground black pepper, plus more to taste
- 4 cloves garlic, minced
- ¾ cup dry white wine
- 6 tablespoons fresh lemon juice (2 lemons)
- ¼ cup Chicken Stock (page 262, or low-sodium canned)
- 1 tablespoon chopped fresh flat-leaf parsley
- 1 teaspoon chopped fresh tarragon

Place the butter and 1 heaping teaspoon of the minced truffles in a bowl. Use a fork to mix until well combined. Place the butter on a sheet of plastic wrap and form it into a 1-inch log. Enclose the log in the plastic wrap, then put it in the refrigerator until it is thoroughly chilled.

Pat the shrimp dry, then lightly dust them with the flour. Working in batches, heat 2 tablespoons of oil in a large sauté pan over medium-high heat. Add only as many shrimp as fit into the pan in a single, uncrowded layer. (Expect to cook three or four batches.) Season the shrimp with the salt and pepper. Cook the shrimp, turning them so they are golden on all sides and nearly cooked through, about 3 minutes per batch. Transfer the shrimp to a large plate lined with paper towels to drain any excess oil.

Once the shrimp are browned, drain the pan and wipe it clean. Add about 1 tablespoon oil and adjust the heat to medium-low. Add the garlic and cook, stirring frequently, until it is soft and fragrant, about 1 minute. Add the wine, lemon juice, and stock, raise the heat to medium, and bring the liquid to a simmer. Cook the sauce until it is reduced by about two thirds, 4 to 5 minutes. Reduce the heat to low. Cut the chilled truffle butter into small pieces and whisk it into the sauce one piece at a time. Season the sauce with salt and pepper to taste. Return the shrimp to the pan and cook, stirring, until heated through and well coated with sauce. Season with additional salt and pepper to taste. Transfer the shrimp to a platter, sprinkle the remaining minced truffles on top, garnish with chopped parsley and tarragon, and serve immediately.

SHRIMP

Country

Salt and Pepper Shrimp

SERVES 6 TO 8

FOR THE SPICY OIL

3 quarts peanut or other vegetable oil (enough to fill your frying pot to a depth of at least 3 inches)

3 tablespoons chopped unpeeled ginger (a 2- to 3-inch piece)

2 fresh hot chile peppers, split (jalapeño or equivalent)

2 tablespoons black peppercorns

2 tablespoons green peppercorns

1 tablespoon coriander seeds

FOR THE SHRIMP

¼ cup all-purpose flour

2 tablespoons smoked sweet paprika

1½ teaspoons coarse sea salt

¾ teaspoon coarsely ground black pepper, plus more to taste

½ teaspoon medium-hot red chili powder

3 pounds unshelled super jumbo (U20) shrimp, heads removed

Fine sea salt

Small handful of fresh cilantro leaves

New York City, my adopted hometown, has one of the best Chinatowns anywhere. This recipe represents my variation on a traditional Cantonese dish I've encountered several times there. Creating a flavored oil keeps the process streamlined and simple while adding a stimulating jolt of spiciness and heat. You can serve this as an appetizer on its own, or add a side dish of steamed sticky rice or jasmine rice to make it a main course.

INGREDIENT NOTES Shrimp are generally classified as "colossal" if there are fewer than 15 per pound or "super jumbo" if there are fewer than 20 per pound, as indicated by the U15 and U20 designations, respectively. If you use U20s, you should have 6 servings of about 9 shrimp, or 8 servings of 6 or 7 shrimp.

To make the oil even spicier, you can chop the spicy peppers without seeding them; just be careful to protect your mucous membranes from a fiery dose of capsaicin (the active ingredient in hot peppers).

Preheat the oven to 200°F.

Place the oil, ginger, chiles, black peppercorns, green peppercorns, and coriander seeds in a large heavy ovenproof pot over low heat. When the oil is warm, transfer the pot to the oven to bake until the oil is fragrant, about 1 hour. Strain the oil and return it to the pot.

Combine the flour, paprika, coarse salt, pepper, and chili powder in a large mixing bowl, and mix well. Add the shrimp and turn them in the spice mixture to coat all over.

Place the oil in a large heavy pot over medium-high heat to a depth of at least 3 inches (the pot should be at least 6 inches deep so the oil level can rise without spillage when the shrimp are added). When a thermometer indicates a temperature of 350°F., or a drop of water sizzles immediately upon hitting its surface, it is ready for frying. (The oil should never smoke before or during the cooking process.) Fry the shrimp in the spicy oil in small batches until crisp and golden brown, about 4 minutes per batch. Transfer the fried shrimp with a slotted spoon to a large platter lined with paper towels to drain off excess oil. Season the shrimp to taste with fine salt and additional pepper (if desired) while still warm. Garnish with cilantro leaves and serve.

SKATE

SERVES 4

FOR THE VINAIGRETTE

1 shallot, minced

2 tablespoons pistachio oil, walnut oil, or hazelnut oil

2½ teaspoons Muscat or sherry vinegar

2 tablespoons chopped pistachios

Fine sea salt and freshly ground black pepper

FOR THE SKATE

4 6- to 7-ounce skate wing fillets

½ teaspoon kosher salt, plus more to taste

¼ teaspoon freshly ground black pepper, plus more to taste

2 tablespoons coriander seeds, ground, or white sesame seeds

Light olive oil or Clarified Butter (page 264), for sautéing

FOR THE GARNISH

2 cups pea shoots, mâche lettuce, or watercress

Pea Purée (recipe follows; optional)

Shinshū-Apple Purée (page 22; optional)

TOWN

Sautéed Skate Wing with Pistachio Vinaigrette

Skate is one of my favorite seafoods because it's sweet, delicate, and somewhat of an underdog (it's scary to look at). I first tasted it in Brittany in the early 1980s and it quickly assumed a permanent place on my list of favorites. Skate fillets are quite thin, so be sure to season them lightly and beware of overcooking. In other words—as with most fresh, light seafoods—a restrained, subtle touch is the key to success. I like to serve this dish with a purée or two. The purées are optional garnishes, recommended if you're putting together a dinner party; you can serve this skate as a main dish with either one, both, or neither.

INGREDIENT NOTES To season the skate wing, I generally use Indian roasted coriander seeds (dhana dal). They may not be easily available (try Kalustyan's online or by phone order; see "Sources and Resources," page 266), so a good substitute is ground coriander seeds or ground sesame seeds.

Golden Delicious apples are specified because they have just the right combination of water content and sweetness—not too much, not too little—for this preparation.

PREPARE THE VINAIGRETTE Place the minced shallot, pistachio oil, vinegar, and crushed pistachios in a small bowl and whisk until well combined. Season to taste with salt and pepper and reserve.

PREPARE THE SKATE Pat the skate fillets dry, season them on one side with the salt and pepper, and lightly dust them on both sides with ground coriander (or white sesame seeds if available). Place just enough oil or clarified butter in each of 2 large skillets to film the bottom of the pans. Place the skillets over medium-high heat. (Alternatively, cook the skate in two batches.) Add the skate and sauté until brown on one side, about 2 minutes. Turn the fillets over and brown the other side, 1 to 2 minutes more. (The "fingers" of skate flesh will pull apart easily when it is done so be careful when you turn or move the fillets.) Transfer the fillets to a plate lined with paper towels to drain briefly, then place them on warm plates.

TO SERVE Dress the pea shoots with about 2 teaspoons of the vinaigrette, then season with salt and pepper to taste. Arrange the pea shoots on a plate next to the skate. Finish each plate with a dollop of warm Pea Purée (if using) and another one of Shinshū-Apple Purée (if using), drizzle additional vinaigrette over the skate, and serve.

PEA PURÉE

Frozen peas work best for this recipe.

MAKES ABOUT 1 CUP

1 cup frozen peas (1 10-ounce package)

1 clove garlic, sliced

2 tablespoons crème fraîche

1 tablespoon chopped fresh mint

Juice of ½ lemon

Fine sea salt and freshly ground black pepper

Bring a small pot of salted water to a boil over high heat. Add the peas and garlic, cooking just until the water returns to a boil. Drain the peas and garlic, and refresh them in ice water. Drain the peas and garlic again, place them in a food processer, and pulse until smooth. Scrape down the sides, then add the crème fraîche, mint, and lemon juice, season with salt and pepper to taste, and pulse to combine well. (I recommend pulsing and scraping down because too much processing—leaving the processor running for the entire puréeing operation—will add air and take away color from the beautiful green peas; it isn't a question of flavor but rather of color.) Return the pea purée to the pot, cover, and reserve in a warm place.

SKATE

Country

Skate in Brown Butter

SERVES 4

FOR THE SKATE

- **2 pounds boneless skate fillets (4 large wings)**
- **¾ cup Wondra flour, for dusting**
- **1 teaspoon kosher salt**
- **½ teaspoon freshly ground black pepper**
- **¼ cup extra-virgin olive oil**

FOR THE SAUCE AND SERVING

- **4 tablespoons (½ stick) unsalted butter**
- **1 cup peeled, seeded, diced tomato (1 medium tomato)**
- **3 tablespoons capers**
- **½ cup flat-leaf parsley leaves**
- **3 tablespoons verjus**
- **3 tablespoons fresh lemon juice (1 lemon)**
- **6 drops Worcestershire sauce**
- **Fine sea salt and freshly ground white pepper**
- **Cauliflower Purée (recipe follows; optional)**

In classic French cuisine, a rich, gelatinous type of fish such as sole, turbot, or skate is often prepared with brown butter (called *beurre noisette,* or "nutty butter," after the flavor it acquires when browned) along with capers and lemon juice. I add just a couple of key ingredients here to keep things interesting. (The cauliflower purée is an optional side dish.) I love the texture and flavor of skate, which some people say is like scallops. It's one of those "poor man's cuts" that when treated right can be as delightful as fancier choices such as lobster or swordfish. Alain Sailhac showed me how to prepare skate the traditional way when he was my chef at Le Cirque. By the way, he's still going strong—teaching at the French Culinary Institute in downtown Manhattan. Whenever I see him, he still busts my chops just like in the old days. Thankfully, some things never change.

INGREDIENT NOTES Skate should smell fresh and mild, with no trace of ammonia; be sure to check this in the market before you buy.

Verjus is raw, unsweetened, French-style grape juice; it has potent natural sugars, a good balance of acidity, and none of the additives that so many mass-market grape juices contain. Regular unsweetened white grape juice is an acceptable substitute.

PREPARE THE SKATE Pat the skate fillets dry. Dredge the skate in the flour, then season generously with salt and pepper. Place olive oil to a depth of ¼ inch in a large skillet over medium heat. Add the skate fillets, skinned side down, in a single, uncrowded layer. (The pan should be large enough to cook the skate in two batches.) Cook the skate, basting regularly with oil, until crisp and golden on one side, about 6 minutes. Carefully turn the fillets over, and cook until the other side is crisp and the flesh is opaque, about 5 minutes more. (Skate is delicate and breaks easily.) Carefully transfer the skate to a warm platter and reserve in a warm place. Wipe out the skillet, add more oil, cook the remaining skate in the same manner, and reserve with the first batch.

PREPARE THE SAUCE Wipe out the skillet and discard the oil used to cook the skate. Place the skillet over medium heat and add the butter. When the butter begins to brown, after about 2 minutes, add the tomatoes. Cook the tomatoes until they begin to release their juices, about 2 minutes, then add the capers and parsley. Reduce the heat to low, add the verjus, and allow the sauce to come to a simmer. Add the lemon juice and Worcestershire sauce; season to taste with salt and pepper.

Transfer one portion of skate fillet to each of 4 warm dinner plates. Spoon sauce over and around the skate, and serve immediately with Cauliflower Purée (if using) on the side.

CAULIFLOWER PURÉE

MAKES ABOUT 3 CUPS

- **1 pound Yukon gold potatoes (7 small), peeled and cubed**
- **½ medium head cauliflower (about 1 pound), broken into small florets**
- **1 cup whole milk**
- **1 cup heavy cream**
- **1 garlic clove**
- **1 teaspoon kosher salt, plus more to taste**
- **½ teaspoon freshly ground black pepper, plus more to taste**

Place the potatoes, cauliflower, milk, cream, and garlic in a medium pot. Season with the salt and pepper, and bring to a simmer over medium heat. Simmer until the potatoes and cauliflower are tender.

Using a slotted spoon, transfer the potatoes, cauliflower, and garlic to a food processor. Add about half the liquid and purée. Add more of the milk-and-cream mixture to attain a smooth purée, then season to taste with additional salt and pepper. Reserve the purée in a warm place until ready to serve. (Alternatively, make it in advance, cool it in an ice-water bath, and refrigerate for later use.)

RED SNAPPER

TOWN

Red Snapper with Pearl Onions

SERVES 6

- 1 750-milliliter bottle dry red wine
- 2 teaspoons truffle oil, walnut oil, or hazelnut oil
- 6 tablespoons neutral vegetable oil (preferably peanut or canola)
- ½ pound slab bacon or pancetta, diced into ¼-inch cubes
- 2 tablespoons sugar
- 30 pearl onions, peeled and halved lengthwise (from root to stem)
- ¼ cup Chicken Stock (page 262, or low-sodium canned; optional)
- 2 teaspoons kosher salt, plus more to taste
- 1 teaspoon freshly ground white pepper, plus more to taste
- 2 tablespoons red wine vinegar
- 3 pounds skin-on red snapper fillets, 1½ inches thick, cut into 6 equal-sized pieces
- 10 to 12 tablespoons unsalted butter

My red snapper dream began when I was very young, but it was very nearly a bust. I ordered it at Legal Sea Foods in Boston when they were out of my usual, which was fried clams. When the waitress brought a skinless white fillet, I remember feeling extremely disappointed because I thought the meat would be red! Red snapper has since become not only one of my personal favorites but generally very popular, widely available, and highly prized for its versatility. You can roast it whole; poach it or grill it; pan-fry, sauté, or roast skin-on fillets; cut the fillets up and make a wonderful ceviche; or even salt it and cure it like salmon. The only challenge is that its firm-textured, lean flesh tends to become dry, which is precisely why this recipe calls for carefully basting the fillets after browning their skin. Although it stands alone as an entrée, I like to serve this snapper on a bed of creamed spinach (page 253).

INGREDIENT NOTE Snapper comes in many different sizes. These instructions assume the fillets are large and thick (about 1½ inches); for smaller or thinner fillets, decrease the cooking time slightly so as not to overcook.

PREPARE THE RED WINE REDUCTION SAUCE Pour the red wine into a medium saucepan over medium-high heat. Simmer until the wine is reduced to about ¼ cup and is slightly syrupy, about 25 minutes. Remove the reduced wine from the heat and whisk in the truffle oil. Set the reduction aside until shortly before serving.

PREPARE THE BACON AND ONIONS Heat 1 tablespoon of the vegetable oil in a large sauté pan over medium. Add the diced bacon and cook, stirring occasionally, until rendered and crisp, about 15 minutes. Remove the bacon from the pan with a slotted spoon and transfer to a large bowl.

Sprinkle the sugar over the bacon fat. Raise the heat to medium-high and cook until the sugar browns, about 3 minutes. (If the pan seems dry add up to 3 tablespoons of water.) Remove the pan from the heat and arrange the onions in the browned sugar in a single layer, cut side down. Return the pan to medium heat and cook the onions until they brown, about 10 minutes. Add the stock (if using) and enough water to cover the onions by about three fourths (about 1 cup of liquid total). Season the onions with 1 teaspoon of the salt and

½ teaspoon of the pepper, cover the pan, and simmer until the onions are tender, about 15 minutes. Using a slotted spoon, transfer the onions to the bowl containing the bacon.

Add the vinegar to the onion cooking liquid. Raise the heat to high and simmer until the liquid is reduced to a glaze, 3 to 5 minutes. Add the onions and bacon, toss to coat with the vinegar glaze, and reserve until shortly before serving.

COOK THE SNAPPER Season the snapper on both sides with 1 teaspoon of the salt and ½ teaspoon of the pepper. Place one very large skillet (or two slightly smaller ones) over medium-high heat. Add about 3 tablespoons of oil to the pan. When the oil is hot, add the snapper fillets, skin side down, taking care not to crowd the fish. Press the fillets flat with the back of a spatula and cook, pressing each fillet flat from time to time, until the skin crisps, about 8 minutes. Add 2 tablespoons of butter to the skillet. Reduce the heat to medium and baste the fish with the melted butter. Cook, basting, until the fish is white and opaque nearly all the way to the top, 3 to 5 minutes. (The sides of each fillet will be white and cooked; the top will still appear pink and translucent.) Carefully turn the fillets over and cook for about 1 minute more. Remove the pan from the heat and keep the fillets warm at the back of the stove.

ASSEMBLE AND SERVE Warm the red wine reduction over low heat; whisk in 8 tablespoons (1 stick) of butter about 1 tablespoon at a time. Season the sauce with additional salt and pepper to taste. Reheat the bacon and onions over medium-high heat until just warmed through. Place a piece of snapper fillet on each plate, arrange the pearl onion mixture around the plate, drizzle with the red wine reduction sauce, and serve.

RED SNAPPER

Country

Grilled Whole Red Snapper

SERVES 4

- **1 $3\frac{1}{2}$- to 4-pound red snapper, scaled and gutted**
- **1 teaspoon kosher salt**
- **$\frac{1}{2}$ teaspoon freshly ground black pepper**
- **1 large lemon, thinly sliced**
- **6 sprigs thyme**
- **$\frac{1}{4}$ pound thinly sliced prosciutto**
- **$\frac{1}{4}$ cup extra-virgin olive oil**
- **4 sprigs flat-leaf parsley, for garnish**
- **1 large lemon, cut into wedges, for garnish**

It seems to me that red snapper was practically invented to be grilled whole. It's got a relatively flat profile, firm flesh, and skin that stands up well to grilling. If anything, you should err on the side of undercooking it, since you can always put it back on the grill to finish the thicker parts if they aren't done. As an alternative to wrapping the prosciutto around the fish, you can stuff it inside the cavity along with the other ingredients. Either way, it helps keep the fish moist and adds flavor. I like to serve a whole fish on a large platter with potatoes that were roasted right on the coals: simply wrap the potatoes in foil and lay them among the coals once the fire is burning well; cook the potatoes while the fire is burning down to the point where it is ready to grill the fish.

INGREDIENT NOTE Have your fishmonger scale and gut the fish; if you caught it yourself, you probably know how to do this, but you can check the instructions opposite just to be sure. One of the great advantages of red snapper is that it comes in handy sizes for whole roasting, and it also has a really eye-catching appearance with its sleek shape and pink-tinged skin.

Rinse the cavity of the snapper with cold water. Dry it with paper towels, then season it with the salt and pepper. Place the lemon slices and thyme inside the cavity. Dry the exterior of the fish thoroughly with paper towels. Wrap the slices of prosciutto around the midsection of the fish, sealing the belly and protecting the meat; leave the head and tail exposed. Secure the prosciutto to the body of the fish by tying it at 2-inch intervals with butcher's twine.

Prepare a grill for indirect cooking (for specific instructions, see opposite). Brush the fish generously all over with oil. Season it generously with salt and pepper on the outside. Place the fish on the side of the rack away from the coals, cover the grill, and cook the fish until crisp on one side, about 18 minutes. Turn the fish and cook it until the meat is opaque near the bone, about 15 minutes more. Transfer the fish to a platter, garnish with parsley sprigs and lemon wedges, and serve. When serving, use the back of a large spoon to separate the flesh from the bones; it will flake off easily in neat fillets.

CLEANING A WHOLE SNAPPER

Scrape all the scales from the fish using the back of a knife or a scaling tool. Rinse the fish thoroughly in cold water and pat dry with paper towels. Using a pair of kitchen shears, cut away all the fins without puncturing the skin. Make an incision in the belly of the fish and remove all entrails.

PREPARING A GRILL FOR INDIRECT COOKING

Light a hardwood charcoal fire in an outdoor kettle grill. Allow the fire to burn for 45 minutes to 1 hour, until all the charcoal is grayish white on the outside and glowing red on the inside. Push all the coals to one side of the grill, cover the grill, and allow them to burn for another 10 minutes. The heat should be low to medium; you should be able to hold your hand comfortably 5 inches above the grill for about 10 seconds. Alternatively, use a gas grill, preheated and set to produce medium heat.

SPAGHETTI

TOWN

Spaghetti with Creamy Leeks and Caviar

SERVES 6 TO 8

- 8 tablespoons (1 stick) unsalted butter
- 1 clove garlic, finely minced
- 4 medium leeks, white parts only, split lengthwise, thoroughly rinsed, and julienned
- 1 teaspoon kosher salt
- ½ teaspoon freshly ground white pepper
- 1¼ cups Chicken Stock (page 262, or low-sodium canned)
- 1¼ cups heavy cream
- ½ cup freshly grated Parmigiano-Reggiano cheese (from a 4-ounce piece)
- 1 1-pound box of spaghetti (DeCecco brand or equivalent quality)
- 6 ounces osetra malossol caviar
- 3 tablespoons chopped fresh chives (1 small bunch)

The first occasion that comes to mind for this dish is New Year's Eve. I either serve fine caviar on toast with rosé Champagne or this pasta, which, if you're planning on drinking a lot of bubbly, is a great way to soak it all up. Caviar is a celebratory treat; you're going to lavish it on special people for an extraordinary occasion. If your special friends turn on you, have some crispy bacon bits ready to sprinkle on the pasta instead of the fancy fish eggs. (Seriously, though, if you want to create a less expensive variation without foregoing the richness and elegance of this recipe, that's the way to go.) Use a gold or pearl spoon to add generous dollops of caviar to each steaming mound of sauced pasta as it's served at the table; prior to this little ceremony, make sure the caviar is plenty cold.

INGREDIENT NOTES Of the three principle types of genuine caviar (sturgeon roe)—beluga, osetra, and sevruga—osetra is considered just a notch below beluga in quality and prestige. The eggs are gray or brownish gray in color and not as large as the beluga ones. *Malossol* is a Russian term referring to the preservation method for packing and shipping the caviar; it means "little salt." Good malossol caviar features the natural saltiness of the fish and the sea, but does not suffer from an excess of the salt added to preserve the delicate eggs in transit. Since this is a luxury dish and the caviar is presented as a garnish, use the genuine article; if you don't want to spring for osetra, sevruga is a good option, too.

At my restaurants, we use the DeCecco brand of pasta, a very reliable, high-quality durum wheat pasta.

Place 4 tablespoons of the butter in a large, heavy skillet over medium-low heat. Add the garlic and leeks, season with the salt and pepper, and cook, stirring frequently, until the leeks are tender but still a little crunchy, about 7 minutes. Add the stock and cream and raise the heat to medium. Simmer until the liquid is reduced by half, about 15 minutes. Stir in ¼ cup of the Parmesan cheese, then adjust the seasoning with salt and pepper to taste. Keep the sauce warm at the back of the stove.

Meanwhile, bring a large pot of salted water to a boil. Drop the spaghetti into the water, bring it back to a boil, adjust the heat so it maintains a steady boil, and cook the pasta until al dente, about 8 minutes. Drain the spaghetti in a colander.

Return the pan with the leek sauce to the stove over low heat and add the spaghetti. Stir gently until the spaghetti is well coated with sauce. Swirl in the remaining 4 tablespoons of butter, one at a time, then sprinkle with the remaining ¼ cup of Parmesan cheese. Place equal portions of spaghetti in each of six bowls, top each portion with a 1-ounce dollop of caviar, sprinkle generously with chopped chives, and serve.

SPAGHETTI

Country

Spaghetti Primavera à la Sirio Maccioni

SERVES 4 TO 6

- **3 tablespoons extra-virgin olive oil**
- **1 cup sliced mushrooms (from 8 to 10 1-inch white or button mushroom caps)**
- **1½ cups zucchini, in half-moon slices (1 medium zucchini)**
- **1½ cups broccoli florets (1 small head, about ½ pound)**
- **14 thin asparagus, trimmed and cut in 1-inch segments**
- **Kosher salt and freshly ground black pepper**
- **1 tablespoon chopped garlic (1 large clove)**
- **2 packed cups basil leaves, torn into small pieces**
- **1 cup plum tomatoes (2 tomatoes, fresh or canned), peeled, seeded, and chopped**
- **½ cup heavy cream**
- **2 tablespoons unsalted butter**
- **1 tablespoon mascarpone**
- **¼ cup freshly grated Parmigiano-Reggiano (from 1 2- to 3-ounce piece)**
- **¾ pound spaghetti**
- **½ cup shelled English peas (less than ⅛ pound)**
- **¼ cup pine nuts, toasted**
- **2 tablespoons chopped chives (½ of a small bunch)**

Legend has it that famed restaurateur Sirio Maccioni was entertaining the great food writer Craig Claiborne, who had dropped by his house impromptu. Sirio—proprietor of Le Cirque and my former boss—checked in his fridge, found a few ingredients, and pulled together a simple dish of spaghetti primavera, which pleased the somewhat imperious dean of restaurant critics. This primavera (which means "spring" in Italian, for the fresh vegetables in the mix) became the best-selling dish at Le Cirque for about twenty years, and among Sirio's favorites. I did all the prep as a young chef, slicing, dicing, and julienning vegetables; the waiters finished the dish at tableside with a flourish. Each waiter had his own variation, and they'd all excitedly bring samples back into the kitchen for me to taste. Sirio was a bit in love with his own creations and was convinced his version was superior ("I served this to Craig Claiborne!"). I remember very vividly who made the best one, and that's all I'm willing to say—except it wasn't Sirio.

Recently, I made this dish for my engagement party. Later, when I was editing the recipe to include in this book, I realized I had left out the peas. Everybody ate well and enjoyed the dinner, however, which just proves you don't need to get too hung up on every little detail of a recipe to make it work.

Heat 2 tablespoons of the oil in a large skillet over medium heat. Add the mushrooms and sauté them until golden on both sides, about 5 minutes. Add the zucchini, broccoli, and asparagus. Season the vegetables with ½ teaspoon salt and ¼ teaspoon pepper and cook, stirring frequently, until fork-tender, 5 to 7 minutes. Transfer the vegetables to a bowl and wipe out the pan.

Place the remaining tablespoon of oil in the skillet over medium heat. Add the garlic and basil, and cook, stirring frequently, until the garlic begins to color, about 2 minutes. Add the tomatoes and season with ½ teaspoon salt and ¼ teaspoon pepper. Continue to cook until the tomato juices evaporate, about 5 minutes more.

Place the cream, butter, mascarpone, and grated Parmesan in a medium pot over medium-low heat. Season the mixture with additional salt and pepper to taste, and cook slowly, stirring constantly, until the mixture thickens slightly, about 5 minutes; keep warm at the back of the stove.

Bring a large pot of salted water (about 4 quarts) to a boil over high heat. Add the spaghetti to the pot and reduce the heat to maintain a steady, gentle boil. Cook the pasta, stirring initially to keep the noodles from sticking together, until the spaghetti is nearly al dente, 5 to 8 minutes. (The best way—really the only way—to test the doneness of pasta is to fish a piece out of the water and taste it.) Add the peas and cook for 1 minute more. Drain the spaghetti and peas, and return them to the pot over medium heat. Add the creamy cheese mixture, the sautéed vegetables, the fresh tomato sauce, and the toasted pine nuts. Stir to combine well, add the chives, and serve in warm bowls.

STRAWBERRIES

TOWN

Strawberry Vacherin with Passion Fruit–Banana Sorbet

SERVES 6

FOR THE MERINGUES

- 3 large egg whites, at room temperature
- 1 teaspoon fresh lemon juice
- 3/4 cup superfine sugar

FOR THE STRAWBERRIES AND TO SERVE

- 1 quart strawberries, rinsed and sliced
- 2 tablespoons sugar
- Juice of 1/2 lemon
- 1 pint Passion Fruit–Banana Sorbet (recipe follows, or store-bought sorbet; optional)

For those of you who were wondering, *vacherin* is a fancy French name for a meringue cake filled with ice cream or some other delicacy. In this case, I'm using the term to emphasize the special-occasion nature of this dessert, which is certainly several cuts above most of the ways strawberries are usually served. This recipe has two major components—the vacherin and the sorbet. Feel free to take a shortcut and buy the sorbet. There are a lot of really fantastic ones available now in the freezers of supermarkets and gourmet shops. I suggest a good vanilla or buttermilk sorbet.

TIMING NOTES If you choose to make the sorbet, it can be done well in advance and frozen until serving time.

The meringues require 2 hours of slow baking followed by cooling time.

The strawberries need to macerate in sugar and lemon juice for about an hour, which can happen while the meringues are baking.

PREPARE THE MERINGUES Preheat the oven to 200°F.

Line two baking sheets with parchment paper.

Combine the egg whites and lemon juice in the bowl of an electric mixer and whisk on high until they form soft peaks. Still mixing, gradually add the sugar and whisk until a stiff, glossy meringue forms. Using a large spoon, drop 6 mounds of meringue onto the baking sheets; the mounds should be at least 2 inches apart. With the back of the spoon, make a dent in the top of each mound. Place the baking sheets in the oven and bake until the meringues are dry and crisp, at least 2 hours. Remove the meringues from the oven and set them aside to cool.

PREPARE THE STRAWBERRIES Place the strawberries, sugar, and lemon juice in a glass, ceramic, or other nonreactive bowl. Stir gently to mix, then set aside to macerate for about 1 hour.

To serve, place one meringue at the center of each plate. Top with macerated strawberries and finish with a generous scoop of sorbet (if using).

PASSION FRUIT–BANANA SORBET

MAKES ABOUT 4 CUPS

- 8 ripe passion fruit, or ¼ cup passion fruit pulp
- 4 large, ripe bananas, peeled
- Juice of 1 lemon
- ⅔ cup sugar
- 3 tablespoons light corn syrup

Scoop out the interior of the passion fruit, including seeds and pulp. Place the passion fruit pulp and seeds in a strainer, and use a small whisk or wooden spoon to press the pulp and juice into a bowl; discard the seeds. Combine the bananas and strained passion fruit in a food processor and purée. Add the lemon juice and mix well. Transfer the purée to a small saucepan and add the sugar, corn syrup, and 1⅓ cups water. Simmer the mixture over medium heat for 3 minutes. Allow the sorbet base to cool to room temperature, then chill in the refrigerator for at least 2 hours. Process the sorbet in an ice cream maker according to the manufacturer's instructions; freeze until ready to serve.

Country

Sautéed Strawberries with Cracked Black Pepper and Fresh Mint

SERVES 6

- **1 tablespoon salted butter**
- **1½ teaspoons brown sugar**
- **½ vanilla bean, split**
- **2 pounds strawberries, thoroughly washed, stemmed, and quartered**
- **Pinch of cracked black pepper**
- **1 cup coarsely chopped mint (about ½ bunch)**
- **2 tablespoons crème fraîche**

I cooked this recipe on the CBS *Early Show* in a live, outdoor demonstration, and I loved seeing the looks of shock and surprise on the faces of audience members when they realized I was mixing cracked pepper with sweet, fresh strawberries. Instead of the usual sweet/sour contrast, this magically simple recipe uses a sweet/*spicy* combination to elicit the "wow" response. Ripe strawberries are very floral and aromatic; they can easily handle a healthy dose of pepper along with the heady fragrance of the chopped fresh mint. They spend very little time in the pan, just enough to coat them with a sugary glaze.

Melt the butter in a large skillet over medium heat. Add the brown sugar and the vanilla bean and cook until the sugar begins to melt and the butter begins to brown, about 3 minutes. Add the strawberries and cook, tossing or rolling them in the butter, until they are well coated, about 15 seconds. Add the pepper and cook until the berries are warmed through, about 30 seconds more. Add the mint, mix well, and transfer the strawberries to serving bowls. Top with crème fraîche and serve immediately.

SWEET POTATOES

TOWN

Sweet Potato Purée with Caramelized Bananas and Oranges

SERVES 4

- **2 pounds sweet potatoes, peeled and sliced thick**
- **8 tablespoons (1 stick) unsalted butter**
- **1 vanilla bean, split**
- **2 allspice berries**
- **1 cinnamon stick**
- **1 piece star anise**
- **1 orange, quartered**
- **1 banana, peeled and sliced**
- **3 tablespoons maple syrup**
- **½ cup heavy cream**
- **Kosher salt and freshly ground black pepper**

Here's another perennial favorite that's been a staple on just about every menu I've ever devised. It was inspired by Alain Senderens, the great French chef, when he was at l'Archestrate, a Michelin three-star temple of gastronomy in Paris. Most people hesitate for a second, trying to figure out how the banana and orange are going to meld with sweet potato, but they're quickly convinced the second they try this dish. It goes very well with roasted chicken, turkey, or duck.

Cook the sweet potatoes in salted boiling water until very soft, about 20 minutes. Drain the potatoes, then cover and keep warm.

Meanwhile, melt 2 tablespoons of the butter in a large skillet over medium heat. Add the vanilla bean, allspice, cinnamon, and star anise. Toast the spices, stirring occasionally, until they are fragrant, about 3 minutes. Add the orange quarters and banana slices, raise the heat to medium-high, and cook, turning the ingredients regularly, until they brown slightly, about 2 minutes per side. Add the maple syrup to the skillet, lower the heat to a simmer, cover the skillet, remove from the heat, and set aside to allow the flavors to meld for about 30 minutes.

Squeeze the juice from the orange quarters into the syrup mixture, and discard the peels. Remove and discard the spices carefully, making sure not to lose any of the syrup. (Alternatively, place the contents of the pan in a strainer and press down to extract all the juices and preserve all the syrup.)

Purée the cooked sweet potatoes in a food processor, slowly adding the cream and the remaining 6 tablespoons of butter. Add the banana mixture and purée until fully incorporated. Season to taste with salt and pepper and serve warm.

SWEET POTATOES

Country

Sweet Potato Fries with Lemon-Rosemary Salt

SERVES 6

- **3 pounds medium sweet potatoes**
- **1 teaspoon minced garlic (½ medium clove)**
- **1 teaspoon minced fresh rosemary leaves**
- **½ teaspoon cayenne pepper**
- **1 teaspoon fine sea salt**
- **Grated zest of 1 lemon**
- **3 to 4 quarts peanut oil, for frying**

My friend the gifted chef Anne Rosenzweig used to make sweet potato fries at her restaurant Arcadia, which is where I remember first having them in the late 1980s. This is my attempt to match Anne's artistry, with a zesty Middle Eastern twist in the form of lemon and cayenne. I like to serve these alongside a nice piece of grilled chicken or marinated flank steak hot off the barby, or make a big plate of them to eat with a juicy burger, washed down with cold beer. Note that when making fries, it's important to use plenty of oil at the hottest possible temperature (just below its smoke point) and to not overcrowd the pot.

Wash and brush the sweet potatoes to remove any dirt, then pat them completely dry with paper towels. (They should be at room temperature for cooking.) With the skin still on, use a large knife to cut them lengthwise into strips ¼ to ½ inch square and about 3 inches long.

Place the garlic, rosemary, cayenne, salt, and grated lemon zest in a large stainless-steel or other nonreactive bowl and stir to combine well.

Fill a heavy, deep pot to a depth of at least 3 inches with oil and place it over medium-high heat until the oil is hot. (If using a pot, it should be at least 6 inches deep; alternatively, use an electric fryer with a built-in thermometer.) The oil is ready when a thermometer indicates a temperature of at least 375°F., or a small drop of water immediately sizzles on contact with the oil. (The oil can be as hot as 400°F., as long as it is below its smoke point.)

Working in small batches, fry the sweet potatoes in the oil until nicely crisp and light brown on the outside, about 3 minutes. Remove them from the oil with tongs or a slotted spoon and allow to drain briefly on a large plate or platter lined with paper towels. Transfer them immediately to the bowl. When all the fries are cooked, toss quickly (once or twice) in the salt-herb mixture and serve warm.

SWISS CHARD

TOWN

Swiss Chard Gratin

SERVES 6

- 3 tablespoons unsalted butter
- 2 tablespoons minced shallots (2 medium shallots)
- 2 cloves garlic
- 2 tablespoons chopped fresh sage
- 2 cups heavy cream
- Pinch of freshly ground nutmeg
- 2 pounds Swiss chard (about 2 bunches)
- 2 tablespoons extra-virgin olive oil
- 2 cups thinly sliced fresh porcini or cremini mushrooms (about ½ pound)
- Kosher salt and freshly ground black pepper
- 2 large Yukon gold potatoes (about 1 pound)
- ¼ cup freshly grated Parmigiano-Reggiano
- ¼ cup fresh bread crumbs
- ¼ cup dried oregano

Swiss chard is beautiful and highly nutritious, a well-respected yet humble green. This recipe is a way to dress it up with several complementary flavor and texture combinations in an elegant presentation. It requires some assembly and attention, but it's well worthwhile. I think of gratins as accident-proof dishes because the melted cheese is probably the best way to cover up in the event of overcooking.

INGREDIENT NOTE Porcini are among the most expensive mushrooms, so for economy's sake feel free to substitute cremini.

Melt 2 tablespoons of the butter in a medium pot over medium-low heat. Add the shallots, garlic, and sage, and cook, stirring frequently, until the shallots are translucent, about 2 minutes. Add 1⅔ cups of the cream and the nutmeg and bring to a simmer over medium heat. Simmer the cream, stirring occasionally, until it has reduced by three fourths, about 20 minutes.

Meanwhile, cut the Swiss chard leaves from the stems (discard the stems or use them for another purpose). Bring a large pot of salted water to a boil. Plunge the chard into the boiling water and blanch, cooking just until bright green and wilted, about 20 seconds. (This helps soften up the cellulose in the chard's leaves.) Drain the Swiss chard and refresh it in ice water. Squeeze any excess water from the chard. Add the chard to the reduced cream and set the creamed chard aside.

Heat 1 tablespoon of the oil in a large skillet over medium-high heat. Working in batches if necessary to avoid crowding the pan, sauté the mushrooms until golden and crisp, 2 to 3 minutes per side. Add the remaining 1 tablespoon of butter, season to taste with salt and pepper, and reserve.

Peel and slice the potatoes into fourteen ¼-inch-thick rounds. Place the potato slices in a pot, add water to cover, season with 1 teaspoon salt, bring to a simmer over medium heat, and cook until fork-tender but not mushy. Drain the potato slices and place them in a small mixing bowl with the remaining ⅓ cup of cream. Season the potato slices with additional salt and pepper to taste, and gently toss to coat them with cream.

Preheat the oven to 375°F. Arrange 12 potato slices on a lightly oiled baking sheet. Arrange a layer of mushroom slices on top of each potato slice, sprinkle with some Parmesan and bread crumbs, and top with a small spoonful of creamed chard. Sprinkle some grated Parmesan and bread crumbs on the chard. Arrange another layer of mushrooms on each stack, followed by another layer of chard and a final topping of grated Parmesan and bread crumbs. Season the stacks with a little oregano. Drizzle a little of the remaining olive oil over each stack and bake until the topping is golden and the ingredients are heated through, about 20 minutes. Using a spatula, carefully lift two gratins onto each plate and serve.

SWISS CHARD

Country

Swiss Chard Sautéed with Garlic and Balsamic Vinegar

SERVES 4 AS A SIDE DISH

2 pounds Swiss chard (about 2 bunches)

2 tablespoons extra-virgin olive oil

2 cloves garlic, minced

Pinch of hot red pepper flakes

3 tablespoons chopped flat-leaf parsley

1 tablespoon balsamic vinegar, or to taste

Kosher salt and freshly ground black pepper

Like a person who's undeniably talented but a little shy and retiring, Swiss chard can use some exciting partners—in this case garlic and balsamic vinegar—to bring out its best traits. I like to serve this dish alongside grilled fish, lamb, or fowl.

INGREDIENT NOTE Swiss chard is part of the beet family: the regular green variety is the mildest; red or rhubarb chard, with green leaves and red stems and ribs, is stronger flavored; ruby chard, which is red all over with just a hint of greenish tinge to its leaves, is the most interesting-looking. You can use any of these chards, according to availability and personal preference.

Thoroughly wash and dry the Swiss chard. Remove the leaves from the stems (the stems can be sautéed separately or discarded). Tear the leaves into 2- to 3-inch pieces.

Warm the olive oil in a large skillet over medium heat. Add the garlic, red pepper flakes, and parsley. Cook, stirring, until the garlic begins to color, about 1 minute. Add a handful of chard to the pan and cook until it begins to wilt, about 30 seconds. Add another handful of chard and allow it to wilt; continue until all the chard has been added. Season the chard with the balsamic vinegar, and salt and pepper to taste. Reduce the heat to low and cook until the chard is tender, about 10 minutes. Adjust the seasoning if necessary, and serve hot.

SWORDFISH

TOWN

Swordfish Steak "Diane"

SERVES 4

- **4 5-ounce swordfish steaks, ½ inch thick**
- **Kosher salt**
- **2 tablespoons freshly cracked black pepper**
- **2 tablespoons extra-virgin olive oil**
- **4 tablespoons unsalted butter**
- **3 shallots, minced**
- **1 small clove garlic, minced**
- **¼ cup Madeira**
- **2 tablespoons Dijon mustard**
- **¼ cup White Beef Stock (page 261, or low-sodium canned)**
- **1 tablespoon Worcestershire sauce, plus more to taste**
- **Juice of 1 lemon**
- **Juice of 1 lime**
- **1 teaspoon fish sauce**
- **1 tablespoon minced chives**
- **Freshly ground black pepper to taste**
- **1 tablespoon chopped fresh chervil**

The traditional version of this quick, simple preparation consists of a beef steak that's pounded thin, browned in the pan, and dressed tableside with a sauce of Madeira, mustard, and butter. I first had it at one of those family treat dinners—I think I remember my main dish from just about every one—at Locke-Ober, an ancient Boston dining institution. The Diane sauce caught my youthful fancy right away; it had a very high Yummy Factor. My modern variation has a couple of key differences: the main ingredient, of course, is fish; and the sauce is lighter, with less butter, but it has several interesting and very flavorful ingredients. The swordfish here is meant to be cut thin—only ½ inch thick—so be careful not to overcook it: just a couple of minutes per side is enough, and you should err on the side of undercooking. If it's slightly underdone, just add it to the pan with the sauce and leave it there briefly, off the burner, allowing it to come gradually to your desired doneness.

INGREDIENT NOTES The fish sauce called for here is the type found in the Asian sections of supermarkets or in Asian specialty markets; it is often labeled "Thai fish sauce."

Genuine Madeira comes from the Portuguese island of the same name located off the coast of Morocco, and it's made by a process utilizing heat and oxidation, two elements that are anathema to most aging wines. The sweetest Madeiras are served as fine dessert wines. In this recipe, you can use either the genuine article or any inexpensive Madeira-style wine.

COOK THE SWORDFISH Season the swordfish steaks generously with salt and the cracked pepper. (The pepper should be cracked in relatively large pieces; it plays a prominent role in the dish.) Place the oil in a large skillet over medium-high heat. When the oil is hot, add only as many swordfish steaks as fit easily into the pan without crowding. (You will probably need to cook in batches or use two pans.) Cook the swordfish until it is nicely browned on one side, 2 to 3 minutes. Turn the fish over and cook until the steaks are just cooked through, about 2 minutes more. Transfer the fish to a large platter, cover loosely with aluminum foil, and keep warm at the back of the stove.

PREPARE THE SAUCE Wipe out the skillet and add the butter; allow it to melt over medium heat. Add the shallots and garlic, and sweat, stirring frequently, until soft, about 3 minutes. Add the Madeira and allow it to simmer for a few seconds. Stir in the mustard, and add the stock, Worcestershire sauce, lemon juice, lime juice, fish sauce, and chives. Pour any juices that have accumulated under the resting swordfish back into the pan; allow the sauce to simmer for 1 to 2 minutes so the flavors can blend. Adjust the seasoning to taste with additional salt, freshly ground black pepper, and Worcestershire sauce. Spoon the sauce over the fish, garnish with chopped chervil, and serve.

SWORDFISH

Country
Pasta with Swordfish Bolognese

SERVES 6

1 pound swordfish fillet scraps (center cut, not belly)

2 tablespoons vegetable oil, such as light olive oil, canola, or peanut oil

1 teaspoon kosher salt, plus more to taste

½ teaspoon freshly ground black pepper

6 tablespoons unsalted butter

4 medium shallots, chopped

4 cloves garlic, minced

1 tablespoon fresh thyme leaves

¼ cup brandy

¼ cup sherry vinegar

1 tablespoon Worcestershire sauce

1 teaspoon smoked paprika

Cayenne pepper to taste

½ cup chopped flat-leaf parsley

1 pound perciatelli, bucatini, or equivalent pasta

½ cup grated Pecorino Romano (from a 4-ounce piece)

Perciatelli ("pear-cha-TELL-ee") are long spaghetti-like pasta shapes with a hollow center. Also known as bucatini ("the ones with the little holes"), they work well with hearty ragù-style sauces like this, as well as seafood sauces such as the classic Sicilian combo of fresh sardines and wild fennel. You can use other meat sauce–friendly pasta shapes, such as shells or ears, but the thick perciatelli are really ideal. The great advantage of a fish-based ragù is that it doesn't require the long, slow simmer—an hour and a half or more—needed to break down and meld the textures and flavors of red meats.

INGREDIENT NOTES This recipe calls for swordfish scraps, which are trimmings from the fillets or steaks displayed at your fishmonger, sold to make kebabs.

I recommend the DeCecco brand of pasta, or an equivalent, reliable high-quality dry pasta.

Cut the swordfish into 1- to 2-inch cubes. Place the oil in a large sauté pan over medium-high heat. Season the swordfish cubes with the salt and pepper and add them to the pan. Cook the fish until lightly brown on all sides, about 8 minutes; drain the swordfish in a colander and discard the oil.

Wipe out the pan and place it over medium heat. Add 2 tablespoons of the butter; when the butter melts, add the shallots, garlic, and thyme, and sweat, stirring frequently, until the shallots are soft, about 5 minutes. (Reduce the heat as necessary to prevent the shallots and garlic from browning.) Remove the pan from the heat and add the brandy; return the pot to the heat and simmer until the pan is almost dry, about 2 minutes. Add the vinegar and simmer for 1 to 2 minutes. Add the swordfish, reduce the heat to low, and simmer the fish in the vinegar until it is flaky and the pan is almost dry, about 6 minutes. Allow the contents of the pan to cool to room temperature.

Pulse the sauce in a food processor, adding the remaining chilled butter 1 or 2 tablespoons at a time. Process only until the butter is well combined. Add the Worcestershire sauce and paprika; season to taste with cayenne pepper and additional salt. Stir in half the chopped parsley, then transfer the sauce to a bowl, cover, and refrigerate until ready to use. (Alternatively, reserve in a warm place and proceed immediately with the recipe.)

If the sauce has been refrigerated, allow it to come to room temperature before serving. Bring a large pot of salted water to a boil. Add the perciatelli to the pot, bring it back to a boil, adjust the heat so it maintains a steady boil, and cook the pasta until al dente, 8 to 10 minutes. Drain the pasta in a colander, reserving some of the cooking water. Transfer the perciatelli to a large bowl, mix in the sauce, adding some of the pasta cooking water to thin as necessary. Stir in the Pecorino Romano, garnish with the remaining parsley, and serve.

TOWN

Tomato-Watermelon Salad

SERVES 6

1 pound heirloom tomatoes (1 large, 2 medium, or 3 small), cut into wedges slightly larger than bite-size

1½ pounds watermelon, cut into wedges slightly larger than bite-size

1 mango, peeled and sliced into wedges slightly larger than bite-size

2 tablespoons coarsely chopped celery leaves

1 tablespoon coriander seeds, crushed

¼ cup extra-virgin olive oil

3 tablespoons chopped fresh dill

2 tablespoons julienned basil leaves

Fine sea salt and cracked black pepper

I do believe I invented this pairing. At any rate, it's been one of my signature dishes since I put it on the menu at Restaurant 44 at the Royalton Hotel in 1987. I was looking for a break from the same old summer tomato salads with onions and basil, and thought of pairing good ripe tomatoes with another seasonal ingredient, watermelon. The combination may seem a little weird at first, but it begins to make a lot of sense when you realize they share a similar watery makeup while offering two interesting contrasts—soft *vs.* crunchy (texture) and sweet *vs.* acidic (flavor). The dill and olive oil, added in judicious amounts, really make this pair sing.

NOTE To ensure success, the watermelon should be chilled (just a few minutes out of the fridge), while the tomatoes should be at room temperature. The salad should be made immediately before serving; if you let it sit, it can turn soupy.

Combine the tomatoes, watermelon, mango, celery leaves, and coriander seeds in a large bowl. Add the olive oil, dill, and basil, and toss gently. Season to taste with salt and pepper immediately before serving. Place equal portions in small salad bowls and serve immediately.

TOMATOES

Country

Penne with Fresh Tomato Sauce

SERVES 4

$1\frac{1}{3}$ cups coarsely chopped fresh, ripe tomatoes (2 medium or 1 large tomato, about $\frac{3}{4}$ pound)

$\frac{2}{3}$ cup heavy cream

1 pound penne pasta

$\frac{2}{3}$ cup freshly grated Parmigiano-Reggiano

$\frac{1}{3}$ cup torn fresh basil leaves

6 tablespoons extra-virgin olive oil (optional)

Kosher salt and freshly ground black pepper

This is a great rescue or bail-out dish. It's delicious, comforting, satisfying, and the perfect antidote to a night out on the town, particularly because it's a "nonrepeater"—that is, it doesn't have any garlic or onions that may come back to haunt you later while you're trying to sleep, or in the morning when you're trying to wake up. The recipe is quick and easy to prepare, and one of my most reliable home meals; it works equally well with fresh tomatoes or tomato confit. It's not necessary to peel and seed the tomatoes, but if you prefer a smoother sauce by all means go for it.

Place the chopped tomatoes and heavy cream in a medium pot and bring to a simmer over medium heat. Simmer the sauce until the cream has reduced by about one third and the tomatoes have dissolved into the sauce, about 10 minutes.

In the meantime, bring a large pot of salted water to a boil over high heat. Add the penne, adjust the heat to maintain a steady boil, and cook, stirring occasionally, until the penne are al dente, 8 to 10 minutes. Drain the pasta, and return it to the pot along with the sauce over medium-high heat. Stir gently while adding the cheese, basil, and olive oil. Season to taste with salt and pepper, and serve immediately.

INSTRUCTIONS FOR PEELING, SEEDING, AND DICING TOMATOES

Make a cross-shaped cut about $\frac{1}{4}$ inch deep in the top (stem end) of the tomato. Drop the tomato in boiling water for about 30 seconds. Place the tomato in a colander under cold running water. When it's cool enough to handle, peel off the skin by hand. Cut the tomato in halves or quarters and use a small spoon to scoop out and discard the seeds.

TRUFFLES

TOWN

Risotto with Black Truffles and Escargots

SERVES 6

FOR THE SNAILS

- 12 canned snails (from 1 7-ounce can), drained and cleaned, juice reserved
- 2 tablespoons extra-virgin olive oil
- 1 medium carrot, finely diced
- 1 medium leek, white part only, thoroughly washed and finely diced
- 1 small celery root, peeled and finely diced
- 8 cloves garlic, minced
- 2 stalks celery, finely diced
- 1 cup dry white wine
- 6 ounces (1½ sticks) unsalted butter, diced and softened
- 2 tablespoons minced black truffle (from 1 small jar)
- ¼ cup chopped flat-leaf parsley
- Kosher salt and freshly ground black pepper to taste

When I first devised this recipe at Restaurant 44 back in 1987, I was pretty excited about it, but I wasn't convinced it would sell all that briskly. On the contrary, it's been one of my bestsellers ever since. The concept was to combine three key ingredients—snails, garlic, and black truffles—all of which grow one inch underground, a terrific trio of subterranean treats. I learned to make a good risotto early in my career at Le Cirque, but it wasn't until 1988, when I assisted with the opening of Bice restaurant in Paris, that I truly perfected the technique under the kind tutelage of Chef Marta Pulini (who was also one of the mother-chefs at Le Madri in Manhattan). *Grazie,* Marta! I learned to take it slowly, add the broth in increments, and taste the rice so it's cooked to the desired consistency. In any case, it should be neither too liquid nor too thick.

INGREDIENT NOTE Carnaroli is the best of the risotto rices; its starch is even and consistent, it soaks up all the juices yet holds its shape and remains firm through the cooking process.

PREPARE THE SNAILS Drain the snails in a colander set over a bowl; reserve their juices for later use. Cut the snails in half lengthwise and set aside. Place the oil, carrot, leek, celery root, garlic, and celery in a medium saucepan over medium heat. Sweat the vegetables, stirring occasionally, until tender, about 10 minutes. Add the snails and wine, and simmer gently over medium-low heat until the liquid is reduced by two thirds, about 30 minutes. Next add the reserved snail juice and simmer for 5 minutes more. Gradually whisk in the diced butter. Add the truffle and parsley, and season to taste with salt and pepper. Keep the sauce warm at the back of the stove, stirring occasionally.

FOR THE RISOTTO

- 2 tablespoons unsalted butter
- 1 tablespoon extra-virgin olive oil
- 1 medium white onion, minced
- 2 cups carnaroli rice
- 1 cup dry white wine
- 5 cups Chicken Stock (page 262, or low-sodium canned)
- Splash of black truffle oil

PREPARE THE RISOTTO Place 1 tablespoon of the butter and the 1 tablespoon of olive oil in a medium saucepan over medium heat. Add the minced onion and sweat until translucent, about 5 minutes. Add the rice and cook, stirring constantly, until it no longer appears chalky, 3 to 5 minutes. Add the wine and reduce, stirring frequently, until almost dry, about 5 minutes. Next add enough stock to just cover the rice (about 2 cups). Simmer, stirring frequently, until the rice is once again almost dry. Repeat, adding another 2 cups of stock, then simmering and stirring the rice until it has absorbed almost all of the stock. Taste the rice. If it is still crunchy, add the remaining 1 cup of stock and cook until the rice is tender but a touch chewy. The rice should be fluffy-looking and softening on the outside but still slightly firm to the taste. The grains of rice should still be distinct—not entirely melded or rendered mushy by the release of their starch—and the liquid holding them together should be somewhat viscous but not gelatinous or gloppy. (Total cooking time for the risotto should be about 20 minutes.) To finish the risotto, stir in the remaining 1 tablespoon of butter and the truffle oil, then season to taste with salt and pepper. Spoon the risotto into warm bowls, ladle the snail sauce on top, and serve immediately.

TRUFFLES

Country

Black Truffle and Smoked Bacon Turnovers

MAKES 24 TURNOVERS

1/4 pound smoked bacon, julienned

2 large white onions, sliced

1 tablespoon chopped black truffles (about 1/2 ounce; use canned, jarred, or fresh)

1 to 2 tablespoons black truffle oil

Kosher salt and freshly ground black pepper

1 1-pound package frozen puff pastry (2 sheets), thawed

All-purpose flour, for dusting

2 large eggs, lightly beaten

In my never-ending quest for perfect pairs and idyllic trios, I've come across a few real winners: onions, bacon, and black truffles is unquestionably one of them. I got the inspiration from my *stage* at L'Auberge de l'Ill under chef Paul Haeberlin. It was a typically wet, miserable January in Alsace, and the only answer to the bone-chilling cold was a recipe like this, with earthy truffles and hearty smoked bacon.

Making the filling for these turnovers is a quick step, followed by the somewhat more challenging procedure of rolling out the pastry and carving the turnover shapes. It isn't complicated, but it does require a bit of precision. What you have to look forward to is a chic, sophisticated finger food that represents the ultimate hors d'oeuvre for holidays and special occasions.

INGREDIENT NOTE Puff pastry is available in the freezer section of most markets; Greek-style phyllo dough, also available in the freezer section or at a bakery or Greek specialty shop, can be used as a substitute.

PREPARE THE FILLING Place the bacon in a large skillet over medium heat and cook until the fat is rendered and the bacon is crisp, about 5 minutes. Transfer the bacon to a plate lined with paper towels to drain. Discard all but enough of the bacon fat to coat the bottom of the skillet. Add the onions and cook over medium heat, stirring occasionally, until they begin to brown, about 20 minutes. Remove the onions from the pan and reserve. Add the bacon to the onions. Add the chopped truffles, mix well, then season with truffle oil and salt and pepper to taste.

ASSEMBLE AND BAKE THE PASTRIES Preheat the oven to 400°F.

Dust a work surface (such as a large wooden cutting board, butcher block, or marble counter) with flour. Roll out one of the sheets of puff pastry into a 14-inch square; the pastry should be about 1/8 inch thick. Cut the square in half. Prick one half of the pastry all over with a fork; this allows the steam to escape during baking so the pastry rises evenly. Spoon 12 small evenly spaced mounds of onion mixture onto the pricked pastry in 2 rows starting about 1 1/2 inches from one edge and ending the same distance from the other. Brush the second half of the pastry with beaten egg. Carefully lift the second sheet and lay it on top of the first one, matching the sides and corners evenly. Run your finger around each mound of filling, pressing out air and sealing the pastry. Using a small round or square cutter (about 2 1/2 inches across) or a sharp knife, cut the dough around each mound of filling, leaving a 1/2-inch edge, to form turnovers. Transfer the turnovers to a baking sheet, pressing and sealing shut the edges of each as you go. Repeat the process with the second sheet of dough and the remaining filling. Brush the turnovers with the remaining egg, then bake them until puffed and golden, about 12 minutes. Serve warm.

TUNA

SERVES 4

FOR THE TARTARE

- **½ pound bluefin tuna fillet**
- **1 lemon**
- **½ cup pitted, diced cherries (about 1 dozen), or 1 ripe plum, pitted and diced**
- **1½ teaspoons toasted pine nuts, roughly chopped**

FOR THE DRESSING

- **1 tablespoon sherry vinegar**
- **1 tablespoon honey**
- **Fine sea salt and freshly ground black pepper**
- **3 tablespoons grapeseed oil**

FOR THE GARNISH

- **2 cups mustard greens (¼ to ½ bunch), leaves only, torn into bite-size pieces, or micro mustard greens or baby arugula**
- **2 teaspoons rosemary leaves, chopped**

TOWN

Tuna Tartare with Cherries and Lemons

When I opened the Blue Door Restaurant at Ian Schrager's Delano Hotel in Miami Beach in the middle of a hot Florida summer, I designed this dish as a heat-beater. At first glance, you might think cherries and lemons are a curious choice to combine with raw tuna. But consider this: just about every tuna tartare recipe is defined by a balance between two key ingredients, one sweet and the other sour. Here the sweet is represented by the cherries and the sour by the lemons, striking an ideal balance.

INGREDIENT NOTES Washington State cherries are the plumpest around, but any sweet, ripe variety will do. Since ripe cherries are only available in a relatively narrow window, you can substitute a ripe plum.

Israeli lemons are sweeter than your average lemon, but use any high-quality ripe lemon.

The tuna should be high grade sushi quality.

PREPARE THE TARTARE Trim the tuna, cutting away any sinew and/or dark spots. Dice the tuna into ¼-inch pieces and place it in a bowl. Peel the lemon. Use a paring knife to trim any pith, and carve out the sections. Dice the lemon sections, and combine them with the tuna. Add the cherries and chopped pine nuts, and stir to combine well.

PREPARE THE DRESSING Place the vinegar and honey in a small bowl, and whisk to combine well. Season to taste with salt and pepper, then gradually whisk in the oil. Season the tuna mixture with salt and pepper to taste, then dress it with 2 tablespoons of the sherry-honey dressing.

FINISH AND GARNISH Spoon small mounds of the tuna tartare onto each of four chilled plates. (For a fancier presentation, use ring molds to shape the tartare.) Using a spoon, smooth the surface of each tartare mound, then glaze each with dressing, using about 1 tablespoon total. Season the mustard greens with salt and pepper to taste. Toss the greens with the remaining dressing and arrange them around the tuna. Sprinkle a pinch of chopped rosemary leaves on each serving of tartare and serve.

TUNA

Country
Crusted Tuna Steaks

SERVES 6

- **3 tablespoons white sesame seeds**
- **3 tablespoons black sesame seeds**
- **1 tablespoon finely grated lime zest**
- **1 tablespoon minced lemongrass, tender inner part only (about a 2-inch section)**
- **1 teaspoon sweet paprika**
- **1 teaspoon ground Aleppo pepper**
- **1 teaspoon freshly ground black pepper**
- **1 teaspoon kosher salt**
- **6 ½-inch-thick tuna steaks (each about 8 ounces)**
- **¼ cup light extra-virgin olive oil or peanut oil, plus additional for brushing**
- **6 lime wedges**
- **1 cup Mayonnaise (page 264, or Hellman's)**

I think this recipe is a stellar example of casual, sophisticated country style—the maximum possible flavor impact from a minimal number of ingredients. The tuna steaks are coated with an eclectic combination of Asian-accented spices; I got tired of sneezing at the same old pepper crust, so I came up with this variation. The preparation is quick, easy, and straightforward. It's served with a simple garnish of lime and mayonnaise, all of which makes it ideal for a streamlined lunch or supper.

INGREDIENT NOTES For the mayonnaise garnish, you can make your own or use Hellman's.

Dried Aleppo peppers, a naturally sun-dried red pepper from the area around the town of the same name in Syria, are available from Kalustyan's (see "Sources and Resources," page 266), as are black and white sesame seeds.

Place the white and black sesame seeds, lime zest, lemongrass, paprika, Aleppo pepper, black pepper, and salt in a small mixing bowl. Stir well to combine. Pour the sesame mixture onto a plate. Coat the tuna steaks on both sides with the mixture.

Place 2 tablespoons of oil in each of two large skillets over medium-high heat. When the oil is hot, add the tuna steaks and reduce the heat to medium. Cook the tuna until lightly browned on both sides (it will be slightly pink in the center), about 2 minutes per side. Transfer the tuna steaks to six plates, and serve with the lime wedges and mayonnaise on the side.

VEAL

TOWN

Poached Veal Shank with Saffron Mayonnaise

SERVES 4

- 4 medium veal shanks ($\frac{3}{4}$ to 1 pound each), cut for osso buco or left whole
- Kosher salt
- 2 tablespoons extra-virgin olive oil
- 2 small carrots, diced
- 1 large turnip, peeled and diced
- 1 parsnip, peeled and diced
- 1 leek, white part only, thoroughly rinsed and diced
- 3 cloves garlic, chopped
- 6 small tomatoes, peeled, seeded, and roughly chopped
- 2 quarts Chicken Stock (page 262, or low-sodium canned), veal stock, or vegetable stock
- 8 tablespoons Saffron Mayonnaise (recipe follows)
- 2 tablespoons unsalted butter (optional)
- Freshly ground black pepper to taste
- 1 bunch of flat-leaf parsley, chopped
- 1 bunch of chervil, chopped

I learned the technique of parboiling or poaching certain meats—including chickens and this cut of veal—from Daniel Boulud, who knows as well as anybody how to make old French cooking new. At Le Cirque, he would make *bollito misto* (mixed boiled meats) in a huge copper pot almost every day. Poaching removes impurities, softens the meats in preparation for braising, and helps extract fat. It's an extra step—strictly optional—but very effective and satisfying in terms of final results. Whole veal shank is a big, bold, succulent cut that responds well to this treatment; it also works with some of the other tougher cuts such as the breast or shoulder. You can prepare this using either whole shanks or shanks cut "osso buco style"; the latter will reduce the cooking time considerably.

INGREDIENT NOTE The most famous version of braised veal shanks is *osso buco alla Milanese,* which traditionally calls for hind shanks cut into sections about 1½ inches thick. (*Osso buco* means "bone hole" in Italian and refers to the fact that the veal legs have delectable marrow inside the bones—truly the icing on the cake.) Another variation, called *stinco,* originated in the extreme northeast of Italy, around Trieste; as in this recipe, it calls for whole braised shanks. It's possible to use the foreleg shanks; they are tougher and contain more gristle, but of course braising easily overcomes these obstacles. For best results, insist on the hind shanks.

Place the veal shanks in a roasting pot or Dutch oven large enough to hold them in one uncrowded layer. Cover the shanks with water, season with the 2 teaspoons salt, and bring the water to a boil over high heat. Drain off and discard the water; reserve the shanks.

Wipe out the pot, place it over medium heat, and add the olive oil. Add the carrots, turnip, parsnip, and leek, and cook, stirring frequently, until the vegetables begin to soften, about 10 minutes. Add the garlic and cook for about 5 minutes more; do not allow the vegetables to color (reduce the heat as necessary). Add the veal shanks in one layer, followed by the tomatoes. Add the stock and enough water just to cover the shanks. Bring the liquid to a boil over medium heat, then adjust the heat so it maintains a low, steady simmer. Cook the shanks, uncovered, until very soft and tender, about 2 hours. (If the shanks are cut osso buco style, you can reduce their cooking time to about 1¼ hours.) Prepare the saffron mayonnaise while the shanks are braising. Allow the shanks to cool to room temperature in the braising liquid.

Remove the shanks from the pot, then strain and degrease the braising liquid. Return the braising liquid to the pot, and simmer over medium-high heat until it has reduced enough to attain some body, about 15 minutes. Swirl in the butter (if using), and season with salt and pepper to taste. Return the shanks to the pot and reheat over a low flame. Place one veal shank in each of four warm shallow bowls, spoon a portion of reduced braising liquid in each bowl, add about 2 tablespoons of saffron mayonnaise on top, garnish with chopped parsley and chervil, and serve.

SAFFRON MAYONNAISE

MAKES ABOUT 1¾ CUPS

Pinch of saffron threads

2 tablespoons dry white wine

2 large egg yolks

2 tablespoons lemon juice (1 small or ½ large lemon)

½ teaspoon fine sea salt

¼ teaspoon freshly ground white pepper

1½ cups extra-virgin olive oil, or a mixture of extra-virgin olive oil with canola oil

Steep the saffron threads in the wine. Place the egg yolks in a mixing bowl with the saffron, wine, and lemon juice. Season with salt and pepper and whisk until well combined. Continue whisking briskly while gradually incorporating the oil. Adjust the seasoning with salt and pepper. Refrigerate until ready to use.

Country Rack of Veal Confit

SERVES 4

- **½ rack of veal (4 chops), trimmed**
- **1 bunch of rosemary**
- **1 bunch of oregano, plus additional for garnish**
- **1 head of garlic, skin on, halved crosswise**
- **1½ teaspoons kosher salt, plus more to taste**
- **1 teaspoon freshly ground black pepper, plus more to taste**
- **1 gallon olive or canola oil**

For a fun change of pace, here's a way to apply the confit treatment—first slow-cooking in oil, then quickly browning just before you serve—normally used for chicken or duck or a heftier cut of meat. Veal is relatively lean and can dry out, which is why this moisture-retaining method works so well. Plus, the meat is browned at the end so you don't sacrifice the delicious effects of caramelization. The oil used for cooking the veal confit is very flavorful and can be saved for up to one week and used for sautéing or basting. Serve this dish with Creamed Spinach (recipe follows), red cabbage stew, baked potatoes in their jackets, or any root vegetable purée. It's also good with a frisée salad dressed with a bracing red wine vinaigrette. If you like, you can split the half rack of veal into chops and cook them the same way; this reduces the cooking time to about 50 minutes.

INGREDIENT NOTES As with lamb, a rack is nothing more than the rib chops still connected, before they are cut apart. A full rack of veal, also known as a rib roast, is four to six pounds and has six bones. My personal preference is grass-fed veal, but some people like milk-fed, which is generally thought of as Italian- or French-style but is actually a process invented by Dutch dairy farmers. Have the rack trimmed by your butcher.

If you use olive oil, choose a lighter type of extra-virgin, such as Monini—not one of the heavier, greener, fruitier ones.

COOK THE VEAL Place the veal, rosemary, oregano, and garlic in a very large heavy pot. Season with the 1½ teaspoons salt and 1 teaspoon pepper, and add enough oil to cover. Warm the oil over medium-low heat until it is just below a simmer. (A candy or frying thermometer will indicate a temperature of about 170°F.) Adjust the heat so it remains just below a simmer. Cook the veal until it is no longer pink, about 1 hour and 20 minutes. (A meat thermometer inserted in the thickest part of the veal will indicate a temperature of about 155°F.) Remove the pot from the heat and allow the veal to cool in the oil. Once cool, remove the meat from the oil, wrap the rack in plastic, and refrigerate overnight. Strain the oil and reserve it in a cool place. (This step is optional; you can proceed directly to serving if you make the dish all in the same day.)

FINISH AND SERVE Remove the veal rack from the refrigerator about 30 minutes before cooking. Cut the rack into chops, each with a bone. Place about 1 tablespoon of the confit oil in a large sauté pan or skillet over medium-high heat. When the oil is hot but not smoking, cook the chops until well-browned, 3 to 4 minutes per side; work in batches or use two skillets. Transfer the chops to a platter, season them with salt and pepper to taste, garnish with fresh oregano, and serve.

CREAMED SPINACH

MAKES ABOUT 4 CUPS

4 bunches of spinach (3 pounds untrimmed), washed and trimmed

2 tablespoons extra-virgin olive oil

3 shallots, finely chopped

3/4 cup heavy cream

Pinch of freshly grated nutmeg

Kosher salt and freshly ground black pepper

Bring a large pot of salted water to a boil over high heat. Add the spinach and blanch just until wilted. Transfer the spinach to a colander, refresh under cold water, and drain thoroughly.

Warm the oil in a skillet over medium heat. Add the shallots and cook, stirring occasionally, until they soften, about 3 minutes. Add the cream and simmer until it reduces enough to coat the back of a spoon, about 8 minutes.

Chop the drained spinach and add it to the cream. Stir in the nutmeg, season to taste with salt and pepper, and simmer gently until the spinach and cream come together, about 20 minutes. (Even well-drained spinach will release juices into the cream; simmer the mixture long enough so it is thick enough to lightly bind.) Adjust the seasoning as necessary with salt, pepper, and nutmeg to taste. Purée the spinach in a blender and serve warm.

WATERMELON

SERVES 4

FOR THE LEMONGRASS SIMPLE SYRUP

2 stalks lemongrass

1 cup sugar

FOR THE WATERMELON GRANITA

5 to 6 cups cubed seeded watermelon (yield from a 5-pound piece of melon)

Juice of 3 limes

4 cups mixed, sliced ripe local summer fruits (peaches, plums, berries, melons, apricots, cherries)

TOWN

Summer Fruit Platter with Watermelon Granita

When I think of ripe summer fruit, I always think of my uncle Simon. He ran a wholesale produce business, working in a giant cement walk-in cooler where the temperature was perpetually 50°F. (which may explain why he always had the sniffles). Every Saturday morning, my dad would drive me over there, and we'd haul home boxes of the best fruits and vegetables. This recipe simultaneously highlights fresh fruit while dressing up the unassuming watermelon, whose flavor can be elusive because it's so diluted.

NOTE The consistency of the granita should be frozen yet granular. Put another way, it should be manageably flaky—not frozen solid like a block of ice. The way to achieve this is to stir the mixture several times during the freezing process.

PREPARE THE LEMONGRASS SIMPLE SYRUP Peel away and discard the tough outer layer of each stalk of lemongrass. Slice all but the dry stringy topmost portion of each stalk into rings. Place the lemongrass rings in a medium saucepan. Add the sugar and 1 cup of water and bring to a boil over high heat, stirring occasionally. Boil just until the sugar is all melted, then remove the pot from the heat. Allow the syrup to steep for 30 minutes. Strain, discard the lemongrass rings, and allow to cool completely to room temperature.

PREPARE THE WATERMELON GRANITA Purée watermelon cubes in a blender and strain through a fine-mesh strainer into a bowl. Add the lime juice and stir to mix well. Add lemongrass simple syrup to taste (a little less than 2 cups). Pour the mixture into a shallow glass or plastic dish and place in the freezer. Allow the granita to freeze for about an hour, then stir it with a fork to prevent it from freezing into a solid block. Return the granita to the freezer and repeat the freezing and stirring process until the granita is completely frozen.

TO SERVE Chill a large serving bowl for the granita by placing it in the freezer. Arrange the cut fruits artfully on a large platter. Spoon the frozen granita into the chilled bowl and serve alongside the fruit platter, pass-around or family style.

WATERMELON

Country
Whole Watermelon Margarita

SERVES 4 TO 6

- **2 3- to 4-pound very ripe round watermelons**
- **½ cup Flavored Simple Syrup (recipe follows)**
- **1 quart high-quality white tequila**
- **½ quart Cointreau or triple sec**
- **Lemon wedges**
- **Coarse sea salt**

How's this for a pure "party" recipe? It's perfect for a hot summer pool get-together where everyone's looking to totally relax. You can have a lot of fun creating variations with rum, vodka, and even all kinds of flavored vodkas. In fact, I first had this watermelon with vodka at a Colin Cowie party; I decided to create my own version with tequila (and I hope Colin doesn't mind). For a bigger party, you might want to make four or five of these "loaded" watermelons, each with the initial of its respective liquor carved into the rind: *T* for tequila, *V* for vodka, and so forth. If you feel mischievous, put a whole fifth of tequila or vodka into each watermelon.

Combine the simple syrup, tequila, and Cointreau in a large pitcher and stir well.

Stand the watermelons on a flat surface. (Trim a small amount off the bottom, if necessary, so they won't roll.) Cut a small hole in the top of one of the watermelons and insert a funnel into the hole. Slowly add half the contents of the pitcher in approximately 1-cup doses, allowing the watermelon to soak up the margarita mixture before adding more. Repeat the process with the second watermelon and the remaining half of the margarita mixture. Replace the cutout plug, wrap the watermelons in plastic, and place them in the refrigerator to marinate for about 8 hours. Slice the watermelons in wedges and place the wedges on a large plate or platter. Feed them to your guests until the desired effect is achieved. Pass around lemon wedges and salt to accompany the watermelon wedges.

FLAVORED SIMPLE SYRUP

MAKES ABOUT 1¼ CUPS

- **½ cup sugar**
- **Juice of 1 lemon**
- **2 tablespoons kosher salt**

Place the sugar in a small saucepan along with 1 cup of water. Bring to a boil over medium heat, stirring occasionally. Remove the syrup from the heat, stir in the lemon juice and salt, and set aside to cool.

YOGURT

SERVES 6

FOR THE PANNA COTTA

- 2 cups heavy cream
- 1¼-ounce (7 gram) packet powdered unflavored gelatin
- 6 tablespoons sugar
- 1 vanilla bean, split
- 1¼ cups plain whole-milk yogurt (preferably Greek, such as Fage)
- 1 tablespoon lemon juice (1 small or ½ large lemon)

FOR THE SPRING BERRY SAUCE

- 2 cups mixed berries (blackberries, blueberries, raspberries, strawberries), halved or quartered
- ¼ cup sugar
- Juice of 1 lemon

TOWN

Vanilla Yogurt Panna Cotta with Spring Berries

Yogurt was like water in my household growing up, and it's still very important on my pantry list. My mom made 6 to 8 quarts a week from buttermilk and her own starter (saved from the previous batch), and positioned containers by every heating unit in the house. We had it at all three meals—especially for breakfast and for after-dinner dessert.

Panna cotta, meaning "cooked cream," is a simple, traditional, silky-smooth cream-based custard from Northern Italy's dairy lands. It's often scented with vanilla, and works great chilled with a topping of berries or stone fruit. It's one of those dishes you taste and invariably come away amazed at how unbelievably delicious the simplest combinations can be. For extra smoothness, richness, and a touch of acidity, I like to add one of my personal favorite ingredients, yogurt. Dark, lusciously ripe berries work best for flavor and color contrast.

TIMING NOTE The panna cotta needs to be refrigerated for at least 2 hours in advance.

PREPARE THE PANNA COTTA Pour ½ cup of the cream into a medium bowl. Sprinkle the gelatin over the cream and set aside for 5 minutes. Combine the remaining 1½ cups cream with the sugar in a small saucepan. Add the vanilla bean and bring the cream to a simmer over medium heat, stirring occasionally. Gradually whisk the hot cream into the gelatin mixture. Whisk until the gelatin dissolves. Whisk the yogurt and lemon juice into the panna cotta mixture, then strain through a fine sieve. Pour the mixture into six 4-ounce ramekins (or small cups) and refrigerate for at least 2 hours.

PREPARE THE BERRY SAUCE Combine the berries, sugar, and lemon juice in a small saucepan and bring to a boil over medium heat, stirring occasionally. Remove from the heat and allow to cool slightly.

TO SERVE Run a small knife around the edge of each panna cotta and unmold onto a chilled dessert plate. Spoon warm berry sauce on top of the panna cottas and serve.

Country Cucumber-Yogurt Frappe

MAKES FOUR 8-OUNCE GLASSES

- **2 English cucumbers, peeled, seeded, and chopped**
- **3/4 cup plain whole-milk yogurt (preferably Greek, such as Fage)**
- **1/2 teaspoon cayenne pepper**
- **Juice of 1 lemon**
- **Tabasco sauce to taste**
- **Fine sea salt and freshly ground white pepper**
- **4 tablespoons chopped fresh dill**

I call this delicious summery drink with a kick "carpet riders' breakfast fuel." In New England, where I come from, the traditional word for a milk shake is *frappe*; in standard food terminology, a frappe is a slushy frozen drink made with fruit juice or some other flavored liquid, and it can be either sweet or savory. On summer days, my grandmother used to make a traditional Armenian drink called *tahn,* with yogurt, ice, and mint, and I would down it by the gallon. This is my updated version.

Place the cucumbers, yogurt, cayenne, and lemon juice in a blender. Add 6 small ice cubes and purée until the mixture attains a milk shake-like consistency; if it is too thick, add 1 or 2 more ice cubes. Season the frappe to taste with Tabasco, salt, and pepper. Pour equal portions into each of four decorative chilled glasses, garnish each serving with 1 tablespoon of chopped dill, and serve.

TOWN

Zucchini and Sweet Onion Tart

SERVES 4

- 3 tablespoons extra-virgin olive oil, plus additional for brushing and drizzling
- 2 large Vidalia (sweet) onions, peeled and thinly sliced
- Kosher salt and freshly ground black pepper
- 2 tablespoons fresh thyme leaves
- 1 pound frozen puff pastry, defrosted
- 4 small "fancy" (smooth and unblemished) zucchini
- 1 large egg, lightly beaten with a fork
- ½ cup pitted Niçoise (or other dark, somewhat dry) olives, roughly chopped
- ¼ cup peeled, seeded, and diced tomato (from ¼ medium tomato)
- 2 tablespoons freshly grated Parmigiano-Reggiano cheese
- 4 small sprigs fresh basil

Here's the ideal summer appetizer course with a chilled glass of rosé or Champagne. It's my lighter, all-veggie version of an Alsatian specialty, *tarte flambé*. Chose very fresh, fancy small zucchini, and make sure to mound the julienned skin segments loosely so they just wilt and soften in the oven but don't truly cook through. The goal is to coax out their natural sweetness while preserving some garden-fresh crunch. The sweet onions, sautéed into a delicious little marmalade to spread over the pastry as a base for the tart, also sing praises to the delights of spring.

Place 2 tablespoons of the oil in a large skillet over low heat. When the oil is hot, add the onions. Season with 1 teaspoon salt and ½ teaspoon pepper and cook, stirring occasionally, until the onions are soft and translucent, about 20 minutes. (If the pan gets dry and the onions begin to brown, stir in about 1 tablespoon of water.) Add the thyme and cook for about 10 minutes more. Set the onions aside to cool to room temperature.

Lay the puff pastry out on a clean, lightly floured work surface. Cut out 4 rounds, each about 5½ inches in diameter. (The best way to do this is to place a saucer upside down on the puff pastry and cut around its edge with your knife.) Place the pastry rounds on a large baking sheet and refrigerate until ready to bake.

Preheat the oven to 425°F.

Cut the zucchini into thin strips (julienne); this is most easily done with a mandoline. Place the julienned zucchini in a mixing bowl, season lightly with salt and pepper, and toss gently. Remove the baking sheet from the refrigerator and brush the tops of the pastry rounds lightly with the beaten egg, then prick the rounds with the tines of a fork. (This helps ensure that they rise evenly.) Spread 1 tablespoon of the cooked onion mixture flat on each pastry round, being careful not to spill it over the edge. Place a loose, fluffy mound of zucchini, 2 to 3 inches high, on each pastry round. Do not flatten the zucchini; it will wilt considerably in the oven. Sprinkle each mound of zucchini with equal portions of chopped olives and diced tomato. Drizzle lightly with the remaining olive oil, and bake until the zucchini is wilted and the pastry very crisp, about 10 minutes. Remove the tarts from the oven, sprinkle with grated Parmesan, garnish with basil sprigs, and serve immediately.

ZUCCHINI

Country

Chilled Sweet-and-Sour Zucchini Purée with Mint

SERVES 6 (MAKES ABOUT 1 QUART)

6 medium zucchini

3/4 cup cilantro leaves

1/2 cup flat-leaf parsley leaves

4 limes

1 teaspoon Muscat vinegar or sherry vinegar

1 1/2 teaspoons honey

6 tablespoons extra-virgin olive oil

Kosher salt and freshly ground black pepper

1/4 cup fresh mint leaves, roughly chopped or torn into small pieces

When I was growing up, the Zakarian kitchen garden in our backyard was full of mint, which grows like a weed. It was also full of zucchini, which grows like mint. Consequently, I was exposed very early in life to every way of cooking zucchini. This is an old favorite, which in fact requires very little cooking and yields a versatile side dish or condiment—part marmalade, part vinaigrette. It works very well alongside steamed or simply grilled fish. Squash in general—and specifically zucchini—can present somewhat of a challenge in extracting its flavor, and I find most zucchini recipes tend toward over-treatment. This one utilizes the grassy, somewhat peppery flavor of cilantro to bring out the zucchini's mild, fresh character; it also benefits from the sweet/sour combo of honey and vinegar.

Cut three of the zucchini in half lengthwise; use a spoon to scoop and scrape out the seedy white centers and discard them. Roughly chop the seeded zucchini shells and place them in a blender along with the cilantro and parsley. Zest and juice the limes. Add the zest and juice to the blender, then add the vinegar, honey, and 4 tablespoons of the oil. Purée on high until smooth, then season to taste with salt and pepper, and set aside.

Quarter, then seed the remaining 3 zucchini. Dice them into very small, neat cubes (*brunoise*), about 1/8 inch on each side. Heat 1 tablespoon of the remaining oil in a large skillet over medium heat. Add half the diced zucchini, and salt and pepper to taste, and cook, stirring frequently, until the zucchini is tender but not yet beginning to brown, about 10 minutes. Transfer the zucchini to a bowl and repeat the process, sweating the remaining zucchini in the remaining oil. Stir the diced zucchini into the purée. Season to taste with salt and pepper, then place in the refrigerator until well chilled. Garnish with the torn or chopped mint leaves and serve.

basics

Beef Consommé

MAKES ABOUT 6 CUPS

- 1/3 pound lean ground beef
- 3 large egg whites
- 1 small leek, white part only, thoroughly rinsed and roughly chopped
- 1/4 cup roughly chopped celery
- 1/4 cup roughly chopped carrots
- 1 cup roughly chopped tomato
- 1/4 cup roughly chopped parsley stems
- 1 1/2 teaspoons black peppercorns
- 1 1/2 teaspoons fine sea salt
- 2 quarts beef stock, chilled (see White Beef Stock recipe, below)

Place the ground beef, egg whites, leek, celery, carrots, tomato, parsley stems, peppercorns, and salt in a medium pot. Add the beef stock to the pot and turn on the heat to medium-high. Stir constantly until the beef and eggs are thoroughly mixed into the stock and steam begins to rise. Reduce the heat to medium-low. Very gently simmer the consommé without disturbing it. The beef, eggs and vegetables will form a solid "raft" on the surface of the stock. Allow the consommé to simmer over low heat until the liquid bubbling up through the raft is clear rather than cloudy, about 20 minutes. Line a sieve or strainer with a large paper coffee filter or a cheesecloth and position it over a bowl. Remove the consommé from the heat and ladle the liquid into the lined strainer, gently pressing down on the raft. The consommé can be stored in the refrigerator for up to 4 days.

White Beef Stock

MAKES ABOUT 4 QUARTS (16 CUPS)

FOR THE SPICE SACHET

- 2 whole cloves
- 4 juniper berries
- 2 pieces star anise
- 1 teaspoon white peppercorns
- 1 teaspoon black peppercorns
- 6 allspice berries
- 1 dried bay leaf

FOR THE STOCK

- 5 pounds beef oxtails, cut about 1 inch thick
- 1 cup roughly chopped celery
- 1 cup roughly chopped carrots
- 2 cups roughly chopped onions
- 2 medium tomatoes, roughly chopped
- 1 head of garlic, halved crosswise

PREPARE THE SPICE SACHET Place the cloves, juniper berries, star anise, white peppercorns, black peppercorns, allspice berries, and bay leaf in a piece of cheesecloth. Gather the cheesecloth into a bundle and tie it shut with a piece of kitchen twine.

PREPARE THE STOCK Place the oxtails and the sachet in a very large pot. Add enough water to cover, about 6 quarts. Bring the water to a simmer over medium-high heat, then reduce the heat to maintain a steady low simmer. (Do not boil the bones; the water should be just hot enough so it steams and moves gently without a lot of bubbling.) Use a ladle to skim off any froth or fat that floats to the surface. Simmer the pot for 3 hours, skimming regularly. Add the celery, carrots, onions, tomatoes, and garlic, and simmer for 1 more hour. Remove the sachet and strain the liquid through a chinois (china cap or fine-mesh strainer) into a 1-gallon container or several smaller containers. Allow the stock to cool, then cover and refrigerate until ready to use. The stock can be kept in the refrigerator for about five days if you boil it once a day or frozen for up to six months. Always boil stock prior to using it.

Chicken Stock

MAKES ABOUT 4 QUARTS (16 CUPS)

FOR THE SPICE SACHET

2 whole cloves

4 juniper berries

2 pieces star anise

2 teaspoons white peppercorns

2 teaspoons black peppercorns

6 allspice berries

2 dried bay leaves

1 teaspoon coriander seeds

8 sprigs thyme

FOR THE STOCK

2 raw chicken carcasses, trimmed of excess fat and roughly chopped (necks and feet are fine)

1½ cups roughly chopped onion

1 cup chopped carrot

1 cup chopped celery

Of course, it's always better to have a container of your best homemade chicken stock available. Using solid, well-prepared ingredients will make a big difference in your final outcome. But nowadays, there are a lot of very good store-bought alternatives for homemade stock—canned, in cartons, and frozen. So if you shop wisely, that shortcut won't cost you much in terms of quality results. If you're buying canned, buy the low-sodium type; it's always easier to control the seasonings by adding your own salt to taste rather than incorporating ingredients that have added salt.

PREPARE THE SPICE SACHET Place the cloves, juniper berries, star anise, white peppercorns, black peppercorns, allspice berries, bay leaves, coriander seeds, and thyme in a piece of cheesecloth. Gather the cheesecloth into a bundle and tie it shut with a piece of kitchen twine.

PREPARE THE STOCK Place the chicken carcasses in a very large pot. Add enough water to cover, about 5 quarts. Bring the stock to a simmer over medium-high heat, then reduce the heat so the liquid simmers gently. Simmer the stock for 2 hours, skimming and discarding the foam and fat that rise to the surface. Add the spice sachet, the onion, carrot, and celery and simmer for 1 more hour. Remove the sachet and pass the stock through a fine strainer into a 1-gallon container or several smaller containers. Allow the stock to cool, then refrigerate until ready to use. The stock can be kept in the refrigerator for about five days or in the freezer for up to six months. Always boil stock before using it.

Fish Stock

MAKES 3 TO 4 QUARTS

FOR THE SPICE SACHET

- 2 whole cloves
- 4 juniper berries
- 2 pieces star anise
- 1 teaspoon white peppercorns
- 1 teaspoon black peppercorns
- 1 teaspoon ground coriander
- 6 allspice berries
- 2 dried bay leaves

FOR THE STOCK

- 1 tablespoon extra-virgin olive oil
- 2 to 3 pounds raw fish carcasses, including heads (gills removed), roughly chopped
- 1 cup chopped leeks, white part only
- ½ cup chopped celery
- ½ cup chopped parsnips
- 1 cup dry white wine
- Grated zest of 1 lemon
- Grated zest of 1 lime
- 1 teaspoon white peppercorns
- 1 small bunch of thyme

Use white fish, such as bass, cod, or halibut. Avoid oily fish, such as salmon or mackerel.

PREPARE THE SPICE SACHET Place the cloves, juniper berries, star anise, white peppercorns, black peppercorns, ground coriander, allspice berries, and bay leaves in a piece of cheesecloth. Gather the cheesecloth into a bundle and tie it shut with a piece of kitchen twine.

PREPARE THE STOCK Place the olive oil in a large pot over medium-low heat, add the chopped fish carcasses, and sweat, stirring constantly, until any meat remaining turns white and begins to fall off the bones and the liquid given off by the carcasses begins to dry up, about 10 minutes. Add the leeks, celery, and parsnips, and sweat for 5 minutes more. Continue to stir, lowering the heat as necessary so the ingredients do not begin to brown. Add the wine and simmer until the pot is dry, about 10 minutes. Add enough cold water to cover the bones, 3 to 4 quarts. Add the spice sachet, lemon zest, lime zest, white peppercorns, and thyme. Raise the heat and bring the contents of the pot to a simmer. Reduce the heat and simmer very gently, skimming any froth or residue that floats to the top, until the stock is flavorful, about 20 minutes. Do not stir the bones or the stock will become cloudy. Turn off the heat, skim the stock carefully, and allow it to sit for 10 minutes. Ladle the stock into a fine-mesh strainer set over a large bowl. Chill the stock, then cover and refrigerate until ready to use. The stock can be kept in the refrigerator up to five days or it can be frozen and kept for up to six months. Always boil stock before using it.

Clarified Butter

MAKES ABOUT 1½ CUPS

1 pound (4 sticks) unsalted butter

There are a number of variations on the procedure for making clarified butter, but the end result or goal is always the same: to eliminate the milk solids, which cause the butter to burn and spit when frying or sautéing foods at higher temperatures.

NOTE Clarified butter is available in Asian or Indian markets under its Indian name, ghee.

Cut the butter into ½-inch slices and place it in a medium saucepan over medium heat. Allow the butter to melt and then come to a boil; this should take about 5 minutes. Skim off any foam that rises to the top. The butter should sizzle and crackle; throughout the process, make sure the heat is never so high that the bottom of the pan starts to brown or blacken. Lower the heat to keep the butter at a slow, steady boil for another 15 minutes, continuing to skim any surface foam. The bubbles in the butter will become smaller and smaller, ultimately the size of a pinhead. Allow any residual milk solids to settle to the bottom of the pan. Carefully pour off the pure, clear, oily butterfat into a holding container, leaving all solids behind. (At this point, you can pass it through a tea strainer or other fine-mesh strainer just to be sure it's completely clear.) Allow the clarified butter to cool to room temperature, cover, and refrigerate until ready to use.

Mayonnaise

MAKES ABOUT 1½ CUPS

2 large egg yolks

½ teaspoon Dijon mustard

2 tablespoons fresh lemon juice

Kosher salt to taste

1½ cups extra-virgin olive oil

Place the egg yolks in a mixing bowl with the mustard and lemon juice and whisk until well combined. Season with salt and continue whisking briskly while gradually incorporating the olive oil. Place in a glass or other nonreactive container, cover, and refrigerate until ready to use.

Alternatively, the mayonnaise can be mixed in a food processor.

Pasta Dough

MAKES ABOUT 2½ POUNDS

- **4 cups "00" pasta flour (see Ingredient Note), or unbleached all-purpose flour, plus additional for sprinkling**
- **6 large eggs, lightly beaten with a fork**
- **1 tablespoon fine sea salt**
- **1 teaspoon white distilled vinegar**

The easiest and best way to roll out pasta dough is to use a simple pasta machine; old-fashioned hand-cranked ones are best.

INGREDIENT NOTE The pasta flour used to make homemade dough in Italy is called "00" (*doppio zero,* or "double zero"); it is a fine-grained flour with less gluten than most standard types sold in the United States.

Mound 4 cups of flour on a clean work surface. Use a fork to form a large well in the center of the mound. Pour the eggs into the well. Add the salt to the well with the eggs and begin to swirl the eggs against the walls of the flour well with the fork until a doughlike ball is formed; the mixture will still be very clumpy. Drizzle the clumpy ball of dough with the vinegar and 1 tablespoon of water.

Knead the dough, folding it onto itself, and incorporating any excess flour from the mound as quickly as possible. Knead the dough until it is smooth, elastic, and no longer sticky, adding a little extra flour if necessary, about 10 minutes. Cover the dough tightly with plastic wrap and place it in the refrigerator to rest for at least 20 minutes and up to 24 hours.

Remove the dough from the plastic wrap and flatten it by hand on a flat work surface that has been liberally sprinkled with flour. Roll out the dough to the desired thickness with a rolling pin or in a pasta machine. It is now ready to form into shapes.

Tomato Confit

MAKES 8 TOMATO CONFIT PETALS OR ABOUT ⅔ CUP CHOPPED

- **2 large ripe tomatoes, cored, blanched, and peeled**
- **2 tablespoons extra-virgin olive oil**
- **1 clove garlic, sliced thin**
- **½ teaspoon sugar**
- **½ teaspoon freshly ground black pepper**
- **1½ tablespoons coarse sea salt**
- **8 sprigs thyme**

Preheat the oven to 200°F.

Cut the skinned tomatoes in quarters lengthwise and scrape out the pith and seeds to create a "petal." Place the tomato petals in a bowl with the olive oil and sliced garlic. Add the sugar, pepper, salt, and thyme. Mix well. Lay the tomato petals on a baking sheet lined with aluminum foil. Place a sprig of thyme and a slice of garlic on top of each petal, pour the seasoned olive oil left in the bowl over the tomatoes, and roast in the oven until the tomatoes are concentrated and slightly shrunken, about 1 hour. Allow the tomatoes to cool then store in a sealed container in the refrigerator until ready to use.

SOURCES AND RESOURCES

The Baker's Catalogue
P.O. Box 876
Norwich, VT 05055
Phone: 800-827-6836
Fax: 800-343-3002
E-mail: customercare@kingarthurflour.com
Website: shop.bakerscatalogue.com

ChefShop
P.O. Box 3488
Seattle, WA 98114
Phone: 877-337-2491
Fax: 206-267-2205
E-mail: shopkeeper@ChefShop.com
Website: www.ChefShop.com

Dairy Fresh Candies
57 Salem Street
Boston, MA 02113
Phone: 800-336-5536
Fax: 617-742-9829
E-mail: sales@dairyfreshcandies.com
Website: www.dairyfreshcandies.com

D'Artagnan
280 Wilson Avenue
Newark, NJ 07105
Phone: 800-327-8246
Fax: 973-465-1870
E-mail: orders@dartagnan.com
Website: www.dartagnan.com

Dean & Deluca
Various locations throughout the United States and also in Japan
Phone: 877-826-9246
Fax: 800-781-4050
E-mail: atyourservice@deandeluca.com
Website: www.deandeluca.com

Electrolux
Home Products—North America
250 Bobby Jones Expressway
Martinez, GA 30907
Phone: 877-435-3287
Fax: 706-228-6615
Website: www.electroluxusa.com

FlowerDepotStore
Phone: 877-780-2099
E-mail: dryflowrco@aol.com
Website: www.flowerdepotstore.com

GourmetSleuth
Phone: 408-354-8281
Fax: 408-395-8279
E-mail: help@gourmetsleuth.com
Website: www.gourmetsleuth.com

Kalustyan's
123 Lexington Avenue
New York, NY 10016
Phone: 212-685-3451 or 800-352-3451
Fax: 212-683-8458
E-mail: sales@kalustyans.com
Website: www.kalustyans.com

Murray's Chicken
5190 Main Street
South Fallsburg, NY 12779
Phone: 800-770-6347 (for retail locations; no mail order)
Fax: 845-639-9272
E-mail: info@murrayschicken.com
Website: www.murrayschicken.com

Nando's
c/o Kizulia Trading
1040 W. 18th Street, Suite A205
Costa Mesa, CA 92627
Phone: 949-722-0230
Fax: 949-922-0102
E-mail: nandos4sauces@prodigy.net
Website: www.nandosusa.com

Niman Ranch
1025 E. 12th Street
Oakland, CA 94606
Phone: 866-808-0340
Fax: 510-808-0339
E-mail: info@nimanranch.com
Website: www.nimanranch.com

Perks Peri-Peri Inc.
1 Boston Post Road
Milford, CT 06460
Phone: 888-737-5773
Fax: 203-882-5649
E-mail: sales@PerksPeriPeri.com
Website: www.perksperiperi.com

Petaluma Poultry
P.O. Box 7368
2700 Lakeville Highway
Petaluma, CA 94955
Phone: 800-556-6789
Fax: 707-763-3924
Website: www.petalumapoultry.com

Sahadi's Specialty Foods
187 Atlantic Avenue
Brooklyn, NY 11201
Phone: 718-624-4550
Fax: 718-643-4415
E-mail: sahadis@aol.com
Website: www.sahadis.com

San Francisco Herb Co.
Phone: 800-227-4530
Fax: 415-861-4440
E-mail: info@sfherb.com
Website: www.sfherb.com

Whole Spice
292 North San Pedro Road, Suite B
San Rafael, CA 94903
Phone: 415-472-1750
Fax: 415-276-4768
E-mail: support@wholespice.com
Website: www.wholespice.com

Wolferman's
P.O. Box 15913
Shawnee Mission, KS 66285
Phone: 800-999-0169
Fax: 800-999-7548
E-mail: wolf@wolfermans.com
Website: www.wolfermans.com

ACKNOWLEDGMENTS

I want to acknowledge and offer my most heartfelt thanks to the following people (in no particular order) for their generous help and support in my efforts to make this the best cookbook I could write.

My sole sponsor, Electrolux, whose products, professionalism, and support for this book I cherish.

Margaret, my spectacular wife—I cannot imagine being without her—for her incredible honesty, energy, and intelligence, along with her wonderful sense of humor. She has made me a much better man in a very short time.

John Johnson, my executive chef at Town, whose talent, compassion, care, and friendship for ten years have been invaluable to me. I could not have done this book without his help and dedication.

My business partners, Michael Callahan, Huy Chi Li, Robin Leigh, and others, for their belief in my dreams and for financing them in full.

Adam Block of Block Associates, who has put me on the path to success in this difficult profession and is a loyal and wonderful friend.

Scott Feldman of Two12 management, a close friend and business associate whom I trust for his uncanny sense of timing and vision for the projects and directions I should pursue.

Luci Levere, my pastry chef at the time of writing, for her one-of-a-kind pastries and remarkable sense of taste and balance with desserts. She brought a wonderful presence to the kitchens at Town for four special years.

To all the team members of Town, whose support, loyalty, and passion is evident every day when they amble into our beautiful restaurant—especially sous-chefs Chris, Thomas, Ben, Amabele, Abdul, Jameel, Vandana, and many, many more.

My good friends for their advice, criticism, kindness, and patience in putting up with me when I get in my foul moods, which is sometimes too often: Tony Fortuna; Paul Guzzardo, for his constant spot-on advice and business acumen; Linsey Snyder; Nick Mautone; Joseph Lucas; Fran, Marie, Debra, and Harris Williams; Bobby Flay, the real thing; Tom Colicchio; Michael Schlow; my good friend Ira Drukier, for his constant support and genuine kindness; Dr. Harold Langlois, for encouraging me to follow my gut instincts and pursue my dreams; and Jonathan Morr, my one and only Sam.

Graziano from Valentino, for making me always seem well dressed.

My brother, George Zakarian Jr., for his love and thoughtfulness, and especially my sister, Cynthia, whose selflessness, dedication, and love while caring for my mother during her fifteen-year struggle with cancer should be a model of compassion for everyone. She is truly a gift to me as a sister and role model.

David Gibbons, for his commitment to hearing and getting my voice. He is a uniquely talented food writer who made me laugh during the sometimes tricky process of self-exploration that one tends to undertake when writing a first book. I look forward to more collaborations with him in the near future.

My agent, Jane Dystel, the consummate pro and another great advisor.

My editors, Rica Allannic and Chris Pavone, who signed up the book, shepherded it, and spearheaded the fabulous publishing team at Clarkson Potter.

Cathy Young, an extraordinary young woman and talented chef who tirelessly tested every one of these recipes.

Quentin Bacon, the best there is in food photography.

All the great chefs I've had the pleasure of working with, learning from, and now can proudly call my colleagues and friends—first among them Alain Sailhac, Daniel Boulud, Jacques Maximin, and Alain Passard.

INDEX

Note: *Italicized* page references indicate photographs.